CONQUERING HEROINES

Conquering Heroines

How Women Fought Sex Bias at Michigan and Paved the Way for Title IX

SARA FITZGERALD

University of Michigan   Ann Arbor

ISBN-13: 978-0-472-03788-9 (print)
ISBN-13: 978-0-472-12704-7 (ebook)

2023   2022   2021   2020   4   3   2   1

"Unless we record our history, it will be lost."

—JEAN L. KING, 1994

CONTENTS

Illustrations follow page 182

TIMELINE OF HEW INVESTIGATION
AND AFTERMATH

September 24, 1965—President Johnson signs Executive Order 11246, prohibiting racial discrimination by federal contractors.

July 1966—University of Michigan is investigated for its compliance with Title VI of the 1964 Civil Rights Act, prohibiting racial discrimination in programs that receive federal aid.

October 13, 1967—President Johnson signs Executive Order 11375, prohibiting sex discrimination by federal contractors.

October 13, 1968—Executive Order 11375 takes effect for federal contractors.

June 1969—U.S. Department of Health, Education, and Welfare (HEW) (now the Department of Health and Human Services) conducts compliance review of the University of Michigan's minority hiring practices.

1969—University of Michigan adopts affirmative action plan addressing racial discrimination.

January 19, 1970—President Nixon nominates G. Harrold Carswell to the U.S. Supreme Court.

January 29, 1970—U.S. Rep. Patsy Mink and National Organization for Women (NOW) President Betty Friedan testify before the Senate Judiciary Committee in opposition to the Carswell nomination.

January–February 1970—Ann Arbor women organize a chapter of FOCUS on Equal Employment for Women to oppose the Carswell nomination.

January 31, 1970—Women's Equity Action League files its first sex discrimination complaint against a U.S. university, in this case the University of Maryland.

March 1970—HEW investigators visit Harvard University to review potential racial discrimination in hiring.

April 1, 1970—Black Action Movement strike ends as the University of Michigan sets goal of 10 percent black admissions.

April 8, 1970—Senate rejects Carswell nomination.

April 12, 1970—Kathleen Shortridge's investigation of sex discrimination at the University of Michigan is published in the *Michigan Daily*.

May 27, 1970—FOCUS on Equal Employment for Women files sex discrimination complaint against the University of Michigan with the U.S. Department of Labor.

June–July 1970—U.S. House Education and Labor Select Subcommittee on Education holds hearings on sex discrimination.

August 17–21, 1970—Team from the Chicago regional office of HEW's Office of Civil Rights conducts investigation of the University of Michigan.

August 31–September 4, 1970—HEW team returns to Michigan campus for further investigation.

September 12, 1970—Helen Hornbeck Tanner writes HEW, detailing her battle to get hired by the U-M History Department.

September 20, 1970—U-M Zoology Professor Margaret Davis writes HEW, detailing her battle for a salary increase.

Late September 1970—University of Michigan President Robben Fleming meets with HEW regional officials.

October 6, 1970—HEW investigator Don Scott writes Fleming, setting 30-day deadline for the University of Michigan to modify its affirmative action plan to address sex discrimination.

October 7, 1970—Fleming responds to Scott, saying it is unlikely that the University of Michigan can meet that deadline.

October 10–11, 1970—University of Michigan holds a teach-in marking the centennial of the admission of women.

October 13, 1970—University officials issue press release, disclosing HEW's deadline and ultimatum.

October 14, 1970—U-M's Center for the Continuing Education of Women (now the Center for the Education of Women) holds symposium marking the centennial of women's admission.

November 6, 1970—The *Michigan Daily* discloses that HEW has held up a contract between U-M's Center for Population Planning and the U.S. Agency for International Development to provide family planning services to the government of Nepal.

November 10, 1970— University of Michigan officials meet with HEW regional officials in Chicago.

November 20, 1970—*Science* magazine discloses the key findings of the HEW investigation.

December 4, 1970—HEW investigator Scott advises Fleming that the University's response is still "unacceptable."

December 8, 1970—Fleming pledges to submit a revised affirmative action plan within 90 days; sends telegram to HEW Secretary Elliot L. Richardson, asking him to release held-up contracts while the outstanding issues are resolved.

December 31, 1970—University concludes negotiations with HEW and reaches agreement over how to proceed.

January 1971—The University of Michigan and HEW announce "historic" agreement to address sex discrimination.

January 13, 1971—U-M's Commission on Women holds its first meeting.

January 26, 1971—Cheryl Clark files sex discrimination complaint against the University of Michigan, citing salary inequities.

March 8, 1971—University files revised affirmative action plan with HEW, including goals and timetables for hiring women over next three years.

May 17, 1971—Lucille I. Matthews, deputy director of HEW's Chicago regional civil rights office, notifies Michigan that its affirmative action plan is "incomplete."

May 28, 1971—University Complaint Review Committee rejects Cheryl Clark's complaint on a 2-1 vote.

Mid-November 1971—PROBE files a new complaint with HEW, charging that Michigan is acting "in bad faith" in implementing the goals and timetables.

December 1971—U-M's Vice President for Academic Affairs Allan Smith orders a review of the salaries of all women, instructional and non-instructional, on the academic staff.

December 17, 1971—University officials announce a consulting firm will review the job classifications for more than 5,000 professional and administrative employees on its three campuses.

February 4, 1972—HEW officials return to Ann Arbor to discuss the status of Michigan's affirmative action plan.

February 9, 1972—U-M's Commission for Women releases critical "cluster" reports prepared by subgroups of female employees throughout the university.

February 25, 1972—Michigan announces it is awarding salary increases to 100 women, effective February 1, 1972.

May 1, 1972—U-M departments ordered to begin advertising academic openings.

June 2, 1972—U-M Astronomy Professor Anne Cowley files complaint, alleging sex discrimination regarding her position and salary.

June 23, 1972—Education Act of 1972 signed into law, including "Title IX," barring sex discrimination at colleges receiving federal support, and amending the Equal Pay Act to include women in professional and administrative jobs.

July 1972—On appeal, Michigan agrees to raise Cheryl Clark's salary.

October 27, 1972—Kenneth R. Mines, HEW's new Chicago regional civil rights director, tells Fleming that Michigan has still failed to meet its commitments to the agency.

May 4, 1973—Mines again reiterates that the University of Michigan has not corrected the "deficiencies" in its plan.

July 1973—Michigan sends HEW revised goals and timetables for 1973–76, makes the plan public in October.

October 1973—Complaint Appeals Committee rejects Anne Cowley's grievance and remands tenure decision to U-M's Astronomy Department, which again rejects her appointment.

January 1975—Regents approve the appointment of Connecticut College Dean Jewell Cobb as dean of U-M's College of Literature, Science, and the Arts. Cobb rejects the offer after Zoology Department refuses to grant her tenure.

1985—Linda S. Wilson named vice president for research of the University of Michigan.

April 1, 2002—Mary Sue Coleman becomes president of the University of Michigan.

A NOTE ABOUT LANGUAGE

The 1960s and 1970s were a time of rapid changes in American society, and those changes included the kind of words that were used to describe persons of color and women. In quoting from historical records or persons from that time, the author has, with one exception, used the original words, recognizing that many would not be considered acceptable today. Her goal was to accurately capture the history and attitudes of that time—and thus some of the barriers that these persons faced.

PROLOGUE

The spark that fueled the wildfire was a nomination to the U.S. Supreme Court, a white male from Florida named G. Harrold Carswell.

On January 19, 1970, President Richard M. Nixon had reached back into the pool of southern federal judges to fill a vacancy on the high court. His first nominee, U.S. Circuit Judge Clement Haynsworth, had been rejected by the Senate two months before. Carswell was a younger judge, a relative newcomer to a different federal circuit court.

There was much to question in Carswell's record, and his opponents quickly found it. There were the statements he had made about white supremacy when he ran for the Georgia legislature in 1948. There were the cases in which he had ruled against the interests of organized labor. There was the high rate at which his district court opinions had been overturned by appellate courts. In the midst of the confirmation battle, Republican Sen. Roman Hruska of Nebraska did the nominee no favors when he observed that "even if he were mediocre, there are a lot of mediocre judges and people and lawyers. They are entitled to a little representation, aren't they, and a little chance?"

But there was something else. A few months before, Carswell had joined his fellow jurists in declining to hear the case of a woman named Ida Phillips, who was denied an assembly-line job at Martin Marietta Corporation because she had preschool-aged children.

January 29, 1970, the third day of Carswell's confirmation hearings, marked the first time in American history that women challenged a federal judicial nomination because of the nominee's positions on sex discrimination. Democratic Rep. Patsy T. Mink of Hawaii told the Senate Judiciary Committee that Carswell's nomination was "an affront to the women of America." She went on to charge that "male supremacy, like white supremacy, is equally repugnant to those who believe in equality." When Republican Sen. Marlow Cook of Kentucky pointed out that ten other judges on the circuit court had agreed with Carswell's decision to deny a full-court review, lawyer Mink replied, "Yes, I am well aware of that, Mr. Senator. But the other nine are not up for appointment to the Supreme Court."

Mink was followed by Betty Friedan, then the president of the National Organization for Women (NOW). Friedan observed that more and more sex discrimination cases were working their way through the courts. She contended that Carswell would be "a sexually backward judge" who would deny the cases a hearing before the Supreme Court.

Dr. Jo-Ann E. Gardner, an experimental psychologist at the University of Pittsburgh, also sought to testify. Gardner said she represented FOCUS on Equal Employment for Women, what she described as a bipartisan national coalition with chapters in several cities. "In 1948," she observed in her prepared remarks, "the people of this country were not sensitive to the dreadful inequities produced by white supremacist statements. Today, in 1970, the people are generally unaware of the dreadful inequities that result from parallel but more subtle male supremacist beliefs."

In Ann Arbor, Michigan, a newly minted lawyer and Democratic activist got wind of Gardner's efforts and decided to organize a FOCUS chapter there. Back then, Jean King later recalled, "Ten people were enough to form an organization." She invited a few friends to meet in the living room of her modest home on Sunnywood Drive, a shady street west of downtown. Their first goal was to support Gardner, who, King remembered, "planned to travel to Washington and chain herself to a chair in the Senate hearings. . . ."

On February 3, a story on the front page of the *Detroit Free Press*'s "For and About Women" section spotlighted King and FOCUS's "cross-country telephone campaign" through which members were calling two friends and urging them to send a telegram to their senators, protesting the nomination. They were then supposed to recruit more friends to join the opposition network.

"We feel that there is a real groundswell of indignation among women of all ages and political preferences," King and Mary Yourd, her Republican co-chair, were quoted in another news story, "and we want this indignation to become visible to the men who decide whether Carswell could make fair decisions for all Americans, men or women, white or black."

Carswell's confirmation vote was delayed.

On March 31, King distributed instructions to her troops in Michigan, urging them to send telegrams to Republican Sen. Robert P. Griffin, who sat on the Senate Judiciary Committee, and to get friends from other key states to do the same. King noted, "It will cost you about $3.00 for one phone call and a wire. That is less than a penny a month for the 30 years Carswell may spend on the Court unless he is rejected by the Senate."

On April 5, a letter from Mary Dabbs appeared in the *Michigan Daily*, the University of Michigan's student newspaper. Dabbs was a mother of two who, ten years before, had been turned down for a secretarial job in Atlanta because she had scored too high on an IQ test. Identifying herself as a FOCUS member, Dabbs urged *Daily* readers to phone key senators to oppose the nomination. "The next great moment in the history of the Supreme Court may be when it decides whether or not women are persons under the Constitution," she wrote. "Carswell is most unlikely to make a useful contribution to those deliberations."

Three days later, the Senate rejected Carswell's nomination by a bipartisan vote of 51 to 45.

The battleground now seems so familiar, that it can be hard to remember what a different time that was. 1970. Fifty years had passed since American women had won the right to vote. More than a hundred years had passed since Congress had approved legislation to create public land-grant universities, open to both men and women.

But, as *New York Times* columnist Gail Collins wrote of that time, " . . . it seemed that once women had gotten the right to vote, they never got anything else. There was an endless list of ways they were discriminated against or treated unfairly, from lower salaries to inferior facilities for girls' sports in public schools to the different—and less generous— way that Social Security benefits were computed on women's wages. Few people seemed to think all this posed much of a problem. Many of the women who experienced the most discrimination took it for granted; those who didn't saw little possibility for major change."

And universities, those bastions of progressive values and liberal thinking at mid-century, turned out to be no better than most other U.S. institutions when it came to defining the roles women were expected to play.

Throughout the first half of the 20th century, women earned college degrees and went into the workplace in growing numbers. But when World War II came to an end, so did all of those gains. As GIs returned to campuses to finish their degrees, more than one college recognized the veterans' wives with a "PhT" certificate—short for "Putting Hubby Through." When women did earn legitimate degrees, they were advised that their ultimate goal should still be marriage and children.

Adlai Stevenson, twice the Democratic presidential nominee in the 1950s, delivered the 1955 commencement address at Smith College and began by poking fun at the lofty themes of most graduation speeches. "But for my part," he went on, "I want merely to tell you young ladies that I think there is much you can do about that crisis in the humble role of housewife—which, statistically, is what most of you are going to be whether you like the idea or not just now—and you'll like it!"

Stevenson continued, telling the graduates that they "may be hitched to one of these creatures we call 'Western man,' and I think part of your job is to keep him Western, to keep him truly purposeful, to keep him whole. . . . This assignment for you, as wives and mothers, has great advantages. In the first place, it is home work—you can do it in the living room with a baby in your lap, or in the kitchen with a can opener in your hands. If you're really clever, maybe you can even practice your saving arts on that unsuspecting man while he's watching television." It was important work, Stevenson asserted, no matter how well educated they were, to assure the defeat of totalitarianism.

W. K. Jordan, president of Radcliffe College in the same era, welcomed entering women students by telling them that their education would "prepare them to be splendid wives and mothers and their reward might be to marry Harvard men." In his 1950 book, *Educating Our Daughters*, Lynn White, Jr., president of Mills College, the all-women school in California, proposed a new curriculum that would prepare a woman to "foster the intellectual and emotional life of her family and community." He called for college courses in home economics that would teach his students the "theory and preparation of a Basque paella, of a well-marinated shish kebab, [and] lamb kidneys sautéed in sherry."

As Betty Friedan, a member of the Smith Class of 1942, approached her 15th reunion, she and two classmates prepared a survey to assess their class's attitudes about the education they had received. Her findings uncovered a widespread sense of dissatisfaction, and led her, in 1963, to write *The Feminine Mystique* and call out "the problem that has no name."

When she was at Smith, Friedan recalled that she had met future Yale president Kingman Brewster when they were both editors of their campus newspapers: "There was something in the way that the men like Kingman Brewster were expected to do big things in society and that expectation propelled them to do it. I don't think that this could possibly have been true at Smith. It was still too much of a freaky thing for women to do anything at all, and then it wasn't that big. Sure you might have been expected to go on and get your PhD and do the academic thing—that was about it. . . . The Smith education was geared to produce very intelligent wives of executives and other prominent men, who would do traditional community service."

Feminist Gloria Steinem, who followed Friedan in the Smith Class of 1956, recalled, "The justification of education for women which I heard at Smith, and the one I myself used to justify why I was there. . . was that educated children could only be produced by educated mothers. . . . There was an attitude of apology all the time, so that everybody was proud of having four times more male faculty than female faculty, and saying, 'Well, it's all right to educate women because they're going to be mothers.' There was no sense that we were going to be anything else. There was also no preparation for the kinds of discrimination we would meet if we did try to get a job—no one ever told us anything, at least not that I can remember. We were taught that our education was terribly important, but the Vocational Department still suggested jobs as researcher and so on, and didn't object to recruiters who asked only if we could type."

When Hillary Rodham Clinton spoke on behalf of her classmates at her 1969 commencement ceremony at Wellesley, she mused, "The question about possible and impossible was one that we brought with us to Wellesley four years ago. We arrived not yet knowing what was not possible. Consequently, we expected a lot. Our attitudes are easily understood having grown up, having come to consciousness in the first five years of the decade—years dominated by men with dreams, men in the civil rights movement, the Peace Corps, the space program—so we arrived at Wellesley and we found, as all of us have found, that there was a gap between expectation and realities." Among the "impossibilities" Clinton and her classmates had encountered was the chance to earn their degrees from Harvard. That university did not admit women as regular undergraduates until after Clinton had moved on to law school.

And that barrier was not unique to the Ivy League. The University of Virginia first admitted black students to its undergraduate programs in 1955. But it was 15 more years before it made the same concession to women.

As some women of the post-war generation pursued advanced degrees and teaching jobs at universities, they found that if they encountered sex discrimination—if they even understood what that word meant—they had few ways in which to fight it. As Congress began addressing discrimination against blacks in the mid-1960s, its southern members figured out that the easiest way to kill a civil rights bill was to build in protections for women. Consequently, as Congress debated the Carswell nomination in the first months of 1970, this was the landscape that women faculty members faced:

- The Equal Pay Act of 1963 exempted professional and executive women, including women teachers, faculty, and administrators at all levels of education in the United States. The exemption had been supported by the bill's woman sponsor as the price she had to pay to win passage of the legislation.

- Title VII of the Civil Rights Act of 1964, which prohibited job discrimination based on race and sex and other criteria, excluded employees "in their educational activities."
- Title VI of the same law barred discrimination based on race, color, and national origin in federally assisted programs but did not include discrimination based on sex.

The University of Michigan was no different from many other campuses at that time—and in some ways, worse. Although it admitted its first woman in 1870, around the time the land-grant colleges were founded, it had a longer history than most of the country's other public universities. Since it opened its doors in 1817, it had promoted the same kind of clubby male atmosphere found at the eastern Ivy League schools, viewing itself as a sort of "Harvard of the West," as "the West" was then defined.

Barbara Newell arrived in Ann Arbor in the late 1960s as executive assistant to the new U-M president, a position that made her the university's highest-ranking woman administrator. But she still remembered her first visit two decades earlier, when she was in high school and her father was teaching at Amherst. "My father was invited to lecture and we were to stay in the Student Union," she recalled. "We found the Student Union, and Dad said, 'Well, here, why don't you get out and go in and register and I'll find a place to park the car.' Logical. So my mother and I got out of the car, went to the front door of the Student Union, and were told to walk around the building." Women were not permitted to use the front door of the Michigan Union until 1954. "So *that*," Newell recalled, "was my introduction to Ann Arbor."

Later, after she assumed a leadership role on women's issues, Newell observed, "I had the sense that there was an awful lot of Ann Arbor that was like that front door. It just didn't open for a long, long time."

In 1969, Michigan women still could not get a lifetime membership in the Union because the facility's 1904 Constitution prohibited it. Nor did the Science Research Club, a university fixture since 1902, accept women members. As for the hallowed ground of Michigan Stadium, the rules had just been loosened a bit. In the fall of 1969, dogs were permitted on the field for the first time, but women and children still were not. *Michigan Daily* staff member Sara Krulwich was confronted by security officials when she sought to shoot photographs of a football game at the start of that season. Women would still be barred from the Michigan Marching Band for three more years.

But change, when it finally came, was rapid, so rapid, in fact, that it was easy to forget how challenging the battle had been.

The Carswell nomination helped the friends in the Ann Arbor chapter of FOCUS find their voices. The judge's defeat gave them a sense of power. And within a matter of months, they would be among the many women around the country who were making new headlines of their own.

1

The Eureka Moment

"It was just the way things were."

Bernice Resnick was a bright graduate of Erasmus Hall High School in Flatbush, New York, when she entered Brooklyn College in the 1940s. Her parents had planned to name her Beryl, but the doctor transformed it into Bernice on her birth certificate. In Yiddish, that translated into Bunya, and, as a result, everyone called her Bunny. She was smart and curious, a whirling dervish. It was not until Bunny entered school that she learned what her real name was.

Bunny was the girl who wanted to do everything at school: change the inkwell, operate the slide projectors, serve as a crossing guard. But those jobs, her teachers told her, were not for girls. Looking back, she reflected, "I must have been quite conflicted about being bright and being female, fearing rejection from males who very often were not as bright as myself." Yet she loved school and "the intellectual life." "For many years," she said, "I used to think of my brightness as either my 'gifted curse' or my 'cursed gift.'"

When she applied to college, she recalled, "It was openly known that women needed higher grades and test scores in order to be accepted. No one complained. . . ."

In 1930, Brooklyn College had become the first public coeducational liberal arts college in New York City. Bunny majored in psychology and graduated cum laude in 1948. She moved on to the City College of New

York, earning a master's degree in clinical and school psychology. The college's undergraduate programs were still not open to women.

She worked as a research fellow at City College, and then, like most women of her generation, she got married—at the age of 22—to a guy named Jerry Sandler. Within a few years, they had two daughters and moved to Bloomington, Indiana. Bunny Sandler applied for the doctoral program in psychology at Indiana University but was rejected. She was told she did not have enough research experience; the department head subsequently hired her as his own research assistant.

Nine months later, the Sandlers moved to Ann Arbor, where Jerry pursued a graduate degree and went to work for the University of Michigan Broadcasting Service, following his interests in the brand-new world of educational radio. Bunny was admitted into the School of Social Work as a part-time student, but after completing 18 hours of coursework, she was expected to switch to full time. She tried it for two weeks, but with two toddlers at home, she decided she had to quit, which was "the only time" she dropped out over the course of her academic career.

In 1963, when her girls were older, she took a course in psychology and then applied for the doctoral program in that discipline. But those plans were derailed when her husband took a job as head of the radio division of the National Association of Educational Broadcasters, and she followed him to Washington, DC. Many months later, she inquired about the status of her application. Again, she learned, it had been rejected.

But she was still undaunted. Now in her 30s, she applied to the University of Maryland. Again she was rejected. This time she was advised that the university rarely accepted women in its doctoral programs, particularly "older" women. But after meeting the chair of admissions at a social gathering and impressing him with her determination, she was admitted into the Department of Counseling and Personnel Services.

Sandler had been interested in doing her thesis on the career decisions of young women, but her adviser would not permit it. "Research on women is not real research," he told her.

While she worked on her doctorate, she taught part-time in the Psychology Department. Teaching was a first love, and she thought she did it well. After she earned her PhD in 1969, she continued to teach part-time at Maryland and another institution, earning less than $5,000, she recalled, for a total class load of 21 credit hours.

The University of Maryland was expanding rapidly with the arrival of the baby boomer generation, and that included the Psychology Department. There were seven new positions, and Sandler hoped she might get one because some were supposed to go to recent PhDs and there was no prohibition on hiring the department's graduates. But she was crushed when she was not even considered. She turned to one of her male colleagues to try to find out why.

"Let's face it," he told her, "you come on too strong for a woman."

Those words, she later recalled, would eventually change not only her own life, but, in short order, the lives of millions of American women and girls. And, she also conceded, "I don't think I would have noticed if they'd said, 'you come on too strong.' The problem was that phrase 'too strong for a woman.'"

But first she went home and cried: "I blamed myself for speaking up a few times at staff meetings. I blamed myself for discussing professional issues with faculty members. I regretted my participation in classes as a graduate student."

Then her husband asked, "Are there any strong men in the department?"

"They are all strong," she replied.

"Then it is not you," Jerry reassured her. "It is sex discrimination."

Despite her supportive husband, Sandler was not ready to apply that label to her own situation. "Like many women at that time," she explained, "I was somewhat ambivalent about the women's movement and halfway believed the press descriptions of its supporters as 'abrasive,' 'man-hating,' 'radical,' and 'unfeminine.' Surely I was not like that."

Reflecting on reporters' later description of her personality as "peppery," Sandler said, "What has stood me in good stead is that I'm quite good at being firm but not abrasive. I rarely, if ever, vent my anger in public meetings and I was sufficiently 'socialized' to be pleasant, etc., so I think, if anything, I probably smile too much and am not as nasty as I sometimes would like to be."

But on that day, the rejection stung. And in quick succession, there were two more of them. Sandler recalled, "A researcher spent nearly an hour of his interview with me explaining why he wouldn't hire women because they stayed home from work when their children were sick. (That my children were in high school was deemed irrelevant.) Subsequently, an employment agency counselor looked at my résumé and told me that I was 'not really a professional,' but 'just a housewife who went back to school.'"

She could no longer rationalize the problem away.

The men "insured that my eyes would never be closed again," Sandler reflected. "I would 'notice' that there had never been a woman with tenure in my department, although a woman would be hired, stay for two to three years, move on, and be replaced by another woman, who would go through the same cycle. I would 'notice' that the male doctoral students in my department went on to good full-time jobs while the women students had no offers, or were only offered temporary and/or part-time jobs." She remembered being turned down for a prestigious merit scholarship "because I was married, and the male it was given to 'needed' it more than I did."

"What had happened to me has happened to many women. We simply did not ascribe any pattern to experiences such as these I have mentioned," explained Sandler. "It is only in retrospect that we see them for what they were: a pattern of experiences based on overt and subtle discrimination."

When things went wrong in her life, Sandler turned to what she called *bibliotherapy*, reading up on a problem to try to solve it. Although she had never been interested in becoming a lawyer, she began studying anti-discrimination laws. "Knowing that sex discrimination was immoral," she recalled, "I assumed it would also be illegal." But she discovered what many of her academic peers were learning: they had no protections under the new civil rights laws.

As part of her review, she read a report published by the U.S. Commission on Civil Rights. She recalled thinking, "I'll read up on what the civil rights movement has been doing because maybe there's some strategies there that can make sense that can be used with women."

In retelling the story in later years, Sandler did not identify the report, but it was likely *Jobs & Civil Rights: The Role of the Federal Government in Promoting Equal Opportunity in Employment and Training*, written by Brookings Institution economist Richard P. Nathan and published by the Civil Rights Commission in April 1969.

Chapter 4 of the report, titled "The Contract Compliance Machinery," reviewed the enforcement history of Executive Order 11246, issued by President Johnson on September 24, 1965, to prohibit job discrimination by federal employers. The executive order, it noted, "also requires that federal contractors take affirmative action 'to ensure that applicants are employed, and that employees are treated during employment, without regard to their race, color or national origin.'"

A footnote was appended to that statement, and "being an academic," Sandler said she was often drawn to footnotes. She turned to the back of the report and read: "A ban against discrimination based on sex was added effective October 1968."

Sandler frequently recalled that she "shrieked" when she read the footnote. It was, in her telling, "a genuine 'Eureka' moment." She recognized that "since most universities and colleges had federal contracts, they were forbidden from discriminating in employment on the basis of sex." There was "a legal route," she said, but "few people knew it at the time."

In fact, Johnson had actually issued the revised executive order, Number 11375, on October 13, 1967, but contemporary news accounts had focused on its prohibition on sex discrimination in federal workplaces. The new requirements on federal contractors took effect a year later. Up until then, the Labor Department's Office of Federal Contract Compliance (OFCC) (currently called the Office of Federal Contract Compliance Programs) had directed its attention to construction contractors and their record on hiring minorities, working out agreements such as the so-called Philadelphia Plan, which addressed the situation in that city. In addition, the department had been slow in issuing regulations to enforce the new requirements. (Sandler later discovered that before she learned about the executive order, Betty Friedan (author of the ground-breaking book *The Feminine Mystique* in 1963) had, in fact, made "a passing reference" to it in a speech Friedan delivered at Cornell University.)

As the Civil Rights Commission's report observed:

The machinery for implementing Executive Order 11246 is widely dispersed and little known even within the Federal Government. It cuts horizontally across the entire Federal establishment. Altogether the Federal Government in March 1967 employed 228 full-time equal employment specialists for Federal contracts and 40 specialists on a greater than half-time basis. These submerged emissaries for equal employment are not unlike thousands of other Federal bureaucrats working for causes to which they are personally, as well as professionally, committed. But what makes the contract compliance specialist's job stand out is that he is designated to achieve a policy objective which frequently conflicts with the basic function or functions of the agency by which he is employed.

Sandler recalled that, at the time, she was "totally naïve" about politics. Her political experience was limited to voting, making a few small contributions to candidates, and serving once as a poll watcher.

After shrieking over her discovery, she began to question herself. "I said I must have read it wrong. There's a mistake here somewhere. This can't be. Somebody would have noticed," she said.

But Sandler's mother had taught her to ask questions. "If you don't know something, you can't learn until you ask," she recalled her mother telling her. "All they can say is 'no.'" So Sandler placed a phone call to the Labor Department. She was fortunate, she recalled, "that the secretary I spoke with put me through to a fairly high official" in the OFCC.

Vincent Macaluso came to Washington in the early 1960s, after combat in Italy during World War II. He served first on a labor policy advisory committee in the Kennedy Administration and then for the Committee on Equal Employment Opportunity, the predecessor to the Equal Employment Opportunity Commission. He joined the Labor Department in 1965 and was serving as assistant director of the contract compliance office when Sandler phoned.

"Franklin Delano Roosevelt was my hero," Macaluso recalled in an interview late in life. Growing up during the Depression, he said, "I was fired up by arguments with my father, who was a Republican. And it just appalled me that we had all these unemployed people and the Republicans weren't doing anything about it except talking about charity."

Macaluso invited Sandler to come talk. Once again, her insecurities kicked in. She thought, "Oh God, he must be coming on to me. How am I going to handle this? Do I really want to do this?"

But she mustered her courage and went to his downtown office. "He's been waiting for someone to do this," she recalled. "And he's so happy to see me. And we talk about filing a complaint. I have no law training whatsoever at that point. But he secretly teaches me about what the executive order means."

For many years, Sandler protected Macaluso's identity when she recounted the story. He was a civil servant, she recalled, without any authority from his political bosses "to be proselytizing this way. . . . Bureaucrats aren't supposed to promote."

But in Sandler, he had found an eager acolyte. "I know as soon as she contacted me, I figured, 'This is going to be great if she really will go through with it,'" said Macaluso. "Of course, she didn't know what she had, and why should she? These are the intricacies of bureaucrats."

Macaluso explained to Sandler that she didn't have to file a lawsuit—all she had to do was make a complaint. "You can write one letter to one university," he told her, "and you can write the same letter to 270 universities because they all . . . take from the federal till. So that's your opportunity."

In fact, Macaluso himself drafted the template that Sandler used for all the complaints she filed. He also coached her on how to get members of Congress to apply pressure on Nixon administration appointees to get them to follow through.

Before Sandler managed to track down Macaluso, she had joined the Women's Equity Action League (WEAL). WEAL was founded by Ohio attorney Elizabeth Boyer in 1968, after Boyer became alarmed by NOW's focus on abortion rights and its protest tactics. WEAL was, in Sandler's words, "a more 'middle-of-the-road' group which would appeal to more 'conservative' and larger groups of women." It focused on issues involving legal and tax inequities, education and employment; members of Congress, lawyers, and a judge were recruited for its early board of directors. By the end of 1969, it had chapters in 22 states.

Sandler said she would never have joined NOW at that point "because it picketed and looked very radical to someone like myself who was just discovering that perhaps there was indeed discrimination. I hadn't even heard of the word *feminist.*"

Macaluso drafted the first complaint, which cited discriminatory practices at all U.S. colleges and universities with more specifics about the University of Maryland. He said Sandler would need some evidence, but told her "just figure out the numbers of women in each department." She compiled the figures for Maryland by reviewing the staff directory and then visiting departments when the gender of faculty members was ambiguous. "It was about as inelegant data as you could get," she recalled.

The complaint was filed on January 31, 1970—two days after Friedan and Mink testified to the Senate committee. Sandler prepared it, and WEAL President Nancy E. Dowding, a counselor at Cuyahoga Community College in Cleveland, signed it—with some nervousness, Sandler recalled. Macaluso told Sandler it would help if she had a title, so she made one up: "chairman of WEAL's Action Committee on Federal Contract Compliance." It was a committee of one. Sandler said she decided that "I'll never be in academe again," but because she could fall back on her husband's financial support, she knew she had "a luxury that some women did not."

At the time Sandler was still teaching part time, but she decided to give that up. "If I came on 'too strong for a woman,' I would never be 'good enough' for an academic career," she recalled. "In that sense there was little to 'give up'; I certainly had no sense of sacrifice."

In its initial three-page letter, WEAL called on Labor Secretary George P. Shultz to "instruct the Office of Federal Contract Compliance to insist that *all* Federal agencies doing business with universities and colleges enforce the Executive Orders which have been completely ignored. We know of no meaningful compliance efforts that have been undertaken." WEAL asked OFCC to "institute an immediate *'class' action* and *compliance review* for *all* universities and colleges receiving Federal contracts. We ask that as stated in the Executive Orders, *universities end discrimination* and *take affirmative action* 'to ensure that applicants are employed, and that employees are treated during employment, without regard to . . . sex.'"

The letter said that in Maryland's College of Arts and Sciences, "nine out of the 15 departments examined had no women who were Full Professors, although all had women in the lower academic ranks." The complaint said the same pattern persisted among college administrators. In Maryland's School of Education, it noted, only one department—Special Education—was headed by a woman. In the College of Arts and Sciences, only the Department of Dance was headed by a woman. "In fact," the letter concluded, "the *proportion* of women in college and university leadership positions is *lower now* than it was 25 or even 10 years ago" (italics in original).

The letter was accompanied by 80 pages of documentation. Sandler found two other studies of faculty women, one done by political scientist Jo Freeman at the University of Chicago and the other by Columbia University's Women's Liberation, that showed the same reality: the higher the rank, the fewer number of women, in addition to large disparities when the percentage of women who had earned doctorates was compared with the percentage of women faculty members. Sandler filled out the complaint with "other bits and pieces, and quotes. . . ." Macaluso, she noted, "had said that quantity was important since most people wouldn't read it but would assume that if it was thick, it must be documentary."

"It was a time of no Xerox machines, no Kinko's," Sandler remembered in 2011. "The only institutions with Xerox machines were government, big corporations, universities, and big non-profits." She prevailed on someone who worked for the Ford Foundation to make 100 or 200 copies—her recollection varied—on the foundation's copy machine.

Another focal point of women's activism at that time was Catherine East, who had served as technical adviser to Kennedy's Presidential Commission on the Status of Women and helped to write its seminal 1963 report. Sandler recalled that East had access to a copier and free government postage. "She was the great center of the women's movement. . . a great source of information and of putting people together."

Women used that old-fashioned device, the telephone, to contact each other. Still, Sandler recalled, "long distance calls were expensive back then." She had never met a feminist before, and she confided to Macaluso that if East or Boyer had turned out to be "nasty or mean-spirited," she would have "dropped out of the women's movement."

But that didn't happen. Instead word spread quickly, through informal networks, women's conferences, and a few media outlets. "I quickly became an expert," Sandler said, "not because I really knew that much then, but because what I did know was so much more than anyone else at that time."

After she filed the initial complaint, a Maryland colleague asked why she couldn't "'be a lady' about the whole thing." She responded "rather angrily," she recalled. "'I've been a 'lady' for over 40 years and where has it gotten me?' I would never care about being 'lady-like' again."

Nearly 50 years after Sandler and Macaluso collaborated on the first complaint, the admiration that they felt for each other shone through when they sat for separate filmed interviews with journalist Sherry Boschert, just a few years before they died. They both took conspiratorial glee in recalling the hiring revolution they had hatched together.

"Bunny was such a . . . wonderful activist . . . such a sparkplug," Macaluso said. "She just took off with it."

"I just wanted to change the world," he concluded. "And I had a lot of fun."

Sandler said Macaluso was "a fair-minded attorney by training." Having worked for the government and the nonprofit world, he was "coming from a different place," Sandler noted. In addition, he was "a very decent human being."

Asked why she felt Macaluso was motivated to help her, Sandler responded matter of factly: "He has daughters."

2

The General

No one would have been surprised if Jean King had met Bunny Sandler when the Sandlers passed through Ann Arbor in the early 1960s. The town was half the size it is today, and they were both young mothers, trying to find an outlet for their advanced degrees and professional dreams.

While Sandler dabbled with courses in the University of Michigan's School of Social Work, King took low-level jobs all around the university. Well-educated women joined the League of Women Voters, where they could discuss important issues, educate voters, and speak up—politely—at city council meetings; one of its presidents came up with the idea for the Center for the Continuing Education of Women (CCEW) (now called the Center for the Education of Women), and lobbied it through to reality.

But King and Sandler would not meet for nearly a decade—after Sandler found her footnote and King found a home in the Democratic Party. They would work together to put Vincent Macaluso's strategy to work against the college that held the second-largest volume of federal contracts, the University of Michigan (U-M).

Jean Ledwith was born in 1924, four years before Bunny Resnick, and the older of two daughters with a mother who worked outside the home. Ida Resnick helped her husband run their women's sportswear store in Rockaway, New Jersey. Like Bunny Resnick, Nettie Ledwith studied psychology, earning a doctorate from the University of

Pittsburgh before going on to write about using Rorschach tests to evaluate children.

Like Sandler, Jean King was, by all reports, a precocious girl, who skipped half of the first grade and graduated early from Mt. Lebanon High School outside of Pittsburgh. Her athletically inclined mother wanted her to take up sports. "But," King later recalled, "I was younger, shorter, and smaller than my classmates, so I wasn't competitive. . . ." But she brought a competitor's zeal to all other aspects of her life.

After King graduated, her parents made her return to high school for a fifth year, during which she studied typing, mechanical drawing, and French. Then, in September 1941, she moved to Ann Arbor to enroll at the University of Michigan.

She started as a chemistry major, but three years later switched to English. However, King believed her years of math and science courses served her well: "I learned to think like a scientist," she remembered. "That was helpful for a lawyer, since the scientific standard of proof is much higher than the legal standard."

After living for a year in a residence hall, she joined Zeta Tau Alpha sorority and moved into the sorority house. In June 1943, she moved into Muriel Lester House, one of the campus's first student co-ops. While she was there, she met John King, an engineering and naval architecture student who was living at another co-op three blocks away.

Over Thanksgiving break, Jean had what may have been her first major confrontation with the university when she was suspended for two months after she and John hitchhiked to her home in Pittsburgh. She appealed to an assistant dean, who told Jean she could resume her studies if she and John agreed to get married. They did—on December 11, in front of the fireplace at Lester House.

By then the United States was deep into World War II, and in 1944, Jean followed John to his wartime job at Terminal Island in California. She stood by him when he was jailed for eight months at the federal prison in Danbury, Connecticut, for holding fast to his beliefs as a conscientious objector.

The Kings preserved the letters they wrote each other while John was behind bars. Years later, when Jean granted a historian permission to quote from them, she wrote: "This is not a period of our lives that we discuss very much; generally not at all since it was painful and we would just as soon forget it. I, for one, have never reread the letters since I thought it would hurt."

After the war, the Kings returned to Ann Arbor and earned their degrees. Over the years, she worked for the university in a variety of jobs, as a waitress in her dormitory, an assistant in the Chemistry Department's library, a clerk for the Detroit Area Project, an editor for both the University Press and the Survey Research Center, an office manager for the Engineering Research Institute, an interviewer of engineering students in danger of flunking out, and a secretary in the Psychology Department.

She later recalled, "I worked all over the university. . . . I knew the university pretty well. And I knew the hiring system, so I came to this with a lot of experience. . . . I wouldn't say that I had good sources of information and contacts. I had opportunities to observe. Nobody was feeding me any information. I was drawing my own conclusions."

In another interview, she said, "I knew how scarce women faculty were. I knew how they were generally treated, and how they were talked about by their colleagues. I certainly knew how. . . female graduate students were treated." King recalled that the only female instructor she had had at Michigan was Marie Hartwig, who taught her to play golf on the field behind her dormitory.

During that same time, King earned a master's in history, writing her thesis under the supervision of longtime U-M Professor Sidney Fine. A few years later, in 1957, John King went to work as an engineer for Ford Motor Company, designing seatbelts and other safety equipment until he retired nearly 30 years later.

Three children, a boy and two girls—Andrew, Nancy, and Sally— quickly followed, with Jean giving birth to their last child at age 37, comparatively late for the women of her generation.

In 1948, before her children were born, King had worked for five years as secretary to Theodore Newcomb, a social psychology professor. She recalled that the most she earned in one year was $2,000—the equivalent of $21,000 in 2019 dollars. One of the frequent "bullet points" in her list of grievances against the university was that women in clerical jobs were paid such low salaries that many of them could qualify for food stamps.

Newcomb founded the doctoral program in social psychology at Michigan and chaired the department until his retirement 25 years later. He and King worked together during the depths of the McCarthy era, and he shared King's progressive politics. In 1956, when U-M President Harlan Hatcher removed three faculty members under pressure from the House Un-American Activities Committee (HUAC), Newcomb challenged both Hatcher and HUAC in a stirring speech to the faculty senate. At the time, Newcomb himself was on HUAC's lists because of his own memberships in leftist groups in the 1930s.

King later recalled that she "studied the University through Ted." Social psychology, she noted, was a liberal discipline at a time when the rest of the university was more conservative. As Newcomb's secretary, she learned his key contacts in other departments and which ones shared his political views. "Secretaries," she declared a half-century later, "have no power, but they know a lot." The academic world, she came to learn, was different from the legal or corporate world, which women could be taught to navigate. "Academia is a secret society. And its secrets are not shared easily," she noted.

King also was well positioned to observe, objectively, how the department's lone female faculty member was treated. "I could see what she was going through," King later recalled.

As a child during the Depression, King had visited relatives in the impoverished rural South; her daughter Nancy later recalled that her mother had "a keen sense of outrage" when she encountered societal wrongs. King noted that Newcomb didn't set out to train a liberal activist, but their association helped shape her political interests.

Unlike the apolitical Sandler, King found an outlet for her outrage in the Democratic Party. In 1957, she became a precinct captain and was proud when her work was recognized by the local party organization. When a pregnancy kept her from going door to door, she relied on her Republican counterparts to keep track of her new neighbors. In 1964, the Kings and the Newcombs were among the Ann Arbor Democrats who took out a *Daily* ad endorsing Wes Vivian, who upset the incumbent Republican member of Congress the year Johnson defeated Republican Sen. Barry Goldwater in a landslide.

In its inaugural issue in spring 1972, *Ms.* magazine coined the term "Click Moment" to identify that point in a woman's life where something happens that first sparks her feminist consciousness. King had a "Click Moment" of sorts when she attended the 1964 Democratic National Convention as a volunteer. She recalled overhearing Ann Arbor Attorney Peter Darrow, a convention delegate, "make a crack" about Millie Jeffrey, then the United Auto Workers' top-ranking woman. King said she decided that she would have to earn a law degree if she wanted to "be taken seriously."

"I wanted credentials in order to be able to tell people what to do and to make them do it," she explained. Jeffrey, she recalled late in life, had been susceptible to Darrow's ridicule because she "didn't have an academic degree." (Jeffrey actually *had* earned both bachelor's and master's degrees from top-ranked universities, but probably did not flaunt them in her union-organizing work.)

Armed with letters of recommendation from Newcomb and Fine, King was admitted to the University of Michigan Law School's Class of 1968 at the age of 41, about the same age her mother had been when she went back to college. There were only 10 women in the class of 327 students.

Not much had changed around U.S. law schools in the decade since Ruth Bader Ginsburg had entered Harvard's. The Michigan Law School still had no women professors, and King recalled that she could go for three weeks without passing another woman in the halls of its Gothic-style buildings. "The women students did not organize themselves in any way, and in my first year we were often ignored by our teachers," King noted. "In Civil Procedure, I sat every day in the third row and always put my hand up to answer a question. I never once got called on."

In King's memory, only one of her professors treated men and women students the same: Thomas Kauper, who began teaching antitrust law around that time and was 11 years younger than King. "He was so different from all the others," she recalled. "It was a surprise."

Jean Campbell, the first director of the university's CCEW, later recalled that King was among the women the center had helped in its early days. "I remembered that we helped her get 'part-timeness' in the Law School when she wanted to go back to Law School," said Campbell.

King, she said, was possibly the first if not the only part-time student in the Law School at that time. "It was that kind of thing that we were doing a lot of in the beginning, taking an individual woman and helping her take the next step, as we used to say," Campbell explained.

If King started as a part-timer, it does not appear that she stayed that way for long. She was, however, the oldest student in her class, roughly twice the age of the others. But she viewed that as an advantage. "I was much more sure of myself," she recalled. Many of her professors, she thought, were like her husband. "I understood middle-aged men. I did not see them as authority figures."

King earned good grades and made the editorial staff of the *Law Review* each of her three years. At the time, the American Trial Lawyers Association (ATLA) (now the American Association of Justice) gave an award to a graduating student at the law school the association's president had attended; in 1968, when Samuel Langerman was the ATLA's president, it was the University of Michigan's turn. King received a $500 award as the outstanding graduate for her "scholarship and academic achievement, responsible leadership in student affairs, and demonstrated concern for the problems of American society." When he presented the award, Dean Francis A. Allen said, "Coincident with her very successful and productive Law School career, Mrs. King has continued to be intensely active in school, civic, and political affairs. She has indeed demonstrated a sincere concern for the problems of her community, state, and nation."

King, notably, accomplished all of this while raising three children under the age of ten. She always credited her husband for his support, and specifically his help with child care.

As Sandler was trying to land an academic appointment, King was trying to launch a legal career. She began studying for the bar exam and commuting to Lansing to jobs in the state government. She was involved with redrafting the state's Motor Vehicle Code and, as a staff member to the governor's Commission on Law Enforcement and Criminal Justice, reviewed bail reform initiatives to see how they could be adapted for Michigan.

She was also moving up the ladder of the Michigan Democratic Party—and experiencing some of the same frustrations that women were encountering in the civil rights and anti-war movements. By 1968, she had risen from precinct captain to Fifth Ward chairman to Washtenaw County Executive Committee to State Central Committeewoman. Following the Democrats' tumultuous convention in Chicago that summer, the party convened a commission to discuss party reforms. King fumed that after a year's worth of discussion, the commission's first report ignored the concerns of women, as well as blacks and students. It "never got around to discussing women," she recalled a few years later.

King drafted a resolution, calling for the party to achieve equal representation of women at all levels. But when she presented it at the Washtenaw County Democratic Convention in December 1969, no woman joined in supporting her. "I couldn't find a single woman to speak for it—not because they didn't believe in it, but because there just weren't very many women who would stand on their own two feet and speak out," King noted. Washtenaw County Democrats actually approved the resolution, but the state convention failed to advance it. The following year, King led the formation of a Women's Caucus in the Michigan party, the first of its kind in the country.

King learned important lessons in the process: "It was an inside/inside operation. There was not much retaliation which could be taken against Democratic women." The party, King explained, relied on the labor of women, and party leaders did not want the negative publicity associated with denying them top party jobs. "The HEW effort was an outside/inside operation and had to be," said King.

Party women, King later recalled, faced the same problem that women in academia did: They were isolated and had no way to share their experiences. "That needed to be overcome, too," she realized.

As the new decade began, women were moving from neighborhood coffee klatches to national conferences to share their stories. And at a conference in New York City, Jean King found out about the legal strategy that a like-minded woman who had never gone to law school was starting to pursue.

3
The Complaint

"At the end of the 1960s," Bunny Sandler recalled nearly four decades later, "the women's movement is only a few years old. There is little awareness of sex discrimination throughout the nation. The words *sexism* and *sexist* have not yet been invented, nor the words *sexual harassment* or *date rape*. Even the words *sex discrimination* have only just entered the lexicon. . . . There is not much interest in women's issues except from a few women, a few small women's groups, and a few men of good will, and some negative members of the press. . . . There are no newsletters dealing with women's rights and discrimination. There are no conferences on women's rights and discrimination. I remember talking to someone, saying, 'Wouldn't it be great if there was a conference that was just about women?' Thus, it is difficult for women both to gather and to share information."

But that was about to change. In the spring of 1970, Jean King traveled to New York City for the founding meeting of the Professional Women's Caucus. Sandler spoke, as did future U.S. Supreme Court Justice Ginsburg. Ginsburg was teaching law at Rutgers University after experiencing her own problems trying to find an appropriate job. When Rutgers students founded the *Women's Rights Law Reporter* that year, she served as their adviser.

Sandler recalled that as television cameras began rolling, someone mentioned that women weren't allowed to be camera "men." One of the men called out that it was because the cameras were too heavy for women to carry. Sandler said that a woman on stage who was of "medium or even small height rushed over to the cameras and grabbed one from the men and raced across the stage amidst much cheering and shouting from the audience of women."

Sandler and King made a good team. While both were short in stature, their skills and personalities complemented each other: Sandler was the academic, King, the lawyer. While Sandler fretted that she probably "smiled too much," King considered herself to be "a bomb-thrower." They both recognized that, in King's words, "women are afraid of confrontation. They have been so punished for standing up for themselves."

After she filed her complaint, Sandler sent out copies with a short press release to media outlets. On March 21, 1970, in an issue focused on education, the *Saturday Review* ran a short item on page 77 in a "Schools Make News" section:

> The Department of Labor has been requested to force an end to alleged discriminatory practices against women by all universities and colleges doing business with the federal government. In a formal complaint to Secretary of Labor George P. Shultz, the Women's Equity Action League . . . accused the institutions of higher education of wholesale discrimination in the hiring and promotion of women faculty members and requested the department to enforce presidential orders forbidding sexual discrimination.

Unlike the other publications, the magazine included Sandler's name and address as a contact.

Along with her conference appearances, she recalled, "it was enough to open the dikes." She advised the women who contacted her to collect what data they could about their university, and after they sent it to her, she filed a complaint against that university on their behalf.

By May, specific complaints were filed against 43 colleges and universities. They were, in a tally published in *Science* magazine, "public and private institutions, rich and poor, Northern and Southern: Harvard; City University of New York; the universities of North Carolina, Tennessee, Pittsburgh, Boston and Maryland; Rutgers; Southern Illinois; Brandeis; Massachusetts Institute of Technology; Smith; Amherst, Radcliffe; and a group of small colleges—DePauw, Marymount College in New York, Clarion State College in Pennsylvania, and others."

By now, Sandler was getting help from Ann Scott, a professor of English at the University of Buffalo (now the State University of New York at Buffalo). After founding the Buffalo chapter of NOW, Scott became the national organization's "federal compliance coordinator" and joined Sandler in encouraging women to gather the information that would back up complaints. Sandler recalled later that Scott lived in Baltimore, not far from where Sandler lived in Washington's Maryland suburbs, making it easy for the two women to work together and lobby federal officials. A Boston area NOW chapter had been the party to file the complaint against Harvard.

King returned to Ann Arbor, fired up by the strategy Sandler had outlined in New York City. But she felt she didn't have the time to pursue a complaint against the University of Michigan. She was commuting an hour to Lansing, organizing Democratic women, raising three children, and planning the next step in her legal career.

CCEW, she thought, was the logical organization to bring the complaint. But, she later recalled, "I didn't recognize then that some things have to be brought from the outside because the insiders are relatively helpless and easily squashed. I later understood that if [the center] had attempted to bring a federal complaint, it would have lost its funding in six months."

The center was then the most visible campus institution addressing women's concerns, but it had only recently secured a permanent line item in the university's budget. Its director, Jean Campbell, was married to Angus Campbell, the director of U-M's Survey Research Center who was about to become head of its powerful parent, the Institute for Social Research (ISR). She was a member of the same generation as U-M President Robben Fleming and thought to be a woman to whom he listened.

But Campbell also knew what Michigan women were up against. After CCEW opened its doors in 1963, she reached out to "the gatekeepers," the associate deans of the university's colleges, to let them know that the center would be working to help more women enter their programs. "And it was interesting that there wasn't anybody who might have been thought to be on our wavelength. . . not even, especially something like Landscape Architecture, which feared that women would want to design their own gardens and that was it. That really was the attitude from one school to the other," Campbell recalled.

Later, when she contacted William Hubbard, dean of the School of Medicine from 1959–70, about ways to attract more women to the Medical School, she found him to be "very sympathetic, very much interested, but we immediately realized that he was talking about physician's assistants and we were talking about doctors!"

"Jean Campbell," King noted later, "wouldn't have lasted five minutes" if she had been involved with the complaint. Filing it "made the university very angry. Anybody connected with it was in jeopardy." So, King figured, "I had to do it myself."

Around the country, the drumbeat about sex discrimination on campuses was growing louder. In March, 1970, 12 people testified before the House members of Michigan's Joint Senate-House Labor Committee, charging that the state's public universities discriminated against women in admissions, scholarships, counseling, placement, and staff policies. In a March 23 letter, Arthur M. Ross, then U-M's vice president for state relations and planning, responded to a query from the chairman of the House committee. By including 392 teaching fellows in his tables, Ross suggested that women represented 19 percent of the faculty of the College of Literature, Science, and the Arts (LSA), the university's largest unit. His charts did note, however, that across the university, there were only 46 women who were full professors. He also highlighted the work of CCEW to make the case that the university did not discriminate.

But across the country and in Washington, the voices of Sandler, Scott, and other faculty women were starting to be heard. As the U.S. Senate continued to wrestle over the Carswell nomination, Democratic Rep. Martha Griffiths of Michigan took to the U.S. House floor, criticizing the government's failure to enforce the executive order as it applied to sex discrimination. Griffiths was then a member of WEAL's national advisory board, and Sandler provided Griffiths with most of the background for her speech. Three weeks later, the government launched a contract compliance investigation of Harvard.

In the end, the Michigan women prepared their complaint without any direct involvement by WEAL or NOW. Only a handful of women worked on it. King could not remember whether she held another meeting or simply telephoned the friends who had attended her first FOCUS meeting to get their approval to file the complaint under the group's name and use their individual names with the press. The women included Marge Brazer, an economist and Democratic Party activist who was married to Harvey Brazer, an economics professor who had served in the Kennedy administration; Louella Cable, a biologist with the U.S. Fish and Wildlife Service, and Gertrude Drouyer, both members of the Business and Professional Women's Clubs; Margaret Klamp, an officer with the Ann Arbor League of Women Voters; and King's "best friend," Ruth Schelkun, a mental health professional whom King later recalled "had talked me through law school." Drouyer, who worked for the library that became the Bentley Historical Library, was the only university employee publicly identified with the group.

The sole Michigan professor who worked on the complaint—but was not publicly identified with it—was Elizabeth Douvan, a psychology professor. Douvan had been hired as a lecturer in 1958 after earning her doctorate at Michigan and working at the Survey Research Center. King had known Douvan since she was a graduate student, and Sandler had met her when she lived in Ann Arbor. As a full professor and holder of an endowed chair at the time of the complaint, Douvan was then one of the highest-ranking women in LSA. Douvan's name appeared on a list of FOCUS members found in King's papers, as were the names of six more women, only one of whom, Kate Bolton, was shown with an Ann Arbor address.

Sociologist Zelda Gamson, who worked with Douvan and considered her a mentor, said she knew that the professor had worked on the complaint. "I think she lent legitimacy to it," she said. Douvan, she recalled, "was a very good political operator within the University. She liked these guys." The professor, she said, was "very sophisticated" and "elegant in her speech." She "knew how to put herself together." But, Gamson said, Douvan was also "very left-wing." Like Ted Newcomb, she had been friends with the professors who had been expelled from the university during the McCarthy years. "She was," Gamson added, "a very kind person but very tough minded."

Douvan likely met King through her connections to Newcomb. In 1999, Douvan recalled that "there were places in the University that were better for women. And I happened to be in one of them. The Psychology Department was very advanced. We had three or four women by the time I became a faculty member."

But Douvan knew that was not the case in most departments. "I think it's hard to recognize that because there were so few women and because the atmosphere was chilly, we were just glad to have a place where we could do our work," she noted.

Douvan recalled that King "was alarmed when she discovered how much. . . how consistently women were paid less than men on the faculty. So she called a group of women together and we decided it was time to do something."

Douvan lent her statistical expertise to the preparation of the complaint. "We wanted it to be as accurate as possible," King noted. " . . . We were dropping this bomb."

In tutoring Sandler, Macaluso had stressed the importance of enlisting the support of members of Congress, and Sandler passed that strategy along to her lieutenants. King recruited Mary Yourd, a 55-year-old "Republican feminist well known in her party" to the group. Yourd had been active in efforts to repeal Michigan's restrictive abortion laws and was a member of the Michigan Women's Commission. Yourd was the daughter of a suffragist and a 1938 graduate of LSA.

Yourd's husband, Kenneth, had been assistant dean of the Law School when he died suddenly in October 1969. King remembered that Kenneth Yourd had arranged for her to receive a $250 grant at the end of her first year of Law School. In recalling Mary Yourd's involvement in the complaint, King never mentioned that Yourd had been widowed only months before the complaint was filed.

Douvan recalled Yourd as "a lovely, independent Ann Arbor citizen." She was "the most charming, warm, loving—and angry woman. I mean, she was pissed off!" King recalled that Yourd once suggested they should wear white gloves to a meeting, and King confessed she didn't own a pair. King remembered Yourd, who was ten years older than she was, as "considerably older. We would operate differently." Most importantly, they moved in different political circles. They agreed that a member of Congress would, in King's words, "respond better to an approach from a member of his party," and divided up their work accordingly.

Douvan echoed King's memory that the first gathering of FOCUS was very informal: "Jean just called a few old friends and said, 'Would you come by my house on Saturday . . .?' We were mainly going to talk about the fact that the women on the faculty were not paid what the men were, and didn't get the same kinds of opportunities, the glass ceiling, blah, blah, blah. So we all took the bit. . . ."

"And then it was decided by Jean, I think, or maybe by Jean and Mary, that women on the faculty would not actually do the signing of the complaint," she said. "Because at that time women on the faculty were very vulnerable and there was no reason why they could not just be fired by the department."

Throughout April and May 1970, King and Yourd worked, with input from Douvan, on gathering statistics about women employees and the status of students. On April 12, that job became easier when the *Michigan Daily* published a lengthy feature story in its Sunday magazine section under the provocative headline, "Women as University N-----Or, How a Young Female Student Sought Sexual Justice at the 'U' and Couldn't Find It Anywhere."

The article was written by Kathleen Shortridge, who was working on a master's degree in journalism and had researched the topic for a seminar on investigative reporting. An earlier version had appeared in a Journalism Department publication. Then Shortridge expanded her research, cleaned up a few statistical errors, and found a wider audience in the pages of the *Daily*.

Shortridge claimed no responsibility for the article's headline, an apparent word play on a statement the artist Yoko Ono had made the previous year: "Woman is the N----- of the World." In the end, Shortridge's reporting provided much of the statistical detail that was included in the complaint. "Nobody was at all defensive about these things," she recalled. "It was easy to get information . . . . The patterns were just quite clear."

The article began:

You won't find 'sexism' in the dictionary, but if you did, the definition would read like this:

> Sexism—n. 1. a belief that the human sexes have distinctive make-ups that determine their respective lives, usually involving the idea that one sex is superior and has the right to rule the other. 2. a policy of enforcing such asserted right. 3. a system of government and society based upon it. sexist, n., adj.

Shortridge went on to write:

> "You shouldn't be too harsh in judging the University for dis-
> criminating against women," more than one administrator has
> told me. "After all, the whole culture has that orientation and
> practical reasons exist for it."
>
> I'll grant the University reflects cultural attitudes; it also
> perpetuates and helps form them. Practical reasons help ex-
> plain sexism, but don't excuse it. Most people don't realize that
> a locker room mentality pervades the University, so the first
> step in changing discriminatory policies is to show that they
> exist.

Shortridge went on to chronicle her own experience, backed up by
statistics and jaw-dropping quotations from oblivious male administrators and professors. Shortridge noted that in four years at Michigan,
she had taken only one class taught by a woman. The numbers supported that: According to figures from the Office of the Vice President
for Academic Affairs, women represented only 4.3 percent of full professors, 10.8 percent of associate professors, and 1.2 percent of assistant
professors—or only 4.8 percent if the top three professorial ranks were
combined. Shortridge noted that that number fell well below wom-
en's 13.3 percent share of recent PhDs who were looking for academic
jobs.

Shortridge reported that 40 percent of "instructors" were women,
but that those were considered "dead-end jobs," held by persons who
did not hold a doctorate and had no plans to get one, many of them in
medical fields such as nursing and physical therapy.

Shortridge then highlighted the university's anti-nepotism policy,
writing, "Just as peasants tend to marry peasants, professors often tend
to marry professors."

But the university's official personnel rulebook stated that no person should be assigned to a post from which he or she might affect
the performance or promotion of a family member. That was generally interpreted to mean that departments could not hire spouses. The
result, Shortridge said, was that women often had to go talk to Eastern
Michigan University or Oakland University if they wanted a teaching
job.

Noting that much of the university's personnel decision-making was decentralized, Shortridge observed that individual attitudes could have a disproportionate impact on how women were treated. She cited these stories from academic women:

- The director of an institute told a psychology professor: "I rarely promote women. Men have better use for the extra money."
- A department head in LSA: "I don't like having women around because then I can't tell my dirty jokes."
- An English professor: "All these uppity women need is a better sex life."

One key discovery of Shortridge's reporting was that the university had a quota, based on gender, governing its first-year admissions policies.

Decades later, Shortridge could still recall her interviews with members of the admissions committee, all of whom were men: "I said, 'It's interesting because every year you seem to admit about 48 percent girls and 52 percent boys (men and women as we say now).' [The article actually reported that the split was closer to 45–55 percent.] He said, 'Yes, yes.' And so I said, 'So why do you suppose that is?' And he said, 'Well, I think they're probably more qualified.' So I said, 'Well, yes, but look at the data. Their grades are lower. Their SATs are lower.' . . . And finally he just said, 'Well, I think we just feel that's the right way to do it.'"

G.C. Wilson, executive associate director of admissions at that time, noted that in the 1960s, the proportion of women among qualified applicants "began to creep up, and it became apparent that unless something were done, women would soon outnumber the men in the freshman class. The Literary College was particularly interested in maintaining at least 55 percent males in the entering class." As a result, it was explained, the Admissions Office began admitting men who were less qualified than women applicants.

When Shortridge asked why it was important to maintain that split, Wilson puzzled over his answer before suggesting that men provided more support to the university in their contributions, work, and recruiting efforts. He also said they performed better and were more likely to finish their studies.

He then suggested that Shortridge speak with John E. Milholland, a psychology professor who sat on the admissions committee, and who provided what she described as her "least cordial" interview. But she and Milholland eventually discussed how the policy evolved. He explained that when the committee realized that women were about to outnumber men, "the automatic reaction of the members was that steps must be taken to prevent this 'overbalance.'"

"We just felt maintaining parity was a good policy," Milholland told her. "It was just a feeling in our bones. I don't know that we ever discussed it at all."

Upon further reflection, Milholland suggested several rationales. Men were culturally disadvantaged (less mature, lower grades) and consequently needed more help. Once admitted, men performed better. And men were the breadwinners and needed an education more. Shortridge obtained data demonstrating that women students had higher grade point averages and that only 60.8 percent of men who had entered Michigan in the fall of 1965 had graduated by 1969, compared with a 76.5 percent rate for women.

Shortridge also sarcastically observed that the concern about "disadvantaged" students apparently did not extend to the Medical School, where there were only 204 women among 1,583 students, or the College of Engineering, where there were only 89 women in a student body of 4,397.

Shortridge did acknowledge areas where she failed to find patterns of discrimination. The Placement Service required recruiters to follow federal anti-bias laws. She found no discrimination in the awarding of financial aid. And when she reviewed how women graduate students had fared in the $4,000 Rackham Prize competition, she found that they had done "startlingly well." They received a higher percentage of departmental nominations and a higher percentage of the prizes than their share of the student body. To make it that far, these women students were thought to be exceptionally well qualified. Dwight E. Durner, assistant to the dean of graduate fellowships, observed: "I've met a lot of these women, and they're qualified, serious scholars. They're aggressive. They're hustlers. And they're doing very well as far as research grants go."

But Shortridge noted that the hiring picture was not likely to improve quickly because universities were entering "an economic slump," and administrators acknowledged that the policy of "the last hired, first fired" applied to women.

Shortridge quoted Barbara Newell, an economist who was then serving as acting vice president for student affairs: "Women are traditionally marginal workers. They're hired with soft money grants (as opposed to appropriations), whose source cannot be depended on from year to year and they're non-tenured. As research funds get cut back, there will be a disproportionate loss of women."

Others observed that there was now a glut of PhDs seeking jobs, and the Placement Service was having trouble finding positions for graduates. Byron Groesbeck, then dean of U-M's Rackham Graduate School, said that as departments received less money, they would probably admit more men "who are more likely to finish, less likely to drop out and have babies."

Newell was a protégé of Fleming's, and, Shortridge said, the first woman to reach the Big 10's vice presidential ranks. (Shortridge noted that the number of top administrative jobs available to women had already declined because Michigan had just eliminated the anachronistic position of dean of women.)

Newell observed to Shortridge that women who were interested in administrative appointments could aspire to become a department head. But, she noted, that job is becoming "increasingly hellish, and the academic and professional rewards of the position are dropping. Now you see more women getting the post."

Shortridge concluded her article by quoting sociologist David Reisman:

> Even very gifted and creative young women are satisfied to assume that on graduation they will get underpaid ancillary positions . . . where they are seldom likely to [advance] to real opportunity. A certain throttling down occurs, therefore, both in college and later on, which then, in the usual vicious circle, allows men so mindful to depreciate women as incapable of the higher achievement.

Sandler's efforts had already gained enough traction around the country that Shortridge's article included a warning to university administrators. She cited the executive order and said that violating it "could theoretically result in cancelled government contracts, a threat which might make most university administrators eager to mend their ways."

Shortridge recalled that when King "learned that I was pulling together data that could be the basis of the complaint, she contacted me about it." In addition to lending her research and writing skills, Shortridge served as FOCUS's press contact when the complaint was filed six weeks after her article was published.

There was no shortage of things for the women to cite in making their case. Nearly 30 years later, King reeled off a long list:

> . . . [W]e cited the lack of women faculty (including none in the Law School and, as I recall, none in the Medical School), the low salaries of women faculty, the failure to hire and to promote women faculty. . .the lecturer ghetto for women faculty, the discrimination against women in graduate school (as I recall there were no women graduate students in math and I know there were no women faculty in math and that is only one program), the lack of scholarship, grant, and other financial support for women students, the very low rates of admission for women to professional schools (law and medicine), the lack of gynecological services at Health Service, the lack of varsity sports for women students and the otherwise very weak athletic program for women students, the low salaries for women staff from janitors to administrative assistants including women employees at the U-M Hospital. . . .

> We may have complained about student organizations which excluded women, including honor societies—but that may have come later. We probably complained about counseling (both by faculty and by the University's counseling services)— women students steered to sex-stereotyped jobs and sex-stereotyped graduate training. We probably also complained about the lack of women administrators at the U, the lack of women deans, department heads, the lack of their representation on important University committees. We may have complained about the total lack of women cheerleaders and women in the band.

But what became known as "the HEW complaint" was a two-page letter, focused solely on the university's hiring and admissions policies. The May 27, 1970, letter to then-Labor Secretary George Shultz called on him to "instruct" the contract compliance office "to insist that *all* federal agencies doing business with the University of Michigan enforce" the executive orders. The complaint cited the admissions quota and the lagging number of women who were hired after earning doctorates. It also asked the department to "investigate reports that highly educated women are employed by the University in clerical positions but expected to do administrative and supervisory work for clerical pay."

In noting that only 6.6 percent of professors were women, the complaint said that figure "does not give a true picture of the University. Nursing, for example, is traditionally a female profession. Forty of the university's 182 faculty members of professorial rank are in the School of Nursing. When the faculty of the School of Nursing is omitted from the calculations, women comprise only 5.3% of the university's professorial staff."

Perhaps most shockingly, the complaint said that of the more than 900 persons at the professorial rank in "the huge College of Literature, Science, and the Arts," only 34 were women. The pattern persisted in other disciplines that traditionally attracted more women: Only 6 out of 100 professors in the School of Education were women, only 12 out of 58 professors in the School of Social Work, and only 3 out of 14 in the School of Library Science.

While attention was naturally drawn to women faculty members, the university actually employed far more women in non-teaching jobs. The inclusion of their concerns in the original complaint helped ensure it would have a more far-reaching impact.

King and Yourd signed off on the letter with their home addresses and said they could provide the names of persons "who will testify in support of this complaint." They also sent a copy to Robert Finch, then secretary of the U.S. Department of Health, Education, and Welfare (HEW) (now the Department of Health and Human Services; the education piece moved to the Department of Education).

FOCUS also followed Sandler's media strategy: Send the complaint first to the newspapers rather than to the university. As Sandler explained, ". . . why give the university time to respond publicly? This way they would get a call from the newspaper saying, 'Charges have just been filed against you in terms of sex discrimination.' They wouldn't know what to do because they hadn't seen it. Sometimes they would say things they shouldn't.'"

King acknowledged that "the coordination of our filing and newspaper publicity was deliberate on our part." Copies were sent to reporters in Detroit and Ann Arbor with a press release Shortridge had prepared.

In her release, Shortridge quoted from Rep. Griffiths's floor speech:

> . . . most of these institutions discriminate outrageously against half our citizens—women. They neglect and disregard their potential talent. They place innumerable obstacles and hurdles in the way of academic women. Is our nation so rich in talent that we can afford to have our universities penalize the aspirations of half of our population? Should the Federal Government close its eyes to such unjust discrimination and continue to provide the billions of dollars that help to support those unjust practices?

In the *Detroit Free Press*, the story merited an eight-column headline in its women's section. A university spokesman said administrators would have no response until they had seen the complaint. The *Daily*, meanwhile, played the story on page 1.

In her press release, Shortridge wrote: "For the last decade, according to G.C. Wilson, Executive Associate Director of Admissions at the University of Michigan, the Office of Admissions has adjusted requirements to insure that an 'overbalance'—that is, a majority—of women would not occur in the freshman class." Although Wilson had described the policy and made his share of potentially embarrassing quotations, it was actually John Milholland, a member of the admissions committee, who had used the word *overbalance* in Shortridge's original *Daily* story. When the *Daily* called Wilson for a response, he said he could "not recall" saying such a thing and that "the requirements for admission are the same for everyone."

Shortridge responded in a letter to the *Daily*, saying she had first interviewed Wilson in February and returned a few days later because she wanted to make sure that her facts were correct. "I said, 'Mr. Wilson, I wanted to be sure I have some points straight. Are some less qualified men admitted in preference to more qualified women in order to maintain sex balance in the freshman class?' Mr. Wilson replied, 'Yes, that's right.'" She said she had retained the notes from her interviews.

On June 4, the *Free Press* published the university's short, formal response: "We shall try to do better." The article quoted a university spokesman as saying that the complaint was particularly appropriate at this time because the university was about to celebrate the centennial of the admission of women: "We have had and will continue to have this year, various celebrations of outstanding women of Michigan." Statistical information demonstrating higher male than female enrollment and faculty is, he said, a reflection of a "general situation" in society.

"The society as a whole tends to be male dominated although this situation has been changing and surely we can anticipate further progress toward equal treatment," the unidentified spokesman said. He highlighted the fact that the university had a woman dean, a vice president, and a regent—and might be the only coeducational college in the country that did. However, he said, "This only begs questions legitimately raised." The reporter noted that the dean in question led the School of Nursing and the vice president was serving on an acting basis.

But it was summertime in Ann Arbor. And for the time being, the complaint was easy for top administrators to ignore. Although the "action minutes" of the university's executive officers for the month of June suggest they were still trying to identify a possible site for a campus day care center, there was no follow-up action item related to the complaint. At the July 7, 1970, meeting, under an item labeled "Employment of Women," Allan Smith, vice president for academic affairs, was supposed to "proceed on determining average salary of women in each of the schools and colleges."

But King and others were continuing to gather information for the day when the federal government came calling. In June, she got a job in Ann Arbor as a referee with the Washtenaw County Juvenile Court, a time, she recalled, "when we were doing a lot of heavy work on the complaint." One of her summer interns was an African-American law school student named Saul Green. King said she "constantly sent Saul on errands" related to the complaint. Years later, he served as the U.S. attorney for the Eastern District of Michigan during the Clinton administration.

Looking back, King acknowledged later that a university president "really doesn't have any power to change hiring and so forth unless he really, really tries extremely hard. But the departments and the colleges are very stubborn. And depending on what generation those deans come from . . . it can be really very difficult to change their culture. That's the reason this administrative complaint was necessary." Then she added with a chuckle, "We'd still be there if there hadn't been something to do."

4
The Times

The HEW complaint broke into the headlines during a two-year period that, by any measure, was arguably the most tumultuous period in the University of Michigan's long history.

John Papanek, a *Daily* sports editor who went on to reach the top ranks of American sports journalism, captured the climate he found when he arrived on campus in the fall of 1969:

> Thanks to so much of what our upper classmates had done and gone through during the crucial run-up years of '66 to '68, September 1969 seemed, to us at least, to be the launch date for every kind of freedom imaginable—social, sexual, cultural, musical, academic, pharmaceutical—and nobody could tell us what we could *not* do, least of all the stuffy University administrators in the brand new brick fortress built to house and protect them from us, or the bureaucrats who thought they ran things from Lansing and, for that matter, Washington, DC.
>
> From September through November '69, the University raged and seethed in an endless series of battles, running from cold to very, very hot—between students and administrators; students and landlords; students and other students; students and police; administrators and faculty; townies and the University community. Just as Richard Nixon would gaze out his White House window and wonder whether the heaving sea of pro-

test-ors and pacifists would ever go away, or at least get haircuts, so too did University President Robben Fleming, an otherwise lovely, anti-war liberal former labor relations expert, wonder how and when his worst nightmare would ever end.

In his memoir, *Tempests into Rainbows: Managing Turbulence,* Fleming dealt at length with his strategies for managing student protests. Of returning to campus from a vacation at the end of his first year, he wrote: "We did not know it at the time, but the problems would not peak until the spring and summer of 1970. . . ."

In a 2001 interview, Barbara Newell recalled:

During my entire time at the University of Michigan, the social environment was so yeasty, that there was really hardly a moment for reflection. It's hard to really convey that. But the day I walked into the Student Affairs Vice President's Office, I went a little early, and when I got there, I discovered that the rugby team was sitting in my office, in a sit-in, demanding that I do something about the paving of a rugby field. And I only had three sit-ins that day.

In an interview a half-century later, Newell recalled, "We were measuring success or failure of our job by whether somebody *died* on campus, not by the quality of the education being offered. That is a horrible thing for an educator to be saying."

Looking back at campus protests that took place in the 1800s, Fleming observed:

What those events tell us is that when we place large numbers of young people in a relatively small geographic area and subject them to a steady regimen of study, there are going to be occasional outbursts. Students are in the prime of their physical energy, they are removed from parental restraints, they are not yet fully mature in their judgment, they find a certain joy in challenging their elders, and alcoholic stimulants are bound to contribute to unruliness.

What made this later period different was not the fact that there were problems, but that serious unrest in the larger society came on top of what might be described as the "normal" agitation. We were involved in an unpopular war in Vietnam, we were engaged in civil unrest over racial differences, and protesters had learned the advantages inherent in the tactics of civil disobedience. On top of that, our values were changing. There were severe strains on the traditional family structure; drugs, particularly marijuana, had entered the scene; premarital sex was no longer the taboo it had once been; and respect and civility were lacking.

The 1969–70 academic year began with students jamming a Regents meeting to demand a student-controlled bookstore. Later that day, Fleming joined Rennie Davis, a founder of Students for a Democratic Society, at a teach-in on campus where they both called for an end to the Vietnam War. (In his memoir, Fleming revealed that he had known Davis and his parents since Davis's childhood, but did not want to "ruin his reputation with the activists" by acknowledging their friendship.) Demands for the bookstore culminated with a sit-in at the building that until recently housed the top adminstrators.

The protest was finally broken up in the early hours of September 26, when Fleming called in state and local police to evict the demonstrators; 107 of them were arrested.

On October 15, hundreds of students traveled to Washington to participate in the Moratorium to End the War in Vietnam, while another 20,000 protestors gathered in U-M's football stadium. A month later, an even larger protest was staged in Washington; this time at least 12,000 Michigan residents marched in a state contingent. On December 1, the first Vietnam-era draft lottery was held, impacting the future of every eligible male student over the age of 19.

On March 11, 1970, students from around the country met in Ann Arbor for a teach-in that launched the first nationwide Earth Day a month later. And on March 19, after the Regents approved a plan for increasing black admissions that leaders of the Black Action Movement (BAM) found unacceptable, the organization called for a student strike, vowing to "Open It Up or Shut It Down." Among their key demands were increasing the proportion of blacks in the student body from about 3.5 percent to 10 percent (their share of the Michigan population), recruiting more black faculty and administrators, and providing more financial aid to black students. After 18 tumultuous days, the university agreed to set a "goal" of 10 percent black enrollment and to take other steps to increase the number of blacks on campus.

All across the country, campuses were erupting in rage and frustration. On February 25, the Bank of America branch near the campus of the University of California at Santa Barbara was burned during a melee between students and police. On April 15, dozens were injured when students and police clashed during an anti-war rally in Harvard Square. After President Nixon announced on April 30 that he was expanding the Vietnam War into Cambodia, more protests broke out. On May 4, four students were killed and nine injured by National Guardsmen in a protest at Kent State University in Ohio. Eleven days later, two more students died and 12 were injured at Jackson State College (now University) in Mississippi. In late August, a physics researcher was killed when a bomb was set off in Sterling Hall at the University of Wisconsin–Madison by four men, protesting that university's military research.

That summer, Nixon appointed a Presidential Commission on Campus Unrest, which asked colleges to report the number of incidents that had disrupted "the normal functioning of the institution." On August 24, James Brinkerhoff, who as director of business operations was in charge of campus security at Michigan, tallied 13 episodes for 1967–68, 19 in 1968–69, and 42 in the 1969–70 academic year.

Fleming arrived in Ann Arbor in September 1967, just weeks after riots had broken out in black neighborhoods of Detroit, leaving 43 persons dead. The next spring Martin Luther King Jr. was assassinated, sparking riots in other American cities. By the end of 1968, the Kerner Commission reported, the country "was moving toward two societies, one white, one black—separate and unequal."

Newell recalled that when she and Fleming arrived from the University of Wisconsin, he asked her to work on trying to increase the minority presence on campus. She said the two of them met with "all of the department heads and all of the deans, one on one, to find out what people saw as their problems and where they were going." The university, she noted, was just 50 miles from Detroit, and "the proportion of blacks . . . in any category was just shameful. And something had to be done. It was a tinderbox."

In his memoir, Fleming observed, "Against this background, it was not surprising that some of the black students, faculty, and staff at the University of Michigan began to organize and to campaign for changes in the status of blacks at the university." University administrators were "well aware," he said, "of the need to take action in some of these areas long before" he arrived on campus. "Nondiscriminatory programs with respect to the employment of personnel were in place, as were financial aid programs for disadvantaged students. Still, progress was slow, and, in the mood of the times, faster action was demanded."

Fleming faced a difficult balancing act, managing calls from state legislators and top Nixon administration officials to do something about the student protests. At the height of the anti-war protests in the fall of 1969, Vice President Spiro Agnew declared, "A spirit of national masochism prevails, encouraged by an effete corps of independent snobs who characterize themselves as intellectuals." The next spring, Agnew called out Fleming by name, saying the BAM settlement amounted to a "surrender" and a "callow retreat from reality." He told a Republican fundraising dinner in Iowa that "in a few years' time, perhaps. . . America will give the diplomas from Michigan the same fish eye that Italians now give diplomas from the University of Rome."

With a master's degree in history, Jean King was well aware of the ways in which the struggles of blacks and women had been intertwined over the course of American history and how suffragists had been forced to practice patience in their battle for the vote. King also had had a front row seat on the Democratic Party's own battles over minority rights: At the 1964 convention, she had observed the floor fight over seating an all-white delegation from Mississippi.

Three decades later, King said she would not have filed the HEW complaint if the BAM strike had not been resolved a few months earlier. "I don't want the University to be able to play blacks against women," she declared. She said she did the same thing in politics: "Because that's the usual response, at least it was at that time. Women ask for something and they say, 'Oh, well, you don't want black people to have it?' So strategically, it was better to wait."

At another point, she wrote, "My reluctance to put female discrimination before race discrimination was partly because of the importance I personally place on attempts to alleviate race discrimination and partly because white men will attempt to guilt trip white women who are agitating for relief by pointing out that blacks are worse off." King knew some of the BAM leaders, including a recent Law School graduate, but was not directly involved in the strike.

Sandler also was mindful of the sometimes competing demands of minorities and women. She told a historian that when she first read the Civil Rights Commission's report, "I remember being annoyed because the writer was openly concerned that any emphasis in sex discrimination would take away from discrimination efforts for blacks."

Referring to the enforcement of Title VII of the Civil Rights Act of 1964, the report had said:

> The question must be raised at this point whether [its] twin objectives of banning race and sex discrimination are compatible. Strong tensions exist between proponents of the two and among the various interest groups which seek to influence the [Equal Employment Opportunity] Commission. Although few face the issue squarely, there is the obvious problem that, with the limited staff and resources of the EEOC, efforts devoted to the implementation of the sex discrimination ban detract from the Commission's ability to combat racial discrimination. In even more basic terms, where the Commission is successful in opening up jobs to women, this is likely to draw into the labor force white females who do not now have employment. This, in turn, may mean that jobs which minorities might otherwise obtain are unavailable.

Still, the BAM strike had demonstrated that grass-roots activism could lead to change at Michigan. More than 40 years later, Kathy Shortridge recalled:

> The atmosphere at the University was very exciting back in the later '60's and early '70's. There was lots of organization and agitation around all kinds of issues—the war, the Johnson presidency, child care, and, of course, the Black Action Movement. Most of us had been involved in more than one of these move-

ments, and learned the basic skills of organization through this experience—calling meetings and protests, running a mimeograph machine, etc. I don't recall that BAM had a specific impact on what we did, but it was certainly an important part of the atmosphere that made it possible.

Library Science Professor Rose Vainstein, whose office was near BAM's "command post" on campus, observed that after the BAM marches and strike, "Women began thinking, 'What about us?'"

Like King, many women activists had experienced sexism in their political work. Cynthia Stephens, an undergraduate who emerged as a leader of BAM, recalled, "I was the vice president because in those days, that was what women were." (In 1970, vice chairman *was* the highest-ranking position a woman could hold in both of the major national political parties.)

One thing that was ignored or overlooked by King and other women backing FOCUS's sex discrimination complaint was that HEW was already conducting compliance reviews of Michigan's efforts on minority hiring. Administrators had been monitoring the hiring and admission of blacks since the early 1960s, but the government began tracking their efforts following passage of the Civil Rights Act of 1964 and the executive order barring racial discrimination the following year.

In July 1966, Walter R. Greene, acting regional director of the U.S. Defense Department's Contract Compliance Office in Detroit, had led a compliance review of the University of Michigan, based on Title VI of the Civil Rights Act of 1964, which barred racial discrimination in programs that received federal aid. Greene spent four days talking with officials at 16 university units about their hiring practices. That November, the *Daily* disclosed that Greene had concluded that the university was known as a "large, highly academic school basically for rich white students." At the time, university officials estimated there were fewer than 26 black faculty members or administrators on campus and only 450 blacks in a student body of 31,000. The *Daily* quoted one "University source" as saying that Greene's study "would probably not show any conscious discrimination or non-compliance on the part of the University. 'But discrimination and affirmative racial balance are two different things,' the source added."

As would be the case when they responded to HEW's findings on sex discrimination four years later, university officials did not release the specifics of Greene's report to the public; they also said his study should not be characterized as a formal report to the Pentagon.

In March 1967, Greene sent U-M President Hatcher a list of 16 recommendations he had made to the departments to improve "equal employment opportunities," as well as suggestions for "centralized affirmative action." Among other things, he recommended that the university create an Office of Civil Rights and that each department be required to "develop a written plan of affirmative actions to improve its employment practices in the Fiscal Year 1967–68." Greene recommended an immediate "crash program" for the School of Engineering to address its "exceptionally bad employment practices." Among his creative ideas was a recommendation that the university place recruitment ads in newspapers "having a specific minority group readership," such as the *Wayne Dispatch*, "serving Inkster and Nankintownship [sic]." He also recommended that the Central Personnel Office and other recruiters establish "personal contacts" with "Mr. Hamilton Vanzetti, President of the NAACP and Mrs. Eaglin in the Negro community of Ypsilanti." (Later that year, Greene, an African-American, became deputy director of the Michigan Department of Civil Rights before serving as deputy mayor of Detroit from 1970–73.)

In February 1968, after the *Daily* had spotlighted the university's failure to make progress on hiring blacks, Vice President Smith asked several deans for their own "progress report." William Haber, then dean of LSA, replied that he had polled his chairmen and found "there are no startling achievements." Haber said there were only "three Negroes of professorial titles" in his college and only eight teaching fellows.

Haber asserted that the problem could only be addressed by a long-term commitment to affirmative action. Still, he acknowledged that "the Chairmen are clearly divided over one central question: We have traditionally inquired about whether the person being considered is the best person available. This applies both to academic appointments and graduate student admissions. We are now asked whether we should seek to find the best Negro candidate, even though he might be inferior to a better white candidate."

Haber suggested that the problem could be addressed over the next five years by securing a "'massive infusion' of Negro graduate students." But he said the short-term problem would remain: "My own inclination would be to attract eight or ten Negro professors to the University even if it might require some nominal compromise of traditional criteria. This is sheer heresy. Without it, let's admit that we can get nowhere."

The 1967 executive order did not yet apply to federal contractors' record on sex discrimination, but within seven months, it would. Still, there was no sign that the university was concerned about its record on hiring or promoting women, nor, apparently, was the federal government. From June 23–27, 1969, the Chicago regional office of HEW's Office of Civil Rights conducted a compliance review of the university; by then the Labor Department had assigned HEW the job of monitoring the universities that were federal contractors.

At the end of that HEW visit, Fleming signed a letter committing the university to make changes to the "Equal Employment Opportunity Affirmative Action Program" it had submitted a few weeks earlier. Among other things, the university agreed to provide annual updates on its progress on hiring minorities, strengthen its efforts to recruit minorities, assure compliance with the executive order for subcontractors and vendors holding contracts worth $10,000 or more, and put a discussion of equal employment and the executive order on the agenda of at least one Regents' meeting a year. The university was also expected to report on the "recruitment, appointment and utilization of Negro medical interns and residents."

On July 3, 1969, the *Daily* ran a front-page story under the headline "'U' Employment Policy Praised." The story said: "The University's affirmative action program for equal opportunity employment has been commended by a visiting team of representatives from the Department of Health, Education and Welfare. 'The University has made commendable steps moving in the right direction,' said contract compliance officer Clifford Minton, who visited the University last week along with four other HEW representatives. . . ."

But within a matter of weeks, the tension that would characterize the university's relationship with the Chicago office over the next few years flared up. On August 6, Fleming wrote the office: "It is apparent that a basic misunderstanding with respect to the timing of certain reports has developed. . . ." HEW had asked for some reports to be delivered by August 15; university officials thought they had a year to produce them:

> We could, of course, furnish you with a wholly meaningless report almost instantly. Presumably you do not wish us to engage in that kind of mutual deception. A university is not like an industry, with precise and limited job classifications. The only way one can know what kind of realistic future projections are feasible is to ask literally scores of people in many different areas. We know from much hard effort that in certain areas there are few, if any, minority persons who have acquired the training which the field requires. However sad a commentary this may be on our national history, it does not help to blind ourselves to the facts.
>
> Let us be clear on two things: (1) This University is unequivocally opposed to racial discrimination in any form and will actively work towards the elimination of it, and (2) we will welcome suggestions from any and all sources as to how we can improve our present program. Unfortunately, our critics frequently contend that our performance is deficient, but then decline to give us specific information as to how we can improve. We are at a loss to know how to respond to such charges.

In 2001, when he was nearly 85, Fleming was asked to recall his memories of the HEW compliance reviews. "When that first came out, they were just as badly organized as we were," he replied. Fleming said Michigan had been told "not to record race in our records," but then HEW told the university it wanted employment records tracked that way. "We can tell you with a pretty educated guess," he recalled telling the agency, but "I don't know any way we can tell you quickly."

It appears that HEW backed down on its aggressive timetable, and at the start of the 1969–70 school year, the University Michigan met its commitment to publish a revised affirmative action plan. The *University Record*, the administration's mouthpiece, declared: "Equal Employment Opportunity Affirmative Action Program Outlines University's Positive Anti-Discrimination Efforts." The package began with a statement from Fleming and William L. Cash Jr., a former U.S. Office of Education staff member who was Fleming's assistant for human relations affairs and, at the time, U-M's highest-ranking black administrator: "All members of the University community should be aware of our individual and collective commitment and responsibility in taking affirmative action to promote equal employment and educational opportunities. While most of what is stated in the policy is being implemented, publication of this comprehensive statement of our intentions will serve, hopefully, as both a reaffirmation and stimulant for us all."

The document asserted that U-M was complying with all the requirements of the executive order and would report back to the Chicago office before January 15, 1970. Throughout the document, the university asserted that it would not discriminate on the basis of "sex," along with "race, color, religion, creed, national origin, or ancestry." But there were no specific references to promoting or recruiting women. It also announced the creation of a Coordinating Committee for Human Relations to advise on hiring policies, noting that its members were the "persons most intimately involved with problems of the Negro as they relate to the University." The 11-member committee included only one woman, Nellie Varner, an African-American political scientist who was then assistant to the dean of LSA.

In November 1969, Associate LSA Dean Hayden Carruth reported to Cash the "heartening discovery" that since Haber's earlier review, that college now had 12 blacks in the ranks and 19 black teaching fellows. Carruth included a list of the college's 180 minority employees, breaking them down as "Blacks" or "Orientals." Carruth included summaries of the departmental reports on their efforts to attract minorities, drawing attention to "perhaps the most pungent statement" from the Sociology Department. That department observed that the request for "'. . . . a statement of your specific minority group employment goals, and that you indicate target dates so that future achievement in this field may be measured against definitive criteria' . . . smacks very much of what one might call quotas. . . . Certainly the Department of Sociology does not intend to engage in any practice of setting quotas with respect to race, ethnic status, religion, sex, political identity or any other criterion. At the same time we do not intend to discriminate against any prospective employee with respect to these criteria."

Carruth noted that the departments' attitudes varied widely. The Political Science Department's summary mentioned two persons who would play later leadership roles on issues related to sex discrimination: Its "Special Recruitment" Committee, under the direction first of Professor Don Stokes and then by Varner, had been working on the issue, and department members had reached out to the University of the West Indies in Jamaica and contacts in India, looking for minority candidates.

But from the top of the university on down, administrators continued to view the concerns of blacks and women very differently. A year later, the *Ann Arbor News* published an illuminating interview with Fleming that captured this dichotomy. The interview appeared two weeks after HEW had begun to investigate the FOCUS complaint and Fleming said he was "not alarmed" by the investigation.

"He believes the ferment for women's rights will affect the future men-women ratio of the U-M work force," the reporter wrote. "But he thinks the eradication of sexual discrimination in employment presents more serious problems for enforcement agencies than for employers.

"'It is clear statistically,' he says, 'that in professional fields the personnel is overwhelmingly male, and that is the preference of the market.'

"'The question arises,' he adds, 'whether in a supposedly free economy, market preference should have any weight?'"

Fleming, the article said, had felt for some time that male-dominated professions were shortsighted in excluding qualified women. In June 1967, it said, he had urged a conference of engineering educators to initiate a major effort to recruit women and deplored the "social attitudes" that had blocked it. However, in the article Fleming said that managers' hesitance to hire women professionals could be traced to women's tendency to leave the labor market during their child-rearing years.

"He feels that if the University is found guilty of job discrimination against women, society at large will have to bear the indictment as well," the reporter wrote.

The president saw no parallels between BAM's demands and the complaint by FOCUS, now described as "the Ann Arbor-based organization championing female equality."

The reporter continued: "'In the case of blacks,' he says, 'we are talking about opening up educational opportunities, but when it comes to women, we can't say they haven't had equal opportunity. Their complaint lies in being denied access to certain areas of the labor market.'"

Fleming's own mother had been a school teacher and returned to work when his father died when Fleming was 17. Fleming's wife, Sally, had worked in a variety of jobs in their early married years. He observed, "I was brought up in a family that believed deeply in fairness, courtesy, concern for others, and humility. . . . I had lived for twenty years in academic communities, and I knew a good deal about the habits of the academic world."

In a 2001 interview, Fleming asserted that he had been sympathetic to women's issues because he had two daughters "who wanted to go to school and didn't see any reason why they shouldn't do what men did." (When Fleming arrived at Michigan, his older daughter, Nancy, had just graduated from Beloit College, and his younger daughter, Betsy, was in junior high.) But Fleming still reflected the mindset of white men who had grown up during the Depression years—a description that fit all but one of U-M's vice presidents in the fall of 1970: In the Depression, he said, "companies frequently would fire a married woman where her husband also had a job in order to hire another man because the man was regarded as the breadwinner for the family and most people thought that was fair."

King later observed of Fleming, "He has many good qualities, just sex discrimination is not something that he understands. He was raised in a different way. But, of course, that was true of most of the men then."

In July 1970, two months after FOCUS filed its complaint, Fleming received an extraordinary letter, written by Mary Maples Dunn, a history professor at Bryn Mawr, at the end of her sabbatical year at Michigan. She said her time in Ann Arbor had been full of "pleasure and interest." At Bryn Mawr, she said, "I am a member of the faculty and live in a milieu in which the intellectual and professional equality of men and women is taken for granted." Then her letter took a critical turn:

> At Michigan, I have a claustrophobic sense of living in a man's world, despite the fact that the department of history has been generous but not patronizing. I have missed the companionship of women who share my professional commitments and the problems they bring, and I have become defensive about the professional potential of women who should not need my defense

any more than men do. This, of course, is a personal reaction, and I can't deny the fact that I have often enjoyed getting on my soap box; but until there are more of us, women may not be entirely comfortable on this faculty.

My relations with students have also been interesting to me, and I think more important than my personal reactions to the University as a man's world. In the first weeks of the summer term, many girls came to talk with me. Most of them volunteered the information that I was the first woman professor they had met and studied with, and they were intensely curious about me. They wanted to know how and why I had decided on such a career, whether I am married and have children, whether I neglect my children, how I cope with these multiple roles. It was a novel experience, and I concluded that at Michigan the students have far too few models to suggest to them the wide range of intellectual and professional choices they can make. Furthermore, my conversations with them led me to think that beyond a narrow range of acceptable professional training (principally, which given my experience is admittedly from a small sample, teaching and social work) they have only the vaguest ideas about the purpose of women's education in general and their own educations in particular. Despite the career orientation of Women's Lib, many women will not take up careers even though they are educated in a professionally oriented institution. It seems to me that this is a problem which the university has ignored; it has not thought seriously or with clarity about its responsibilities toward female undergraduates.

The case of graduate students is different. They have made a professional choice; the history department welcomes them and certainly gives them excellent training. Several of the graduate women I have met and worked with seem to me first class, and they will probably be good historians. But as long as hiring policies in LSA do not reflect the increased number of PhD's being awarded to women, one wonders again if the University has clearly and logically thought about female education.

Dunn closed by saying, "this letter is written out of a sense of obligation and responsibility to a splendid university—but not, alas, a perfect one." As an "outsider" about to return to a post at another college, she had a different perspective than other women faculty members—and also greater freedom to "tell it like it is."

To his credit, Fleming wrote Dunn back, praising her "thoughtful" letter and expressing appreciation that she had taken the time to write it. "Moreover, I am conscious that there is a great deal of truth in your perception of this University. We need to make many changes. Not all of them can come at once. But we ought to try, and I shall see that your thoughts are brought to the attention of the right people," Fleming wrote. A handwritten note on the letter indicates it was forwarded to Vice President Smith; Acting LSA Dean Alfred Sussman; and Stephen Spurr, dean of U-M's Rackham Graduate School.

Earlier in his career, Fleming had had the opportunity to reflect on concerns like Dunn's from a different vantage point than that of a university president. In his memoir, he described an arbitration hearing he had conducted in the early 1950s, involving a case in which unionized women janitors had filed a grievance because they were paid ten cents less than the men were. (In a later interview, he identified the company as Allis-Chalmers, the Milwaukee-based manufacturer.) Fleming noted that the company had argued that men did heavier work but that the evidence suggested that was not necessarily true. Fleming said he tried several different approaches to get the company to recognize that it was not evaluating the women's work fairly. When he asked company officials to explain the discrepancy, he said, "They looked at me in astonishment and said, 'But women always get less than men, therefore there is a differential.'" Fleming said he ruled in favor of the women.

Later, when he taught labor law, Fleming said he would ask his classes—all men, except for two or three women—how they would resolve the grievance. Fleming recalled, "They unhesitatingly and overwhelmingly said that the company was right. The main reason seemed to be that 'everyone knew women were paid less than men!'" Fleming cited the case as an illustration of "how blinded we can all be by prevailing attitudes and past practices."

Fleming's reputation for managing student protests had been a major reason he was recruited to be president of Michigan, and as the

1970–71 school year began, he was riding high—at least in academic circles. The *Ann Arbor News* article noted that he "wasn't hankering for instant replays of much that had happened in the past 12 months. . . ."

The reporter noted, "Yet in spite of the clamor and crises that have swirled around him and the institution he heads, Fleming appears to have retained his outward equanimity and inner resilience." Fleming's "national stature," he concluded, "had soared" during the past year. In addition to negotiating an end to the BAM strike, Fleming got some peace-keeping help from Michigan's trimester calendar. As Brinkerhoff, the director of business operations, explained in his response to the Campus Unrest Commission, the university was on break when campuses erupted in protests following Nixon's invasion of Cambodia. "Summer school was starting and there were minor incidents," Brinkerhoff wrote. "If school had been in session, we would have had serious trouble."

Fleming was one of two college administrators who were among the first persons to testify before the commission that summer. In April, he had appeared on "Meet the Press" as a representative of the American Council on Education's (ACE's) Special Committee on Campus Tensions, and in May, he had joined the presidents of Yale and Notre Dame on a special CBS News program entitled "The Campus in Crisis: The College Presidents Speak."

But Fleming's increased prominence came at a price. In late August, nationally syndicated columnists Rowland Evans and Robert Novak wrote that the U-M faculty had "deep misgivings" about the way Fleming had handled "last winter's student crisis." While acknowledging that Fleming had been "widely praised by press and politicians for peacefully settling" the BAM strike, the columnists asserted that "those professors concerned about Michigan's survival as a great university (sadly a minority) privately contend that Fleming's tactics have encouraged more politicization here and set dangerous precedents harmful to academic freedom." The column appeared in the *Washington Post* and locally in the *Detroit News*. Letters to the editor from two high-ranking members of the university community were sent to papers that had run the column and the *Detroit News* subsequently devoted a page of its "Viewpoint" section to responses from several persons, including Fleming. The president also sent Novak an angry letter, labeled "not for publication," detailing what he described as "the gross misstatements of facts."

In his interview with the *Ann Arbor News*, Fleming said he did not anticipate any controversy in the 1970–71 school year that would "snow-ball" into shutting down the campus like the BAM strike had. Asked by the Campus Unrest Commission to state "the most serious problem that your university will face this fall that may lead to campus unrest," Brinkerhoff had responded: "It is difficult to tell. ROTC [the Reserve Officers Training Corps] and recruiting on campus will probably con-tinue to be issues. Black students may be restless about what the Uni-versity is doing for the community. And Environmentalists may feel that the University should take a more active role in various affairs."

Asked what "the federal government" and "state authorities" could do to "reduce the likelihood of disruption or violence on your campus," Brinkerhoff responded that the feds could "re-order priorities so that our serious domestic problems can be attacked," an oblique way of say-ing, "stop the war." As for the state, he replied, "Help us with fund-ing for disadvantaged students, and refrain from imposing restrictive legislation."

Fleming's attitudes toward women and his renewed self-confidence may not have served him well when the HEW investigators returned to campus that August. But even the *Michigan Daily* did not fully anticipate the way women's issues would come to dominate campus life in the coming semester. A news analysis from September 2, 1970, noted that at the start of the previous school year, no one would have predicted that the campus would go on strike over black admissions. The reporter con-cluded that the war in Southeast Asia was likely to remain the biggest cause of concern, but pointed out (correctly, as it turned out) that the American Federation of State, County and Municipal Employees might call for the university's hourly service employees to go on strike. Far-ther down, below a recounting of the concerns of the Gay Liberation Front, the reporter dealt with women's issues. There was no mention of the HEW complaint, but he wrote, "Women's liberation is in much the same 'sleeper' position that the blacks were a year ago—not very unified. Their immediate concern is for a permanent day care center, supported by the University." But, he added, "From the struggle over an issue such as a day care center could come the organization and aware-ness to create a major conflict over the other issues of discrimination against women in employment and admissions."

5

The Summer of 1970

As the FOCUS complaint was winding its way through the federal bureaucracy that summer, it was fueled by two efforts that helped campus women find their voices. One was based in Washington, the other in Ann Arbor.

Democratic Rep. Edith Green of Oregon had been interested in education issues and job discrimination since she arrived on Capitol Hill in 1955. Green had worked as a school teacher and later legislative chairperson of the Oregon Congress of Parents and Teachers before running for public office. During her freshman term, she was appointed to the House Education and Labor Committee, where she stayed for the next 18 years. She turned down opportunities to run for the U.S. Senate, it was said, because she believed her House seniority gave her influence she would not otherwise have as a woman.

"When I first went to Congress," she recalled for an oral history project involving former members of Congress, "a woman would be doing precisely the same work as a man and would be paid a lower salary. A man comes in and is going to be the head of a department; a woman who has been working there for ten years has to train him in order to do the job, but she does not receive the promotion, not would she receive anywhere near the same salary." Upon arriving in the House, Green introduced a bill to establish the principle "that if a woman had the same background and experience and was [doing] the same work as a man, it was only just and right that she should be paid the same amount of money." It took eight years to get the bill passed, and when it did, Green was forced to accept an amendment that exempted professional, executive, and administrative positions—in other words, academic women.

Seven years later, in the spring of 1970, congressional offices representing all parts of the country were beginning to receive letters inquiring about the status of the WEAL complaints. Within her first four months, Sandler claimed to have filed 100 of them. A tally she provided Congress by July listed close to that number, including complaints filed against the entire state university systems of California and Florida (and all of that state's two-year community colleges), as well as the American Psychological Association and the American Personnel and Guidance Association (today called the American Counseling Association). Another complaint was filed against Phi Delta Kappa, the honorary society for educators, whose membership was then restricted to men.

Sandler fleshed out and updated the list of 43 colleges and universities that *Science* magazine had previously reported were the subject of WEAL complaints. The list now included George Washington University; the University of North Carolina–Wilmington; Virginia Commonwealth University; Northeastern University; the University of Massachusetts branches at Amherst and Boston; Tufts; Clark University; Brown; Columbia; the universities of Connecticut, Miami, Georgia, New Hampshire, Rhode Island, Minnesota, and Wisconsin; Wayne State University in Detroit; and Carnegie Mellon.

But complaints were filed against smaller schools, too: Eastern Illinois University; Western Carolina University; Northeastern Illinois State College; Winthrop College in South Carolina; Hartwick College in New York; Frostburg State College and Chesapeake Community College in Maryland; Lincoln University and Susquehanna University in Pennsylvania; Michigan Technological University; Pacific Lutheran University and Western Washington State College in Washington state; and Mercer County Community College in New Jersey. Four subdivisions of Rutgers (Douglass College, its Camden and Newark campuses, and Livingston College) now were named.

Two of Sandler's earliest complaints were filed against two of her alma maters; by summer she had added the third, Brooklyn College, to the list.

The long list provided to Congress noted that on May 28 the complaint filed against the University of Michigan was handled by an organization other than WEAL: FOCUS on Equal Employment for Women.

In Sandler's retelling, Phineas Indritz, a civil rights attorney who served on NOW's first national board and on its legal committee, urged Green to hold hearings on sex discrimination. (In her reports, Sandler said Green had been a member of WEAL's board of directors, but her name did not appear on its letterhead at that time; the names of Indritz and Griffiths did.)

Sandler said Green was reluctant to hold the hearings "because there was little data available and apparently no constituency on whom she could count to testify."

"It was a time when there were no books and only a few articles that addressed the issue of discrimination against women in education," Sandler recalled. "No conferences had been held to examine the issue. There was little research or data and barely a handful of women's studies courses. . . .The issue of sex discrimination in education was so new that I received many letters from women and men asking me if it was true that such discrimination in education existed and, if so, would I send them proof."

The WEAL complaints, however, provided Green with what she needed. Sandler contributed lists of people and organizations who would be willing to testify—"because I knew almost everyone actively working to end discrimination in education"—and Green agreed to draft legislation and hold hearings. The measure, Section 805 of HR 16098, was designed to amend the Civil Rights Act of 1964 to prohibit sex discrimination in federally financed programs and remove the law's exemption for education. It would have also eliminated the exemption for executive, administrative, and professional employees in the Equal Pay Act. And it would have added sex discrimination to the mandate of the U.S. Civil Rights Commission. Green's Special Subcommittee on Education scheduled seven days of hearings in June and July.

Sandler recalled that "witnesses provided horror stories, mainly about women employed on campus, such as departments refusing to hire women, or refusing to promote them or give them tenure; or women who received many thousands of dollars less salary than their male counterparts; or women working full-time as faculty, with no benefits, no office, no salary, because their husbands also taught at the same university." Sandler herself testified, providing an overview of the situation, based on the complaints she filed.

On July 7, Rep. Green wrote King, noting that she had been suggested as a possible witness but that there was not enough time to include everyone. Instead, she invited King to submit "any statement you might like to make on any aspect of discrimination against women, together with any materials on the subject which you believe would be of value." But she gave King a deadline eight days later, and amid a very busy summer, there is no evidence that King sent a response.

Green kicked off the hearings on June 17, 1970; Committee Chairman Carl D. Perkins was present, but only 3 of the 15 male subcommittee members showed up. In her opening statement, Green said, "During the next several days I hope that the various kinds of discrimination in our society will be discussed and will be fully documented, and that this can be made available to the men who run the world." The transcript of the hearing noted that that comment was greeted with "laughter."

The frustrations Green had endured over her years in politics bubbled up throughout the hearings. Later that day, she recalled, "When I first came to Washington, there were four women who entered the Congress that year and all the papers called up and said, 'We would like to take a picture of you.' Every single time they wanted me to be whipping up pancakes or a cake. Finally, I just said, the congressional job is not making a cake perfectly. I will not have any more such pictures! I asked: When you ask a new male Member of Congress to have his picture taken, do you say, 'We want a picture of you painting the window or driving some nails to prove that you are a man?' This is again exemplary of the psychological warfare."

The hearings covered discrimination in fields beyond higher education; among other things, they dealt with issues faced by black women, the sociology of discrimination, sex-segregated want ads, and legal issues. Among those who testified was Virginia R. Allan, who had chaired the President's Task Force on Women's Rights and Responsibilities and was then a regent at Eastern Michigan University.

Allan was called to discuss the task force's report, which had been formally released only the week before. In the fall of 1969, the Nixon administration had rushed to assemble the task force so that some proposals on women's issues could be included in the President's 1970 State of the Union address. The task force completed its work within two months, but none of its recommendations made it into the President's speech. The administration continued to sit on the report for six months, until it was finally leaked to a Florida newspaper.

Only a handful of men testified, none of them associated with a university. During the second round of hearings in July, Green pointedly challenged three high-ranking HEW officials: Peter Muirhead, deputy assistant secretary and associate commissioner for higher education in the Office of Education; Owen Kiely, director of the Office of Civil Rights' Contract Compliance Division; and Preston M. Royster, an equal employment opportunities officer whose job included promoting equity within the Office of Education itself.

Muirhead said he was testifying on behalf of the HEW secretary, but Elliot L. Richardson had assumed that job only the week before. Muirhead began by acknowledging that "the record of educational institutions—particularly higher education—in affording to women equal opportunity, equal status, equal pay has been discouragingly poor." He said that the ACE's annual survey of college freshmen had found that women enter college with "slightly better records of high school achievement" than men. He went on to cite statistics that Sandler and other women had compiled, noting that Cornell maintained a three-to-one ratio of men to women and that Harvard/Radcliffe maintained a four-to-one ratio. In the fall of 1969, the University of North Carolina, a public university, had admitted half of the 3,231 men who had applied, but only one-fourth of the women.

Reviewing the extent of discrimination, Muirhead discussed "contributing factors," such as "lower expectations, institutional practices, lack of day care facilities and so on." But, he said, "the inequities are so pervasive that direct discrimination must be considered as [playing] a share, particularly in salaries, hiring, and promotions, especially to tenured positions. . . . Despite the present belief that in many academic fields there are no women qualified to teach, close investigations have discovered that this is often an untenable excuse."

Muirhead said that during fiscal 1969, HEW's Contract Compliance Division had received and investigated three individual sex discrimination complaints; in two of the cases, the agency backed the complainants and adjustments, including back pay, were made. But since then, he said, HEW had received "85 allegations against over 100" colleges and higher education professional organizations, and "we are now gearing up to undertake compliance reviews in the area of sex discrimination." Compliance reviews, he said, were currently under way at Harvard, Maryland, George Washington University, and Manhattan Community College of the New York City college system.

Kiely testified that HEW had forwarded the Labor Department's recent enforcement guidelines to its civil rights field offices. He explained that public universities were exempted from the requirement to have an affirmative action plan on file, "but in the process of our compliance reviews with any contractor, whether it is a public or private institution, we are bound to investigate the actual patterns and practices and to negotiate for corrective commitments where we find discrepancies."

He added, "If we found there was an exclusion of females from certain job categories, or differences in pay even with the private institutions, they would have to make written commitments on the action they were going to take to correct that problem." Kiely said that HEW was requesting "detailed data on all the job categories, from low to high, including faculty. . . ."

Green challenged the officials on whether they were doing enough to alert university and college administrators about their responsibilities. Muirhead and Kiely acknowledged that their agency had not yet sent colleges information about the executive order's additional requirements and the prospect that they could lose their federal contracts if they did not meet them. But Kiely said the department had worked with "the National Council on Education [sic] and the American Association of Universities" to get them to alert their members.

Green also established the record on how few women could be found at the top ranks of HEW itself: there was only one woman at the highest salary rank below that of the secretary and his deputy: Patricia Reilly Hitt, whom Nixon nominated as an assistant secretary after she served as national co-chair of his 1968 presidential campaign. Across the department, there were only 13 women in the top three civil service salary ranks, and only one woman in the regional offices who earned as much as the third highest salary rank. Royster, an African American, testified that the Office of Education had not yet added a woman to its equal employment staff.

Green's hearings were later heralded as the first time Congress had held hearings on any issue related to sex discrimination. She sarcastically observed that although Muirhead had outlined "so persuasively" the discrimination women endured, HEW had never sponsored a conference or proposed legislation to solve the problem. Like others, HEW opposed the specific amendments that were the focus of Green's hearings that summer because of their potential impact on single-sex colleges.

Although the statistics of higher education organizations were cited, Sandler later wrote that "no one from the official world of higher education testified, although they were invited to do so. An ACE representative told the committee counsel that 'there was no sex discrimination in higher education,' and even if it did exist, it wasn't a 'problem.' Apparently, Rep. Green's bill was not seen as being of much interest to, or having any major implications for, educational institutions."

When the hearings were over, Green hired Sandler to compile and publish a transcript, as well as related documents. The result was *Discrimination against Women,* two volumes totaling 1,261 pages. Sandler recalled that because there was so little written about the employment and education of women, she appended numerous documents, including 14 studies of women in colleges, copies of her complaints, scholarly publications, and magazine articles. The latter included one on the status of women in computing that Jo-Ann Gardner's husband had written for the January 1970 issue of *Computers and Automation.*

It was an encyclopedic rendering of the job and educational world that women confronted in 1970. Amid page after page of dry but painful statistics, it also provided a platform for the underemployed women who testified before the committee or had written about the problem. No one from the University of Michigan testified, but Sandler incorporated some of FOCUS's research into the formal statement she submitted.

"Even in academic areas where women would be expected to be found in substantial numbers, women are conspicuously absent," she wrote. "For example, out of 105 professors in the School of Education at Michigan, only 6 are women. Again, at the University of Michigan, out of 58 professors in social work, only 12 are women; in library science, out of 14 professors, only 3 are women." A hundred years earlier, she noted, women made up one-third of the nation's faculty members; now they represented only one-fourth of the total and "in the prestigious Big Ten schools," 10 percent or less.

And Shortridge's reporting on the admissions quotas was also incorporated; the "overbalance" quote was again attributed to G.C. Wilson, though he may not have been the admissions committee member who had actually used that word.

The transcript of the hearings also captured more of the prevailing male attitudes. On the second day, Democratic Rep. William D. Hathaway of Maine queried a panel that consisted of Sandler; human rights attorney Pauli Murray, then teaching at Brandeis University; and Ann Sutherland Harris, an assistant professor of art history at Columbia University, representing Columbia Women's Liberation:

> *Mr. Hathaway*: The question in simple terms, say there are 10 women and 10 men in a society and there are only 15 openings in a school and we know, statistically, to make it easy, that all 10 men have to get a job and only five of the women are ever going to get a job: Isn't the school warranted in taking more men than women?
>
> *Dr. Murray*: Do you want another answer to that?
>
> *Dr. Sandler*: I think one could almost make the same analogy and see if it holds with blacks, or Negroes, and say, "Well, since so many of them really aren't going to be professionals and many of them are going to be stuck being janitors and cleaners and in low-paying jobs, why waste time educating them?"
>
> *Mr. Hathaway*: I am not doing it on the basis of what has happened before as far as the jobs have gone. I am just doing it on the simple fact that more men than women have to get a job to support a family, no matter what kind of job it is.

Then Rep. Green joined in, repeating what she said was "the most shocking statistic I have seen," namely that in the state of Virginia, 21,000 young women were rejected for college admission and not a single male.

> Mrs. Green: I have seen so many men that never use their
> college education. They train to be engineers, and end up
> politicians! Or they train to be teachers and become real
> estate operators!

> Mr. Hathaway: That might be good training for a politician.

> Mrs. Green: Then, according to the logic suggested of
> not admitting girls because some of them won't use
> their education, he should not have gone to 5 years of
> engineering school! It is a waste of space and money at the
> college. Somebody ought to have made the judgment at
> 18 that persons should not be admitted to an engineering
> school because he will never use that training.

> Mr. Hathaway: From the figures I cite, it is obviously
> discrimination, but I think a college is warranted to have
> a policy that says they will take in slightly more men than
> women, because more men than women are going to be
> required immediately after graduation to get a job and
> support a family and, if they are limited in the number of
> people they can take in, I think they would be warranted
> in that policy.
>
> Obviously many are going far beyond that and take
> in only the very brightest women and take in even the
> dullest men.

> Mrs. Green: Why don't we play God at 13 and decide—as has
> been done in other countries and here 100 years ago—that
> girls are just going to be homemakers and not have them
> go to high school? What Neanderthal thinking.

Murray testified passionately about the experience of black women, saying at one point: "I do not think the male members of this subcommittee can fully appreciate the extent to which women's liberation has taken hold across the Nation if you attempt to view it objectively merely through the facts and figures which have been presented here. Women are appealing, demanding, organizing for and determined to achieve acceptance as persons, as full and equal partners with men in every phase of our national life."

As Sandler summed up:

> Women are denied admission to graduate and professional training programs because of the rather odd and illogical reasoning on the part of university decisionmakers: "If a woman is not married, she'll get married. If she is married, she'll probably have children. If she has children, she can't possibly be committed to a profession. If she has older children, she is too old to begin training." Now it is true that she may very well marry. Many of her fellow male students will do likewise. She may very well have children. Men also become parents, but we do not as a society punish them by limiting their professional development and professional opportunities.
>
> *Essentially our universities punish women for being women.* They punish women for not only having children, but even for having the potential to bear children. Such blatent [sic] discrimination against women has gone virtually unchecked for years. In every sector of university life, women are losing ground.

(Two years later, Hathaway moved up to the U.S. Senate by defeating Republican Margaret Chase Smith, then the longest-serving woman in that chamber.)

After Sandler finished her editing of *Discrimination against Women*, Green won approval to print 6,000 sets of the books, rather than the usual few hundred. The volumes were sent to every member of Congress, with a note attached, and Sandler also sent copies to higher education leaders and organizations and to media outlets.

Sandler recalled, "The hearings probably did more than anything else to make sex discrimination in education a legitimate issue. When administrators or faculty members would deny the existence of sex discrimination in academe, women (and men) could point out that this was not a frivolous issue and Congress itself had held *days* of hearings on this important subject."

Sandler clearly had her ears tuned to the mood on American campuses at the time. "In a little noted development all over the country, on both small and large campuses," she said, "women have begun to form groups across departmental and professional lines. They are beginning to do more than complain. They are examining the role of women on their campuses, and their university's treatment of them."

It was happening at the University of Michigan too.

By the time Rep. Green's hearings started, another group of women was organizing in Ann Arbor to support the HEW complaint. Among the leaders were Shortridge and Jeanne Tashian, who worked as a secretary in the Office of Student Services and later donated many records of the group to U-M's Bentley Library. The group decided to call itself PROBE.

Sandler had always thought that one of the strengths of the Michigan complaint was that King and Yourd were *not* employed by the university. Unlike many of those at other colleges for whom Sandler initiated complaints, the two women did not risk retribution by their employer. At Michigan, Sandler noted, there were women involved "who weren't employed by the university but were married to the university. Their husbands were secure in their jobs. It made a huge difference."

Yet women employees still wanted to play a role. In a flyer that PROBE prepared that summer, it described itself as "a coalition of independent researchers and researchers from various women's groups including FOCUS on Equal Employment for Women and OIUW (Open It Up for Women), a student organization, as well as I.S. and N.U.C. It has been formed for the specific purpose of investigating discrimination against women at the University of Michigan." A later memo also named NOW as a member of the coalition. PROBE said it hoped to compile information for a variety of purposes, including supporting the FOCUS complaint and WEAL's activities in Washington.

In a document distributed later in the fall, PROBE said that publicity around the HEW complaint had provided the "impetus" for its formation: "Since women from more than 100 universities had filed sex discrimination complaints similar to the one at Michigan we anticipated months or years before the Michigan complaint would be investigated. We believed the problems were too serious to wait."

In a later oral history, a PROBE member who preferred to remain anonymous described the group as an "offshoot" of FOCUS. "PROBE was more like the grass-roots implementation of awareness and possible action at the University. And it certainly wasn't the only organization that did that. There were other organizations that did that, too. But PROBE was one of them," she noted.

The other groups, she said, "tended to be associated with what was known at that time as the student left-wing, radical, bra-burning, flaming anti-establishment movement. PROBE was not quite that radical. [It was] more a mixture of people. There were students, no doubt about it, graduate students, a couple of undergrads. There were University employees, quite a number of those of all types."

But, she added, "the deeper any of us got into this, the more 'radicalized' we became because it became obvious that there were underlying societal problems. It wasn't just getting a lousy deal when you went to apply for a job or wanted to apply for a job. It was fundamental societal problems. . . . We were always meeting and talking. . . you just realized there was a lot of fundamental problems in society that had to be addressed along with employment discrimination."

Proposed agendas for the group's early meetings included discussions of activities that could be pursued. Among the ideas were developing surveys of women employees; reaching out to King to explore what legal rights, if any, they had to personnel data; contacting activists around the country; and arranging for office space and letterhead. At a July 9, 1970, meeting, members discussed writing the Regents about the search for a permanent vice president for student affairs; Barbara Newell had held the job on an acting basis. On July 16, the group was one of four groups that spoke during the open part of the Regents' monthly meeting. It distributed its statement on new stationery with the formal name of "PROBE into the Status of Women at the University of Michigan," and used Shortridge's address and phone number. The statement read:

PROBE is a representative cross-section of the female population at UM, and as such, we feel a strong need for women to be in executive positions and involved in the University's decision making process. Quick examination bears out that disturbingly few women hold such positions and have a say in University policy. Yet, the Regental Bylaw, Section 1.14, approved February 1968, does prohibit discrimination in employment by sex, a fact that is underlined by the rising consciousness of the University of Michigan's socially aware student body, not to speak of the whole nation, regarding the conditions of modern women.

The letter referenced the HEW complaint (incorrectly citing Title VII of the 1964 Civil Rights Act as its basis), then went on: "While it yet remains to be proved that the University of Michigan does indeed discriminate against women in employment, it would seem injudicious at this time not to have at least one of the Executive Officer positions filled by a woman on a permanent basis."

Arguably, it would have helped the executive officers to have a woman more directly involved that fall. But PROBE's hopes were dashed before the start of the new school year, when U-M Law Professor Robert Knauss, then the chairman of the Senate Advisory Committee on University Affairs (SACUA), was named to the post. Carol Leland, an official with the College Entrance Examination Board, had withdrawn from consideration early in the two-year search, concluding, according to news reports, that the job was an impossible one. Over the summer, Gretchen Wilson, a graduate student in organization psychology who worked in the Office of Student Services, had also been interviewed. It was thought that Newell could not be a candidate for the permanent job because Fleming had appointed her without seeking the input of a search committee.

On August 4, PROBE wrote Vice Presidents Smith and Newell, and Wilbur K. Pierpoint, vice president for finance, seeking their cooperation in "supplying PROBE with salary and personnel data which would greatly aid the cause and purpose of our organization." In this letter, they described themselves as "a coalition of independent researchers specifically concerned with the problems of women at The University of Michigan." They added, "We have no reason to believe that The University of Michigan is not following the national trend in practices of employment and discrimination against women. We do believe, however, that once the facts are brought to light, the University will take the initiative to correct whatever inequities may be revealed." (Minutes from meetings of the executive officers a few weeks later suggest they began to develop a response, but it was more than four months before officials met with the group to address their questions.)

Overnight, campus women were noticing things that had never bothered them before. The PROBE memo to the vice presidents observed that in the June 15 issue of *UM News*, a photograph featured *six male* personnel representatives who were available to help employees file grievances. The group asserted, "This sort of blatant discrimination is not only insensitive but is insulting to the intelligence of women. How many of these men have ever worked as a secretary, or even as a clerk? How can they be expected to be sympathetic to, or understand the problems of women? . . . Does the University employ any women in the position of 'personnel representative?' If not, we offer our services in helping to recruit the type of women who have the experience and background necessary to gain the confidence and trust of the people who need the services."

In August, the organization's "Bas-Relief Committee" decided to tackle the matter of "The Dream of the Young Woman," a sculpture that was then installed on the State Street side of the LSA Building. The sculpture depicted a bonneted woman holding a baby and managing another child by the side of a covered wagon, while a man dreamed of an ocean voyage. A photograph of the sculpture had illustrated Shortridge's *Daily* article the previous April.

The sculpture was one of 39 bas-relief works that were installed on the exterior of the LSA Building in 1948, the work of Marshall Fredericks, who taught at the Cranbrook Academy of Art. Fredericks had created other works for the Michigan campus, including one called "American Eagle" that was installed at Michigan Stadium.

On August 5, PROBE wrote Fleming that it found the frieze "to be a peculiar representation for the portals of an institution of higher learning. To our knowledge, the University does not offer academic credit for field work in procreation. We would suggest, therefore, that this sculpture be removed. If the University won't unburden itself of the sculpture entirely, perhaps a more suitable location could be found; one suggestion for a more appropriate location is the drop-in day care center at Mary Markley [dormitory]. Alternatively, the University might commission a second sculpture, 'The Young Woman Wakes Up.'"

PROBE said it expected Michigan to take action by August 26, which, it noted, was the 50th anniversary of women's suffrage.

Fleming, however, was not sympathetic. On August 14, he responded, "I do not attempt to impose my personal judgment within the University in the area of art." He suggested that the group contact the dean of LSA. The faculty, he said, "may or may not suggest that it be removed. In either event, I find it difficult to believe that it will have much to say about the question of whether 'the University is concerned seriously about the position of its women students.'"

PROBE followed up with the dean: "We are disappointed that President Fleming did not show us the courtesy of forwarding our request to the proper office. Perhaps he finds our request frivolous; we do not."

In response to Fleming's comment about artistic judgment, PROBE wrote, "It is the subject of the sculpture and not its artistic value which offends us. A beautifully executed 'Sambo' or flawless illustrations of the Kama Sutra might be artistically unimpeachable. Still, their contents would render them so unacceptable to members of the University community that they would not be found adorning the central buildings of the campus."

On October 7, Acting Dean Alfred Sussman responded that the LSA's Executive Committee had rejected their request. To remove the sculpture, he said, would amount to "censorship," and that while it might be justified to remove some works of art, this one did not "represent such a case."

PROBE circulated the exchange of memos with a final note: "If the bas-relief must stay, why not erect a plaque beside it designating it as a historic site? It is definitely a period piece, reflecting both the art and life styles of another era, the fifties, when the most creative thing a woman was allowed to do was to produce larger numbers of overfed or underfed children (depending on her social class)." (The sculpture, later identified by its full name, "Dream of the Young Girl and Dream of the Young Man," remained in place for 34 more years until the LSA Building was renovated and all of the sculptures were removed. This one was moved to the back wall of the Bentley Library, where it can be viewed from the courtyard.)

No one knew it at the time, but as Sussman sent his response to PROBE, HEW's findings were already in the mail to Fleming. Soon PROBE would have more substantive issues to write about.

PROBE continued to focus on distributing documents, bulletins, and data—"the kind of stuff to inform a very wide number of women about employment discrimination and related issues," the anonymous member recalled. "It was grass-roots, not extremely hampered by political philosophy. It was more targeted to 'let's fix this situation here because it's not fair and it's not right and we've got to get people on board. . . .'"

In later interviews, King expressed her view that PROBE was naïve in thinking it would be able to negotiate with Fleming. She had also been concerned that the university would retaliate against the women employees. "It was dangerous for a lot of people in PROBE and they didn't recognize it," she recalled. "The response at that time, and sometimes even now, can be extremely vicious, and women didn't understand that."

"It probably was dangerous," the anonymous PROBE member acknowledged 30 years later. But she said she did not know of any group member who had experienced retaliation. "Most people didn't have too much courage. They were afraid of losing their job or what have you and you couldn't blame them for that. A few of us were very brave, and we just sort of would not regard what would happen to us. We would just do all kinds of stuff," she said.

King, the woman recalled, attended one or two PROBE meetings: "She gave it her blessing. 'Keep it up. That's great. Do it. That's all perfect.'"

It is unclear whether PROBE's outreach led individuals to bolster the FOCUS complaint by sharing their stories with HEW. Still, PROBE helped to bridge the world between underpaid women faculty members and rowdier students. It connected with graduate students, secretaries, and well-educated women who had been forced to settle for a clerical job. And when the HEW investigators eventually reviewed U-M's employment practices, they focused on the secretaries' problems as well.

The PROBE women turned out to be the foot soldiers, who, like King in her younger years, had learned a lot about the inner workings of the university. "In society at that time," the anonymous member recalled, women "were the secretaries and the people who really, we would say, who really did the work. I think one of our major goals was to get secretaries mobilized because we thought they were a very misused group of individuals. . . . They were low-paid, [had] no prestige, [and] very little recognition. Yet . . . many of them did most of the work for their bosses and they had a tremendous amount of information. . . ."

And as the months went on, those low-paid women had the creativity to figure out how to use the university's systems to their own advantage.

"Maybe the hardest thing to understand about 1970," King recalled, "was the lack of contact between women at the University, staff as well as professors. So they couldn't share with each other what was happening to them. They just sort of individually got angry. It wasn't a movement at all."

In her 2001 interview, the anonymous PROBE member said, "One of the most important things about PROBE was the attempt to really do outreach because a lot of the student organizations were very insular. They didn't attempt to do a lot of outreach. They had certain ideas about who was really brilliant and cool and left-wing and that's who they concentrated on, and PROBE was very, very egalitarian. You didn't have to be anything to fit into our mold."

And, on top of it all, the PROBE members enjoyed working together. "We were winging it, thinking about what we could do," the member recalled. "It was a tremendous amount of fun, as was everything in the sixties, compared to [later]. Just exhilarating. The sense of freedom that you just don't get any more. A sense that you were doing something really important, that would make a difference."

6

The Investigation

When he was in the military, Robben Fleming recalled in his memoir, "I had been taught . . . that if you are going to have a skirmish it is better if you pick the terrain!"

FOCUS had launched its grenade onto a battlefield that Fleming knew well. But unlike his earlier confrontations with student demonstrators, this attack featured no rallies, no crowded Regents meetings, and no outside agitators or police clad in riot gear. Still, it *was* a form of guerrilla warfare. And over the coming months, it would involve the skillful use of the media, typewriters, copying machines, access to important in-boxes—and even a few undercover spies.

As the PROBE member later recounted in her anonymous oral history: "Robben Fleming was very clever. He was a very bright, clever guy. . . . But this was one group that he just didn't quite know how to [deal with]. . . . He knew how to negotiate with sweaty union workers and people like that. But. . . a bunch of women? He didn't know how to deal with that. . . . And I don't think anybody else in a position of power knew that, because the idea of women creating an uprising was very unheralded. . . . Especially their own secretaries!"

More than 40 years later, Sandler cited King's political and tactical skills as one reason the Michigan women were more successful than women on other campuses. King, she recalled, had recognized the ramifications of the executive order more quickly than many other women because she had been trained as a lawyer. "She saw the big picture immediately," said Sandler. Because of King's legal expertise, Sandler added, the Michigan data were prepared more carefully than in many other complaints.

In addition, she said, Michigan was unusual in that many supportive women were relatively high placed. They weren't, she said, "the man-hating stereotype." It gave the complaint "much more credibility" and "made a huge difference in how things went internally."

Vincent Macaluso had stressed to Sandler the importance of writing members of Congress to enlist their support. Sandler later recalled that the letters were "a very powerful tool in this kind of situation. You really can affect things when things are new, because they [HEW] didn't know what they were doing. . . . So they didn't have the satisfaction and comfort of saying, 'You know we've been doing this for years, we really know what's best.' They could say that about investigations maybe, but they couldn't say that about leaving women out [of their investigations], and how to do women. They were unprepared to deal with higher education."

King and Yourd followed Sandler's playbook. "Mary was a known Republican and I was a known Democrat, so we split up the congresspeople," King noted. At the time, the Michigan congressional delegation included 19 representatives and 2 senators. "We didn't know when we started that it would mean 84 hand-typed letters," she recalled.

On July 1, George Shultz, to whom the original complaint was sent, stepped down as secretary of labor to become director of Nixon's Office of Management and Budget. Another round of letters were sent to members of Congress after his deputy, James D. Hodgdon, was nominated to replace him. Then the Labor Department referred the complaint to HEW. Another round was sent, urging congressional queries to HEW Secretary Robert Finch. Another round was mailed when Undersecretary of State Elliot L. Richardson replaced Finch on June 24. ". . . We learned that our request for help was forwarded by most Michigan Congressmen to the four succeeding Department heads personally and with alacrity," King noted. These "Congressionals," as she called them, "were hard to ignore and they weren't ignored."

On another occasion, King recalled, "We gradually began to sense that there were a lot of women in Congressional staff jobs (mostly low level, none administrative assistants, mostly anonymous) that were rooting for us. Some of them [were] able to sign their bosses' names. They could at least sometimes put our letters on top of their bosses' piles of mail."

One congressional aide who turned out to be particularly helpful was Muriel Ferris, a staff member to Democratic Sen. Philip A. Hart of Michigan. Ferris, then close to 60, had worked in Washington since the 1930s, before joining the staff of the League of Women Voters. In 1959, she became Hart's legislative assistant, a relatively high congressional staff position for a woman at that time. King recalled that she got to know members of Hart's staff when she lobbied against the Haynsworth and Carswell nominations.

The letters that King and Yourd sent appeared to have some impact, adding another stream to the letters Sandler was generating about other universities.

One of the first members to follow up was then-Republican Rep. Donald W. Riegle, who represented Flint. He wrote the Labor Department on June 10, forwarding a copy of King's letter. William L. Gifford, the department's special assistant for legislative affairs, wrote back on June 23: "We are requesting that the Department of Health, Education, and Welfare conduct a compliance review of the University of Michigan and provide us with a report of findings and recommendations within 60 days. . . . During the course of the compliance review, compliance officials of HEW will contact Miss King and Miss Yourd for any additional information they may wish to furnish."

On July 2, John L. Wilks, director of the OFCC (and Macaluso's political boss), forwarded the correspondence to HEW's Owen Kiely with this note: "Please note the enclosed referral from Congressman Riegle, containing charges of discrimination on the basis of sex by Miss Jean L. King against the University of Michigan. We would appreciate it if you would undertake the action regarding this matter that is outlined in our reply, which is also enclosed."

Other members of the Michigan delegation wrote a bit later and received responses from Secretary Hodgdon. They included Republican Rep. Marvin L. Esch, who represented Ann Arbor; Republican Rep. Philip E. Ruppe, who represented the Upper Peninsula; and Democratic Rep. William D. Ford, whose district included parts of Detroit. Ford wrote that he had received "several letters urging a full and fair examination of the FOCUS complaint."

In addition to cultivating contacts on Capitol Hill, King also developed friendships with key women reporters. It was easy to find sympathetic reporters on the staff of the *Daily*, whose stock in trade was challenging Michigan administrators on every issue they could. (In the first months after the HEW complaint was filed, both men and women covered the unfolding story; university-related sex discrimination later became a regular beat that was assigned to a woman.)

King wasted little effort on the *Ann Arbor News*. "At that time and for many years afterwards," she recalled in 2002, "the *News* was a complete captive of the U-M, feeding on its press releases and rarely going beyond them." Asked to comment, a U-M public relations official at the time thought that judgment was too harsh but acknowledged that the *News* did run most of the press releases the university issued.

At the *Detroit News*, then the more conservative of that city's papers, a man, Russell McCloy, was still in charge of "the Women's Department" and was on the distribution list for CCEW's press releases. But at the *Detroit Free Press*, King had gotten to know two reporters—Eileen Foley and Helen Fogel—when they had covered some of her earlier activities for that paper's women's section.

Women journalists were generally thought to be more sympathetic to the WEAL complaints because they were fighting the same battles in their workplaces. That year, 46 women filed a sex-discrimination suit against *Newsweek*. It was not until 1971 that women were permitted to join the National Press Club and come down from their segregated balcony when they covered "Newsmaker" luncheons there; it took four more years—and several celebrity-studded protests—before Washington's prestigious Gridiron Club opened its ranks to women.

"Subject themselves to little opportunity and low pay," King wrote, the reporters "admired attempts to overcome these same limitations for women employees of the U-M and gleefully reported what we sent them." Unlike women faculty members, "the women reporters were only doing their job, reporting interesting and novel news, so they were relatively protected."

Eileen Foley, then 36, had earned a master's degree in social work from Michigan before joining the *Free Press* in 1968 in what was a typical entry-level job for a woman at the time: researcher for the paper's "Action Line" reader service column. Reporting for the women's pages was a natural next step. Foley later joined the staff of the *Toledo Blade*. At the time of her death, a former colleague recalled that "she had the journalistic instincts to challenge authority and ask tough questions."

Helen Fogel was a few years older; she later moved to the *Detroit News* and became active in The Newspaper Guild (now called The NewsGuild), the union that represented newspaper editorial employees. A union officer later recalled that when women were directed to write for society pages, "Helen rallied for women to cover real news stories. She was someone that was always in the forefront, a real objective writer and an important reporter in the union movement." King first dealt with Fogel when she reported on King's efforts to organize the Women's Caucus in the state Democratic Party. "I remember she asked me in our first phone call about my position on the Equal Rights Amendment, which I then had never heard of," King recalled.

King and Sandler also worked with women reporters from the *Chronicle of Higher Education* to spread coverage of their activities nationwide. The *Chronicle*, King later wrote, "was more important to us [than] any other publication because we knew that almost every academic woman in the United States from community college employees to Harvard faculty had access to, and often read, the *Chronicle*. Thus thousands of U.S. women could gain hope from our success and have a model to strike out on their own."

HEW had previously begun to investigate a complaint filed against Harvard University by Lynda G. Christian of the Eastern Massachusetts chapter of NOW. In May, then-Labor Secretary Shultz told Republican Sen. Edward W. Brooke that HEW had dispatched a team to Harvard "and we expect a report of their findings and recommendations within the next 30 to 60 days." But the investigation there ended up focusing on racial discrimination instead. (HEW had delayed the awarding of federal contracts to Harvard for two weeks over Harvard's initial refusal to let investigators review its personnel files.) A few years later, Sandler wrote that although the Harvard investigation had started with a sex discrimination complaint, HEW had included only three paragraphs addressing that concern in its five pages of findings about racial discrimination. HEW had also been wrangling with Columbia University since January 1969 about its affirmative action plan, but despite complaints generated by Columbia's Women's Liberation, the focus did not seem to widen beyond racial discrimination.

King was pleasantly surprised that federal investigators came to campus within three months—"really the speed of light in federal investigations," she recalled. William Cash, Fleming's assistant for human relations affairs, told PROBE members later that fall that "HEW actually came to review minority groups, but they also had this complaint from FOCUS and decided to investigate it. . . . They come every six months to do a checkout on-site visit. . . . Michigan happened to be the target institution in the Midwest." But King's letters likely made a difference. By the end of July, Clifford Minton, the HEW compliance officer in Chicago, was told to review the FOCUS complaint.

Because Minton was once again in charge of reviewing Michigan's record, the focus could have easily remained on racial discrimination. On August 11, 1970, Cash sent Minton what he described as the university's annual report on its implementation of its affirmative action program. Cash said the report showed "an observable increase in contacts with minority people." It made no mention of women.

Minton had long been engaged in fighting discrimination against blacks. Years later, Sandler recalled, blacks in the enforcement agencies "wanted to work on their own issues. . . . A lot of people didn't take women's issues seriously." Their attitude was, "Now you're taking resources away" from responding to the problems that minorities faced.

In June, HEW had instructed its field personnel to begin including sex discrimination in their contract compliance investigations, whether or not a complaint had been filed. That same month, the Labor Department finally issued the guidelines it expected federal contractors to follow regarding women employees. The guidelines, which had been in the works for two years, dealt with policies specific to women workers, such as maternity leave. But leaders like Sandler complained that the guidelines were too weak.

In *Jobs & Civil Rights*, his report for the U.S. Commission on Civil Rights, author Richard Nathan provided not only Sandler's key footnote but also the results of his survey of contract compliance specialists and how they viewed their roles. Most considered themselves "counselors or advisors to assist the contractor in putting himself in compliance with the executive order," he said.

Nathan concluded, "There appears to be a number of ways in which an employer can 'get by' without too much effort under the present system. This is not to ignore the fact that many employers are sincere and determined about their equal job programs. The point is that, with a cooperative attitude, most employers who choose to do so can circumvent 'suggested' employment policy changes and yet still avoid serious consequences under Executive Order 11246."

Recalling that era, Macaluso said, "We had been working to give . . . anti-discrimination protection to blacks and Hispanics, and they were all male. And now it was quite a different thing . . . starting to draft sex discrimination guidelines. Fortunately, we had a lot of very, very bright women in the organization, and they were able to tell me— sometimes tell me off—just tell me what we males were doing, that was usually, unwittingly, that was just not fair."

From her vantage point, Sandler noted that up to now federal contract compliance efforts had been focused on defense contractors. "In the world of higher education, the people who primarily have contracts with the government are educational institutions and hospitals. . . . And they're not really looking at the executive order very carefully in terms of women, they're looking at it in terms of race," Sandler said. "All of the people who are on their staff came . . . to work for those departments because they cared about racial discrimination. . . . Along I come, and what happens is that they have to look at sex discrimination in educational institutions, and they don't have a clue. First of all, some of them don't care about this issue, some do, but some don't."

As U-M officials got ready for HEW's review in August, the Flemings squeezed in a vacation when they were invited on what was billed as American Airlines' inaugural flight to Honolulu and the South Pacific, including Australia. On August 16, the day before Minton's team arrived for its five-day visit, Fleming wrote an old friend: "Sally and I have had a great summer. . . . Unfortunately, school is about to start."

Minton was expected to bring three colleagues, identified, in an internal note to Fleming, as "Don Shortt," and two attorneys, Esther Lardent and Justine Fisher. Their schedule called for them to meet with Cash their first afternoon in town, although it is not clear that they actually did. The next morning, they planned to meet with the FOCUS representatives.

The visit occurred during the end-of-summer break when the *Daily* was on hiatus. But King's publicity efforts ensured that this summer's compliance review would draw more attention than the last one did. Fogel teed up the investigation with a *Free Press* story the day the team arrived in Ann Arbor: "Bias Probe Will Open at U-M." The women's section story read: "Millions of dollars worth of federal contracts will be at stake" as HEW officials "investigate charges of illegal discrimination at the University of Michigan this week. . . . Failure to eliminate such discrimination is grounds for termination of federal contracts. Much of the university's research and some of its teaching programs are conducted under federal contract."

Fogel noted that the university was "one of more than 100 universities nationally" that had been charged with sex discrimination; she pointed out that the list now included Wayne State University in Detroit.

The next day Fogel continued pursuing the story, and King probably advised her where and when she would be meeting with investigators. King recalled that Fogel "was waiting at the bottom of the stairs" at the Holiday Inn West. King recalled that "Minton went down to the bottom of the stairs and said, whatever he said, whatever she quoted him as saying, that the women didn't have any case. That time those investigators were mostly investigating race discrimination. And they were mostly investigating factories. They weren't investigating universities. The system for hiring people at the university is very complicated. It was very familiar to me. . . . But this guy, you couldn't explain it to him."

At another time, King recalled of Minton, "It was very hard to get him to understand the contours of the University, the grapevine system of hiring, and other esoterics of academia."

Minton told Fogel that FOCUS's allegations were "of a general nature" and that no individual had stepped forward to complain about sex discrimination. His team, he said, "would have to search records to get specifics." Minton said the investigation would include a check of the university's promotion patterns and its recruiting system. Fogel reported that Minton had "great respect for the sincerity of the FOCUS members" but that the complaints were not specific enough to give the compliance team much to work with. Minton acknowledged that the Michigan complaint was the first sex discrimination complaint his regional office had been called on to review and that "he and his team were feeling their way along."

King's frustration with the initial meeting continued to animate her later interviews. Minton was accompanied only by the two "young women," whom, she recalled, "didn't say much but wiggled their behinds on the sofa at appropriate points in ways that were sympathetic to our arguments so I knew at least somebody in the room understood besides us."

Minton, then 59, was nearing the end of a five-year stint with HEW's Chicago office, during which time he had served as field representative, civil rights director, and chief of contract compliance for the office's six-state region. (He continued to serve as a consultant to the agency until he turned 80.) He had had a long history of fighting racial prejudice, starting in Little Rock, Arkansas. His childhood home was burnt to the ground by white supremacists, and at the age of 16, he had witnessed a lynching.

During World War II, he had succeeded in promoting the hiring of blacks—and eventually black women—at Camp Joseph T. Robinson in North Little Rock and later the Arkansas Ordnance Plant in nearby Jacksonville. In 2017, historian Tabitha Orr wrote that Minton "tenaciously needled and cajoled union leaders, government contractors, military officials and local [United States Employment Services] agents to hire black workers." He also marshaled the local black press and interfaith religious leaders to try to break through the employment practices of the Jim Crow South. "But in the process," Orr wrote, "he made powerful enemies who would revoke his draft exemption to rid themselves of him." Minton later left Arkansas for good, going on to serve as director of the Cleveland Urban League's Department of Industrial Relations before becoming executive director of Gary, Indiana's Urban League in 1949.

King's dismissive assessment of Minton's experience with universities may have been somewhat unfair; in addition to visiting Michigan the previous summer, he *had* conducted compliance reviews at other midwestern universities. At 90, Minton self-published a memoir entitled *America's Black Trap: The Roots of the Culture—Case Experiences in Race, Color and Class—in the United States and Abroad.* Minton viewed his time in the federal government through the lens of race and described at length his expertise in combatting race discrimination. In the book, he specifically referenced an investigation he led at the University of Wisconsin in July 1970 and another at the University of Akron in October 1969. Minton wrote that although that university's president, Norman Auburn, was informed that he would be expected to meet with the compliance team at the beginning and end of their visit, Auburn's secretary told Minton that the president was not available and referred him to a subordinate. "This would not have been acceptable even if there had not been evidence that suggested the prearranged appointment had been changed after it was discovered I was a Negro," he wrote.

Minton said he informed Auburn's secretary to tell him "that if he was not available now as per appointment that my team and I would take the next plane back to Chicago. I told her to tell him the review would be rescheduled and that he would be invited to come to our Chicago office and to bring with him the necessary assistants and records. The clearance of more than a million dollars in Federal funds was pending. The secretary left and did not return. Instead, Dr. Auburn appeared. He was conveniently available as needed throughout the 3-day review. Subsequent events during the review strongly suggested that Dr. Auburn did not desire to negotiate with a Negro, and in the beginning he had attempted to discriminate on the basis of race against a government official."

Minton then added, "We did not experience this kind of behavior with Dr. [Edward] Lev[i], University of Chicago, nor with Presidents Robb[e]n Fleming, University of Michigan; Fred H. Harrington, University of Wisconsin; nor with the president of the University of Minnesota or any other college or university."

During Minton's 1970 visit to Ann Arbor, Michigan's public relations department took photographs of him with Fleming, Vice President Allan Smith, and Cash. Within a matter of weeks, the photo appeared in *Info*, a newspaper that served Gary's African-American community, next to a story headlined "Minton Heads Bias Probe Team." The story said, "Although Minton's experience has been in the investigation of minority group discrimination in employment, he said similar practices and remedies tend to apply in sex discrimination."

In his memoir, Minton said he felt he had worked well with high-level university officials to address racial discrimination during his federal career. He made one reference to sex discrimination, writing, "I believe that Federal funds earmarked to expedite closing the gap between white and black opportunity in higher education have been used to help the schools per se more than to help minorities and women."

King recalled that she was "crushed" when she read Fogel's story and Minton's quotations about the extent of discrimination the investigators had found. That day she wrote J. Stanley Pottinger, then head of HEW's Office of Civil Rights in Washington and Minton's superior. She noted that she had heard back from Republican Rep. William Broomfield and expressed her delight that "HEW has moved so promptly on our complaint." However, she went on, "since the investigation has begun we have become very concerned about two of its aspects." She enclosed a copy of Minton's comments and said, "In the present state of the art, sex discrimination is easily demonstrable by pattern, but women are for a number of complex reasons generally unwilling to come forward and [make] a specific charge in relationship to themselves. If your office understands this, would you kindly explain this to the Michigan congressmen and senators. We have been writing them all summer long enlisting their support in getting this investigation. Now they read in the *Free Press* that we are 'sincere' but our complaints are not specific enough."

In addition, King complained to Pottinger that the compliance team did not believe it had the authority to deal with discrimination in admissions, a question that would become a major sticking point over the coming months. King also complained to Minton's supervisor, John Hodgdon, the director of Chicago's regional civil rights office, whom she remembered as "a real mensch." Sandler later wrote that after hearing about Minton's comments, "WEAL immediately telegrammed the secretary of HEW demanding the investigator's resignation."

King also told Sandler about the lack of attention being given to admissions, and Sandler immediately sent a memo to Rep. Green. Sandler offered to draft letters for Green to send to top HEW officials and suggested to King that she call Hart's office to get its help. She tried to reach Kiely, but he was on vacation. His deputy, Roy McKinney, told her that the department was still reviewing whether it had jurisdiction over graduate admissions. Before the investigators had even left Ann Arbor, Hart's office got the same answer when Ferris inquired.

During the visit, the HEW investigators sought to review individual personnel files, a sensitive issue for politically active faculty members.

On August 20, Fleming wrote Minton while he was still in town: "We are conscious of the fact that in accepting HEW grants we have agreed to make our records available for your confidential examination. [Actually, the executive order did not apply to grant recipients.] Nevertheless, we are concerned because some personnel files would contain statements from references who were assured that they were speaking to us for our own confidential information." Fleming then laid out the rules under which Michigan would permit the files to be reviewed, adding that he believed "they are acceptable to your people." His ground rules specified that files could be reviewed only in the office where they were located; that investigators would use numbers to identify individuals rather than their names; that information provided in confidence by off-campus references would be deleted before the file was shared but could be reviewed with the reference's approval; and that any unanticipated problems would be cleared through Vice President Smith.

Ann Larimore and her husband, John Kolars, both members of U-M's Geography Department, were in Turkey that summer and fall doing research. When they returned in December, she phoned a friend in the department, who told her, "'Your files have been taken out of the office by HEW.' That was the first I knew about it. . . .The department at the time it happened did not alert me. It was just told to me by a friend, 'oh by the way. . . .'"

Larimore recalled that she knew nothing about sex discrimination at the time because she had spent much of her early academic career outside of the country and had been fortunate to be offered faculty appointments. She had no idea why HEW would have been interested in her file. But HUAC's investigation still haunted many Michigan faculty members. When she returned to campus in January 1971, the department chairman "told me that he had resisted, as best he could, letting my file leave the filing cabinet. . . . He assumed that that was exactly what I wanted. . . . He said that a 'brassy dame' had come to the department from HEW and demanded my personnel file. . . . Now this man was six foot seven and weighed 250 pounds and he portrayed himself as standing in front of the filing cabinet. And he said that he refused to let her have access to the file and take it out of the department until the President's Office ordered him to do so. And so he called the President's

Office and was told that he had to comply." Larimore did not identify her chairman, but it was Melvin G. Marcus.

Larimore later learned—probably, she said, from King—that investigators had "pulled the files of all married couples employed in the same units in the university," and that her file was reviewed in that process. As an experienced researcher, Larimore observed that techniques had not yet been developed for defining or assessing sex discrimination. The investigators, she noted, "did what would be kind of a standard sociological procedure: 'To compare two people, we'll compare husbands and wives in the same unit.' So they located all the husbands and wives that were employed in the same unit. So it was systematic."

On the last day of the HEW team's visit, the *Ann Arbor News* cited Minton in reporting that "whether or not the team will return to the U-M campus depends on the quantity and quality of information obtained through interviews and records." As the team left town, Fogel reported that it had found no "verifiable evidence" but that they did find "administrative and procedural deficiencies in personnel administration which appear to operate to the disadvantage of women." The story said the team would return within a week to "present their findings and recommendations to university officials after an analysis of the complaints they have received during their week-long study at U-M." Minton said that if deficiencies were uncovered, they would discuss them when they returned. He said they would also discuss their findings with FOCUS.

Minton reiterated that the investigation was the first he had directed at sex discrimination and that it had covered three main areas: academic and managerial assignments, unequal pay, and the use of women overqualified for a job category.

Fogel's story noted that FOCUS was likely to be disappointed that the team was not reviewing admissions policies. However, McKinney again told her that the department was seeking a legal opinion on the matter.

McKinney contradicted what Minton had said at the outset of his visit, maintaining that the department *did* review employment patterns as well as individual cases. More significantly, he said that the FOCUS complaint had "suddenly received very high priority" among the hundred or so complaints that had been filed, but provided no explanation why. He had, of course, just heard from Sen. Hart's office.

It is not clear exactly what happened to Minton after he left Ann Arbor. One account, prepared in 1971, said he "left the Chicago office of HEW in late August, 1970." His name disappears from all future correspondence between HEW and the university. Fleming's office received a letter over his signature in October 1970, but the letter was undated and seemed to be a standard form letter, forwarding the Labor Department's guidelines on sex discrimination.

In his memoir 30 years later, Minton described the investigations at Michigan and Wisconsin in conspiratorial terms, viewing them as "entrapment plans" by white superiors to remove him from his job. "It became clear that rewards had been offered to three members of my staff to throw a monkey wrench into the investigation behind my back. I conclude entrapment was resorted to after other ways could not be found as a basis for putting demerits on my record and filing charges against me," he recalled.

Minton wrote, "The Foxes assigned to guard the Federal Equal Opportunity Chicken House are suggestive with respect to intent and will of the power elite. Significant among the officials appointed to strategic spots in the administration of the Civil Rights Act of 1964 during the 1960s and 1970s were officials who had been skilled experts in surreptitiously enforcing racist discrimination for years. These old foxes did not seem to desire to learn new dog tricks. It was evident that foxes were concerned with maintaining the status quo. Their underhanded manipulations did not reflect prudence aimed at not moving too fast and getting ahead of public disposition. There were high-level appointments of officials in Washington D.C., who had prestigious open-minded images. . . . But too often the operating officers in lower echelons who screwed the nuts and bolts were not true to the oath of office to uphold and promote the laws of the United States."

Minton's account of the Michigan investigation is riddled with misspellings of most of his close colleagues' names. (He references "Don F. Trott," presumably "Don F. Scott," who took over the investigation; Fleming had been expecting a "Don Shortt.") Minton wrote that Hodgdon (sometimes spelled "Hodson") "was shipped out of the Chicago office after a few months on the job," but Hodgdon actually remained as director for several years.

Nevertheless, Minton served at a time of transition from the John-son to Nixon administrations, when many top officials gave lip service to promoting civil rights while dragging their feet on issuing regula-tions and enforcing the laws. It's possible that his HEW colleagues did complain to their superiors about what happened during their campus visits or that superiors had their own concerns after King and others complained. But his colleagues' record in challenging sex discrimina-tion at the University of Michigan suggested they *were* willing to fight hard against discrimination, even if their focus was not, in this particu-lar case, on race.

Minton's younger colleague Esther Lardent—one of the two "young women" on the sofa in King's retelling and likely the "brassy dame," described by Larimore's chairman—already had experience as one of "Nader's Raiders," the young people whose work supported the cam-paigns of consumer activist Ralph Nader in that era. Lardent went on to a distinguished legal career and founded the Pro Bono Institute in 1996. When she was a student at the University of Maryland, she recalled in an oral history, "... Somebody at the school said, 'You know, there's this really interesting thing that the HEW Office of Civil Rights is doing.' They're the ones who look at universities and hospitals and other organizations that get federal money and investigate complaints of discrimination, and it's always been racial but they're now starting to look at discrimina-tion against women. It just seems like something you might really like."

Lardent got a job and began investigating complaints. "It was a very committed group of people," she said. She recalled that she had wanted a job with the NAACP Legal Defense Fund or the Lawyers' Committee for Civil Rights Under Law to work on civil rights issues in Mississippi. But her husband had been admitted to the University of Chicago's Med-ical School and did not want to transfer to a less prestigious school in the South. So Lardent went to work for the federal government there, "something," she recalled, "I never thought I would do."

Lardent regarded her work on the University of Michigan complaint as "the greatest thing I did."

There is no evidence that U-M administrators were unduly con-cerned about what the HEW investigators might turn up—or, in the immediate aftermath, what they had found. But Fogel's first stories did catch the attention of top public relations officials. Fogel didn't mention

Harvard by name, but her suggestion that federal contracts would be held up while a review was in progress likely sparked further digging. After her first story, Joel Berger, who had just returned to his alma mater as director of information services, contacted the head of Harvard's News Office and reported back to his superiors:

> Bill Pinkerton told me this morning that Helen Fogel is incorrect in her assertion that Harvard's federal contracts have been held up by the federal government because of sex discrimination.
>
> The HEW threat for suspensions is present, but only as a threat. Harvard was investigated last spring by the HEW, first on the subject of minorities, but then on discrimination against women. A meeting of HEW people with Harvard officials was scheduled for August 10, but postponed until September when the date interfered with HEW personnel's vacations.
>
> Last spring the HEW asked for access to personnel records at Harvard. This was regarded as a fishing expedition and permission was denied. Harvard agreed to furnish statistics and lists, but not to allow direct access to personnel dossiers.

Berger concluded: "Bill's impression is that the HEW people are tough, but are looking for an action plan they can live with."

The HEW team returned to U-M on August 31, 1970, 10 days after their initial visit, this time headed by civil rights specialist Don Scott, who had previously been an Internal Revenue Service agent. The gap between the visits was longer than Minton had predicted, and it appears that instead of negotiating with top officials, the investigators did more digging.

In between the two visits, women across the nation had staged protests and gatherings to mark the 50th anniversary of women's suffrage. Large rallies were held in New York and Washington; the Associated Press quoted a U.S. senator who called the women's movement "a small band of bra-less bubbleheads." Meanwhile, in Ann Arbor, PROBE and other women's groups organized a late-afternoon picnic and "rap session" at a local park.

By the time of HEW's second visit from August 31–September 4, the fall semester had resumed and the *Daily* was able to catch up with the story. On September 3, the paper reprinted Minton's quotations to

Fogel. Then it said FOCUS and other local groups were asserting that "there are more stones to turn over" in the investigation. "The HEW team is concentrating on individual cases while our complaint was that the whole pattern of admission and employment of women by the University is discriminatory," a FOCUS spokeswoman said.

Shortridge reiterated that it was difficult to come up with individual cases because "Women are rightly hesitant about coming to HEW—they are very vulnerable. We don't necessarily think the talks will be recriminating, but women are still in a difficult position." Underscoring her new leadership role with PROBE, she added, "If women are afraid and have something to report, they should call me."

The story said that on that day, the next-to-the-last of HEW's second visit, the team "will resume interviewing people, going through University files, and hold random spot checks."

One of those interviewed was Rose Vainstein, a professional librarian who had joined the School of Library Science as a full professor two years before. Vainstein's expertise was in the area of public librarianship; she arrived in Ann Arbor with a master's degree after directing the Bloomfield Township Public Library in Bloomfield Hills, Michigan. (Ironically, Vainstein's career had included a stint as a public library specialist in the U.S. Office of Education, one likely reason that 16 years later she still knew the number of the HEW region that handled the complaint.) The Chicago office sent what she described in an oral history as "a legal beagle of some sort" to interview her. Vainstein recalled:

> I don't know how they chose the people that they did, but I was one of the individuals chosen to be interviewed. I know that our dean was very nervous—didn't know what might come of it, didn't know what I might say or not say, and, of course, he would not be privy to the interview.
>
> It was interesting because Region Five came with very pointed questions to me, on the assumption that I had been discriminated against by the School of Library Science, which happened not to be true. The interview was conducted in my office, in such a way, and the questions phrased like, "When did you stop beating your wife?" so that no matter how you answered, you couldn't win. I kept saying I didn't feel *personally* discrimi-

nated against. I came to U-M at full rank, as a full professor with tenure. Nobody in Library Science at that time was paid a decent salary, and I was not being paid any lower salary than anybody else. He was very disappointed. Then he wanted to know whether I was denied secretarial help or office help or student assistant help. We were all denied that. Our budget was quite limited. I think he found me a very unsatisfactory interviewee. I kept saying, "No, I didn't think that was the case." I felt that I had come in at full rank, a full professor with tenure, and I did not have a PhD and that I thought that was a remarkable appointment. And then I looked at him and I said, "And I'm Jewish, besides." I remember precisely, he slapped his hand on his knee and said, "Thank you very for much for the interview," and it was over. I was sensitive to lots of discrimination against women, but what he was trying to get from me was not anything that I could, in all honesty, speak to.

Nevertheless, Vainstein shared the frustrations that many campus women then felt. She said she was sensitive to women's issues, "partially because of my own profession which is librarianship, predominately female, and much like nursing and education are not professions that are either well paid or valued by the power structure. Once you're at a university like Michigan, you begin to see where the power is and where it isn't, and you begin to feel kind of helpless from being able to affect any kind of change."

7
The Rebels

Clifford Minton told reporters that no University of Michigan woman had come forward with a specific complaint. But before the end of September 1970, at least two women did.

Helen Tanner was the wife of Wilson Tanner, a psychology professor, and a mother of four who had earned a doctorate in history from Michigan in 1961 at the age of 45. In September 1970, she returned to Ann Arbor from her husband's sabbatical year to discover the HEW investigators had already left town. A few years before, Tanner had been poised to join the faculty of U-M's Residential College, but in 1968, the History Department rejected her appointment. Back in town, she vented to her friend Jean King about running into a woman who thought she had "a faculty connection." "My basic gripe is that I have not been able to be considered part of the U of M faculty," she wrote.

But Tanner learned that HEW was still accepting complaints. She wrote Hodgdon about her situation and also sent a long-planned letter to Fleming, with a copy of her complaint. She told King that she had been trying to get other women to write Hodgdon: "It's too bad I was not around in August, because I am sure I could have increased the number of signed letters you received."

A specialist in Latin American history, Tanner described to Hodgdon how she had been hired to teach extension courses at university graduate centers around the state and had taken on the responsibilities of a full professor during a one-semester emergency. As she waited for a teaching job, she had served as associate director of CCEW for four years but decided to resign after the History Department rebuffed her because, she said, "I could no longer make speeches, with any honesty, about 'the wonderful opportunities for women at the University of Michigan.'"

She said she was lodging a complaint against both the department and the central administration. The latter "has permitted a highly prejudiced History Department to carry on arbitrary discrimination against professionally trained women for many years. The injustice of my own situation (i.e., being considered qualified to teach graduate students *off campus* but not to teach undergraduates *on campus*) was called to the attention of the Dean of the Literary College and to the Vice President for Academic Affairs in 1968. The evidence of discrimination was obvious, but administrative officials seemed to feel impotent to interfere with 'departmental autonomy'" (emphasis in original). Referring to her time at CCEW, Tanner added, "I wonder how many of the hundreds of women who brought their troubles to my office have told their experiences to you." Tanner sent a copy of her letter to Pottinger, head of HEW's Office of Civil Rights in Washington.

Tanner advised Fleming that she had "told my story in abridged form. . . because I've become convinced that competent women will not be able to teach at the University unless concerted outside pressure is applied. It seems clear that the U of M has become much more liberal in assisting women to *acquire* an education, but the present university system in Ann Arbor prevents a woman from *using* her education on this campus. Although there are isolated successes, the University of Michigan operates in a manner to exclude professionally-trained women" (emphasis in original).

Meanwhile, on September 20, Margaret B. Davis, a zoology professor, sent Esther Lardent a letter, detailing her efforts to get her salary raised to the level of her male colleagues. Davis's battle had made her so angry that she had threatened to file a sex discrimination complaint with the Michigan Civil Rights Commission. What was particularly notable about her decision to write HEW was that she had little to gain by doing so; she had already received a raise.

Davis's letter became Exhibit #5 of the findings HEW sent to U-M, part of the appendices that apparently were never publicly released. It is unclear why HEW highlighted her complaint but not Tanner's. It may have been that they thought her case was more clear-cut, involving dollars and cents, rather than a subjective hiring decision and a "he said, she said" kind of battle. Or it may have been that in directing her letter to Lardent instead of Hodgdon, Davis captured the attention of the younger woman. In any event, the complaints of both women would play out within the university and HEW over the next two years.

In her letter, Davis acknowledged that if she had filed a lawsuit, it would have been "unsuccessful" because she was not covered by current federal and state civil rights laws. "Other women with less self-confidence and with less time and energy to spend on the matter will not press for salary increases, and therefore will continue at a low salary level. There appears to be no commitment on the part of the administration to pay equal salaries as matter of principle," she noted. Davis told the investigators to "please feel free to use my name and salary figures, and to make use of this letter as you see fit."

In his first response to President Fleming, Don Scott bluntly described Davis's "unsolicited" letter this way: "It is a chronicle of events leading to a pay increase of this particular person. It is an example of the University of Michigan's failure to provide equal pay for equal work for its female academic employees."

Davis's story was not unlike many women faculty of her generation. She was born in 1931 and grew up in an academic family in Cambridge, Massachusetts. According to her brother, Kirk Bryan Jr., when she entered Radcliffe, she had to live at home until she won a scholarship that provided her with enough financial support that she could afford to move into a dorm. As an undergraduate biology major, she became interested in paleobotany, the study of plants through geological history. She graduated first or second (reports vary) in the Class of 1953.

Davis pursued graduate studies at Harvard and won a Fulbright Scholarship to spend a year in Copenhagen, studying with Johannes Iversen at the Danish Geological Survey. Iversen was a world leader in the field of palynology, the study of live and fossilized pollens and spores. Davis changed her focus to that field as she finished her doctorate at Harvard in 1957 and pursued post-doctoral research work there under a National Science Foundation (NSF) fellowship and at the California Institute of Technology and Yale. As described in a 1987 issue of the *Bulletin of the Ecological Society of America*, a research approach she

developed while still at Yale had by then become "a standard palyno-
logical technique."

Davis's background, her brother recalled, "gave her the self-confidence to challenge a system at the university that systematically gave a
lower rating to women than to men. She felt the injustice keenly, while
many women were willing to accept it."

Davis followed her husband, microbial geneticist Rowland H. Davis,
who was two years her junior, to Michigan in 1961. She found a job as
a research associate in the Botany Department. A 1972 story in the *Ann
Arbor News* recounted that "she and her spouse had settled in Ann Arbor
and she knew she had to have a job in the area. That, she feels, put her in
a bad bargaining position with her potential employer. And, consciously
or not, she feels the employer took advantage of this."

In 1964, Davis was hired as an associate research biologist at U-M's
Great Lakes Research Division. In 1966, she became an associate professor of zoology, with half of her salary paid by the university and the
other half by research grants—"a cheapie appointment," as she said
someone later described it to her.

"Salary is set by bargaining," Davis told the *Ann Arbor News*, adding
that the employer pays what he feels the market will bear, not what the
employee should earn on her merits. "Men can move. Everyone believes
women can't. I was vulnerable to low wages because I couldn't leave the
University. I was the lowest paid person in my ranking," she said.

Bryan said he felt his sister's husband "did not really support her in
this struggle with the university hierarchy, and that was probably a fac-
tor in their separation at about this time." The couple divorced in 1970.

That September, Davis wrote Lardent on the letterhead of the Great
Lakes research program. She recalled that in May 1969:

> It came to my attention that my salary ($12,200 for the academic
> year 1968–69) was far below the median being paid for associ-
> ate professors. I complained to the Chairman of Zoology, John
> M. Allen, but he said nothing major could be done about it that
> year. He then said he had talked to the Dean, and that perhaps
> something could be done the next year. He stated that there was
> little that he could do, since half my academic year salary is
> paid from a sponsored research grant, and that he therefore had

no control over the rate of pay. I denied this, pointing out that according to the NSF rulings given in their booklet regarding the administration of research grants, salaries are to be paid at the level set by the University. Dr. Allen invoked this excuse again in 1970 although he never asked whether sponsored research funds were available to meet an increase. Finally at my request the Director of the Great Lakes Research Division, David Chandler, emphasized to Dr. Allen that my salary level is set by the Zoology Department. (My research grant is administered through the Great Lakes Research Division.) Dr. Chandler guaranteed to the Zoology Chairman that the increase in pay recommended by the Zoology Department could be met (that is the half that is paid by sponsored research funds) either from my grant or from general funds in the Great Lakes Division. This effectively removed the source of my salary as an excuse for failure to raise my salary to an equitable level.

In March 1970, Allen told Davis that the Departmental Promotions Committee had recommended that she be promoted to full professor. She told HEW he also told her that the "*ad hoc* letters regarding my qualifications were some of the strongest he had ever seen" and that the promotions committee chairman had also told her he was "impressed." A few weeks later, she wrote, Acting LSA Dean Sussman had said that the college's Executive Committee had approved her promotion and that it would be forwarded to the Regents. Sussman, she recounted, had told her that the promotion had passed "with flying colors, not like some others," implying, she concluded, "that the evaluation by the Executive Committee was that I well deserved the promotion, rather than just squeaking into it." As a member of the Botany Department faculty himself, Sussman was particularly well qualified to evaluate the quality of Davis's research.

Davis said that around that time she asked Allen how large a raise she should expect so she could budget enough to cover her new salary when she reapplied for her grant. He said her salary would be set by the dean but that she should expect a raise of about 8 percent.

Davis said she calculated the dollar amount and concluded "this increase would not even raise me to the median for associate professors, much less to the level being paid full professors." She asserted that

"I felt my salary was low because I was a woman, and that I intended to complain to the Michigan Civil Rights Commission." She continued with her story:

> He said he didn't think that would be necessary. What was my salary? I told him it was $13,200, whereupon he burst out laughing and said he would try to do something. Later in the day, he called me to apologize for laughing, but said he couldn't help it because $13,200 was the salary being paid in the department to assistant professors, not to associate professors about to be promoted to full professors.

In April or early May, Davis said Allen told her he had received a letter from Associate LSA Dean Carruth who agreed that her salary was "rather low," but that "he didn't think it could be rectified this year. Perhaps it could be raised part of the way this year, and part of the way next year." She wrote, "I answered that this would not be satisfactory, I needed the money this year."

Davis wrote that at that point, she realized she would have to file a complaint, and she tried to get more information about salary scales. The information was not available, she said, department by department, "an important point since salaries in Zoology are higher than in the LS&A College as a whole." Further, she said, the salary figures reported by the Senate Report on the Economic Status of the Faculty were a year old and did not provide the salary range for each professorial rank.

"However," she said, "through the kindness of someone who had legal access to the salaries in the Department of Zoology I found that the highest salary being paid an associate professor was $16,500 (1969–70)." A handwritten note added, "and the lowest salary for a full professor was $16,000." She said she had asked Chandler to talk with Allen on her behalf, "and repeated to him that if my pay was not raised to an appropriate level, I was going to take legal action against the University." She reported that Chandler spoke with Allen and Sussman and recommended that her salary be raised to between $16,000 and $17,000.

In June 1970, the month after King and Yourd filed their complaint, Allen told Davis her salary would be set at $16,000. She observed that that was the minimum that was paid full professors, but he disagreed, saying that the minimum was $500 less. Although that was contrary to what she had "obtained independently," she said she had "no way of checking the veracity of his statement."

A few days later, Davis called Sussman and said she wanted to talk about her salary. Sussman, she recounted, replied, "Yes, I know, it's unfair as hell." But, he said, something was going to be done about it. He checked his files and then returned to the phone to tell her that her salary was being raised to $16,000. Davis said that was unacceptable, that others in the department with "lesser qualifications" were receiving higher salaries. She reiterated that she was going to write the state Civil Rights Commission.

"He pointed out that it was a large increase," she wrote HEW, "and I replied that starting from zero, a large increase still didn't mean equitable pay. He said that the University was hard pressed this year. I replied that I felt I had made formidable contributions to the economy of the University already by working all these years for such low pay but that I was no longer willing to do it. He stated that something would be done next year. I replied somewhat bitterly that I did not believe him." Davis's letter continued:

> I then went on to say that when I threatened to lodge a complaint against the University, I really meant it. I stated further that it didn't make sense to me that a University that failed to pay women equitable salaries should expend so much energy training women graduate students. What sort of a future would they face? Dean Sussman said sadly that probably they would never receive equal pay. He then stated that he would try to do something in my behalf, adding that because of my research record he could make a better case for me than some other women in the faculty. The implication of this statement was that women faculty salaries will be raised to the level paid men only in cases where they complain, and made a good case. The burden of proof falling on the faculty member means she has to be sure she's better than equal before she can claim equal pay.

Within a day or two, Sussman called Davis back to say that her salary would be increased to $17,000 for the 1970–71 academic year.

Davis could have returned to her lab, smug in the knowledge that she had achieved her goal. But she had gone through a painful year. She recalled 18 months later that she had incurred some animosity because of her complaints, but that "it hurt me far more to be getting the unfair pay. It made me feel inferior. I was sort of cowed because I felt I was not valued very highly. Now I know it was not a reflection of a differential in merit, but a mistake in the system. If you accept it without complaining, you're admitting that you aren't worth very much. It's a matter of self respect. You have to fight back."

Harriet Mills, a professor of Chinese language and literature who eventually learned the details of Davis's battle, recalled, "She was one of these feisty, no-nonsense people who had the credentials to back it up. There were a few, very courageous people like [Margaret] Davis on the faculty. She happened to be a faculty person who fed into this total pot that was boiling. . . ."

A few weeks after Davis was notified of her raise, Fleming mused to the *Ann Arbor News* that in the professional fields, the personnel was "overwhelmingly male," and that was "the preference of the market." The question arises, he said, "whether in a supposedly free economy, market preference should have any weight?"

Davis knew what *her* answer was. And within a few weeks, she decided to tell her story to the federal government.

8

The Findings

The HEW investigators returned to their offices in Chicago, and in Ann Arbor, the women waited. As classes resumed in the fall of 1970, the attention on Michigan's campus turned to football—and whether Bo Schembechler's Wolverines would repeat as Big Ten champions. HEW had already received more than a hundred complaints and had investigated a handful of them. There was no sign this one would be treated any differently.

Sandler recalled that as the volume of complaints was mounting, "higher education is getting a little nervous." But if Michigan's top officials were worried, they were not telegraphing that concern beyond their office doors.

In interviews 40 years later, investigator Esther Lardent remembered very clearly what she and her HEW colleagues turned up at Michigan. "The fact that all of this was so new meant that. . . people didn't couch anything in the files in subtle ways," she said. "We found the most amazing things in there. For example, there was one comment in a file about a very distinguished woman. . . and her husband had accepted an appointment at Michigan, and in the file it said, 'and we're very lucky because she's following her husband, so we can pay her a lot less than we'd have to if she were a man.'"

Lardent was likely recalling Ann Larimore's situation. The young geography professor was blissfully unaware that her personnel file included these comments:

- "Deserves a professorial appointment, and would have tenure in a major department were it not for the fact that she is in the same field (and, in this case, the same department) as her husband."
- "Because her husband is on the departmental staff, we are not able to make use of her considerable skill in all aspects of the departmental programs, but she makes a remarkable contribution in those areas where she can work."

Lardent said she was "appalled" by what the investigators found.

I don't think any of us sort of realized how intense this was, how accepted it was, how wide-spread it was. Women were clearly not taken seriously. They were not viewed as peers. What we would do is literally go through people's credentials, and the credentials would be identical to a man, and they would be seen as second rate. . . or, innately presenting problems and obstacles, and that sort of thing. It was exciting because this had never been done before.

We literally created the model for how the review went. Women were there in greater numbers, and women were applying in greater numbers, and it was just a different kind of discrimination, but it had an intensity to it that was very strong. When I thought about doing civil rights work, I had always thought about it in terms of race. We have such a horrible history that is pernicious and lingering, to this very day obviously, [of] racism in this country, but there was [a] kind of viciousness about this that was really disturbing.

Lardent added that she knew from talking to her medical student husband that sex discrimination was even worse in medical schools. "It really was like a hell week experience for women," said Lardent. "People would do things to try to shock them, you know, with cadavers or sexual stuff. It was pretty brutal, and there were not that many women. It's amazing when you look at the number of women in law school and med school [40 years later] compared to then, you know, it was so different. . . just incredibly different."

It was not reported at the time—nor in most subsequent accounts— that Fleming met with Scott and Hodgdon in late September. In 1971, a case study of the HEW investigation was prepared for Harvard's Institute for Educational Management. The report was done, it said, "as a basis for class discussion rather than to illustrate either effective or ineffective handling of an administrative situation." For an audience of their peers, university officials spoke more candidly about what had transpired.

The study said: "The short meeting ended with agreement that there was substantial disagreement between HEW and the University. Representatives of the University at the meeting felt that Mr. Scott had done 'poor research.' The data was incomplete and lacked the impartiality needed as a base for such serious allegations, these representatives stated. President Fleming asked Mr. Scott to send him a letter detailing HEW's allegations and recommendations."

Scott sent that letter on October 6, 1970. He outlined four broad areas where he said HEW had found:

- The admission of women to doctoral programs lagged behind the proportion of women earning master's degrees.
- The hiring of women for faculty positions lagged behind the proportion of women who had earned doctorates.
- Wage discrepancies existed between men and women in academic positions.
- Sex discrimination also persisted in non-academic employment practices.

Scott was tough and blunt. He reminded Fleming that the Executive Order "requires that the same qualification for employment be applied to both men and women. Many department chairmen who realize that women are underutilized in their departments do not realize they are required by the Executive Order to rectify the situation by affirmatively recruiting women faculty."

After 10 pages of details, Scott wrote, "The above findings established that the University of Michigan is not complying with the requirements of E.O. 11246 and 11375."

He then threw down his challenge: "In order for the University to continue its eligibility to receive government contracts, you must provide a written commitment to stop the discriminatory treatment of women, to erase the effects of this discriminatory treatment and to develop and implement an amended Affirmative Action Program which will insure equal opportunity for women in employment and in treatment during employment with the University. This amended Affirmative Action Program must respond specifically to the findings contained in this letter."

Scott said the amended program "must include detailed plans to take the following precise actions and the dates for completion of the actions." For every item but one, HEW demanded a statistical analysis or goals and timetables, or both:

1. "Achieve salary equity between current male and female employees in every job category" where both men and women currently worked.
2. "Compensate through the payment of back wages, each female employee who has lost wages due to discriminatory treatment by the University." The payment, he said, would need to be retroactive to October 13, 1968, the effective date of the executive order, and, he said, when the university assumed a contractual obligation not to discriminate on the basis of sex. This, he said, would require an analysis of the wages of every woman.
3. "Achieve a ratio of female employment in academic positions at least equivalent to their availability as evidenced by applications for employment by qualified females for these positions."
4. "Improve the ratio of female admissions to all PhD graduate programs in which admissions are connected with specific employment opportunity such as teaching and research assistantships."
5. "Increase the participation by women on committees which involve the selection and treatment of employees both academic and non-academic."

6. "Develop and issue a written policy on nepotism which will assure uniform treatment of tandem teams throughout the University and which will not have the effect of discrimination against the female members of such teams."

7. "Analyze the effect of the past interpretations on nepotism and achieve salary equity and retroactively compensate any person who has suffered such discriminatory treatment because of past interpretations of the nepotism policy."

8. "Assure that female applicants for non-academic employment receive consideration for employment commensurate with their qualifications." The university was also required to "assure that the concept of male and female job classification is eliminated through the recruitment, placement, transfer, and promotion of male and female applicants and employees into occupations from which they have traditionally been excluded."

9. "Assure that all present female employees occupying clerical or other non-academic positions and who possess qualifications equivalent to or exceeding those of male employees, occupying higher level positions be given priority consideration for promotions to higher level positions for which they qualify."

Scott concluded by saying, "An amended Affirmative Action Program must be submitted to this office within 30 days of the date of this letter. We will, of course, evaluate the program you develop to determine whether or not they appear to be acceptable and responsive to the problems we have identified."

HEW's conclusions were shocking in their breadth and critical tone. But the task it put before the university was a daunting one, even if top officials had been inclined to comply. Sue Rasmussen, who was involved with monitoring Michigan's early affirmative action efforts, recalled that it was not until 1978 that the university had computer systems that could accurately generate the kind of employment statistics HEW wanted across the whole institution; until then it could only produce them by contacting individual departments and offices.

Scott's letter was delivered speedily enough that Fleming's response was dated the next day. But his language suggests he was trying to buy time: "Your letter, and the documents which are attached, are lengthy and require analysis. It is probable that there will be points of disagreement between us, some of which may be serious.

"Given the magnitude of the task which your letter would impose upon us, it would seem to me unlikely that an affirmative program of the kind you envision could be generated within thirty days, even assuming we were in complete agreement. Nevertheless, we shall work immediately upon the analysis of your letter and the development of our program."

Fleming then underscored his view that racial and sex discrimination were quite different: "We do not differ with respect to the principle of equal treatment for women. There are extraordinarily difficult problems in establishing criteria for what constitutes equal treatment, and we believe they are quite different from the now familiar problems in the field of race."

Scott's 13-page letter provided statistical back-up for every finding of sex discrimination that HEW had alleged. It backed that up with seven exhibits, totaling 12 more pages, including a copy of the letter Davis had sent to Lardent.

In reviewing how university administrators chose to respond to HEW, one is struck that this was a problem no one was eager to take on. Fleming naturally took the lead, but he was a very busy man. Despite the breadth of the concerns involved—academic hiring, university personnel procedures, graduate school admissions, research contracts, and government relations—administrators remained focused on their narrow silos of responsibility until Fleming gave them a specific assignment. Newell, by then back working as Fleming's executive assistant, sent him memos with suggestions or things she had learned from contacts at other universities. But she recalled that she was "so busy I was up over my eyeballs" and was not a party to all of the executive officers' discussions.

Newell recalled that the way Fleming ran meetings that she attended, "I felt I could speak on anything I wanted to, even 'you've got the wrong trucks.' Not that I would, but I had a feeling that I could talk about any item . . . and people would hear me. I had been around long enough and I was close enough to Fleming, I suppose that's relevant to why I felt perfectly free to speak whenever I wanted to. I do not feel as if I said very much. And most of the negotiating was really done with Smith and

Fleming. . . as I remember it, and I just wasn't a party." Although Newell was given an important role later on, one wonders if the HEW negotiations might have played out differently if she had been put in charge of them from the start.

The defensive posture of the university's male personnel administrators was captured well in a memo that circulated internally three weeks after Scott's letter arrived. At the time, there were, in effect, two personnel offices managing 14,000 full-time employees; the academic side was managed by Charles M. Allmand, who reported to Smith; the university's Personnel Office, led by Russell W. Reister, reported to Pierpont, the vice president for finance. Edward C. Hayes, manager of compensation plans and personnel information systems, and his staff provided technical support to both. But Newell later commented that any suggestion there was centralized management of non-academic appointments was "simply folklore." Most hiring and promoting, she said, was "done through the individual employing units and cleared with the office on a post facto basis."

It fell to Hayes and a colleague named Keith Evans to dissect Scott's findings for Allmand and Reister. A copy of their memo was sent to Smith, Pierpont, and Brinkerhoff, but not to Fleming or Newell.

The memo concluded that Scott's findings were "based on inaccurate and incomplete information, or faulty interpretation of the information, and a lack of understanding of how the University employment processes work."

The memo would not acknowledge that any problems existed or that any of the findings were valid. Instead, it cited the experience of particular departments to challenge the assertions that discrimination had occurred in others. The men found Scott's conclusions "to be without merit and would recommend that the University push for an objective review of these findings with responsible officials in HEW."

The Scott letter began by addressing discrimination in doctoral programs, the issue over which the university fought the hardest and the longest. Scott's letter included data designed to demonstrate that women were not being admitted to PhD programs at the same rate as men. Analyzing the numbers for several departments, HEW found:

- Botany: The number of men in the doctoral program, compared to the number of men working on master's degrees, rose 136 percent, compared with a 7 percent decline for the number of women moving from the master's to the doctoral ranks.
- English Language: Men earning doctorates increased by 16.4 percent, compared with a 63 percent decline for women.
- History: Men earning doctorates increased by 77.2 percent, compared with a 42.6 percent decline for women.
- Germanic Languages and Literature: Men earning doctorates increased by 8.3 percent, compared with a 52.1 percent decline for women.
- Political Science: Men earning doctorates increased by 160 percent, compared with a 27.2 percent decline for women.
- Mathematics: Men earning doctorates increased by 95.3 percent, compared with a 63.1 percent decline for women.
- Chemistry: Men earning doctorates increased by 386.3 percent, compared with an increase of 18 percent for women.

HEW concluded that "women tend to decrease in representation on the PhD level, while men increase significantly." It said that "interviews with some students revealed that females are being discouraged from continuing for PhD training by departmental counseling," confirming "the allegations from the women's group." HEW said criteria for admission to PhD programs involving employment as teaching or research assistants "must be the same for males and females." The executive order, it said, requires "not only nondiscrimination in this area, but affirmative action to overcome deficiencies and underutilization of women" in the university's doctoral programs.

The Hayes-Evans memo asserted that both the university and other federal agencies—including the Internal Revenue Service, the Social Security Administration, and the Wage and Hour Division of the Labor Department—viewed graduate students working as teaching or research assistants "as fulfilling a degree requirement and not as entering an employer-employee relationship. As such, the graduate student is viewed by all the agencies mentioned above primarily as a student and his wages are viewed as student financial aid." In fact, by that fall 100 of Michigan's 1,500 teaching fellows had already organized themselves into a Teaching Fellows Union and were seeking recognition as the teaching assistants' bargaining agent.

The Hayes-Evans memo argued that HEW's "conclusion, or insinuation" overlooks "one major point, the intent of the women at the Master's level. That is, the percentage of women, in relation to men, who want to pursue the PhD. It is a fact, for example, that in a number of the departments indicated women have set for themselves a terminal degree at the Master's level with the explicit objective of teaching in the secondary schools. The only data that would support a case for discrimination against women in the departments shown would be an analysis of the percentage of women who wanted to continue for the PhD degree and the subsequent percentage who did." Of the interviews with students, they wrote, "there is no apparent evidence that the reported confirmation is anything more than unsubstantiated allegations from a few individuals." While they were willing to concede that some women were likely discouraged by departmental counselors from pursuing doctorates, "it is also the case that men are discouraged . . . because in the judgment of the department they could not successfully complete that training."

The officials attached statements regarding admissions policies and procedures for doctoral programs to demonstrate that men and women were treated equally and asserted that they could find "no evidence of any attempt on the part of the investigating group to discuss these matters with the individuals responsible for the admission policies in the Graduate School."

Regarding discrimination against women faculty members, HEW said, "Despite a pool of qualified women applicants and a representative number of women who receive PhD degrees in their departmental specialties, the departmental breakdown. . . show[s] marked discrepancies in the number of women available and women representation on the present faculty." The report cited data from six LSA departments and the Library Science School:

- Botany: 25 percent of the doctoral students admitted for 1970–71 and 17.8 percent of persons who earned PhDs in 1967–68 were women, but only 10.5 percent of the faculty were women.
- English Language and Literature: 41 percent of admitted doctoral students and 27.4 percent of persons earning PhDs were women, but only 7 percent of the faculty. 22.1 percent of "PhD applicants for employment" were women.
- Germanic Language and Literature: 54.5 percent of admitted doctoral students and 23.9 percent of persons earning PhDs were women, but only 8.3 percent of the faculty. 23.9 percent of "PhD applicants for employment" were women.
- History: 16.1 percent of admitted doctoral students were women and 13.0 percent of persons earning PhDs were women, but only 5 percent of the faculty. 6.3 percent of "PhD applicants for employment" were women. (It is worth noting that the chart said three women were faculty members at a time when the department was challenging whether women who were teaching in the Residential College were truly department members.)
- Journalism: 50.0 percent of admitted doctoral students and 15.6 percent of persons earning PhDs were women, but no women were counted as faculty members. (Marion Marzolf was then teaching entry-level courses.)
- Philosophy: 13.4 percent of admitted doctoral students and 9.1 percent of persons earning PhDs were women, but only 3.6 percent of the faculty. 4.1 percent of "PhD applicants for employment" were women.
- Library Science: 83.4 percent of admitted doctoral students and 31.8 percent of persons earning PhDs were women. Library Science was one school that actually showed a greater proportion of female faculty members—42 percent, but the figure that HEW reported was higher than the one Sandler cited in her statement to Congress. 21.5 percent of "PhD applicants for employment" were women.

HEW indicated these personnel practices were contributing factors:

- In interviews, departmental chairmen indicated that their primary recruiting source were professional meetings and conferences, where, HEW said, "much valuable employment information" was exchanged. "This type of recruiting tends to be covertly discriminatory because to persons who are not part of the 'grapevine' most of the information regarding employment possibilities is not available." Since women were not in the top ranks, this kind of recruiting "tends to perpetuate the present composition of the faculty positions."
- Unsolicited applications receive very little consideration or attention. Applications are "filed away without comment, kept for a year, and then destroyed." HEW conceded that this policy would impact both men and women but that it worked mostly against women applicants because their qualifications may not come to the attention of hiring authorities through other means.
- Screening committees, faculty committees, and ad hoc committees assigned with selecting applicants "are almost uniformly made up of all men."
- Interviews with department chairs indicated "a lack of sensitivity on the part of persons who are crucial to the equal employment opportunities for women." There were "indications" that they did not use equal criteria in evaluating men and women. Further, the agency said, department chairmen who realized that women were underutilized did not realize that the executive order required them to rectify the situation by affirmatively recruiting women faculty.

King had complained that Minton had not understood the nature of Michigan's "grapevine" hiring practices. Clearly, the second team did. They acknowledged the frustration of women scholars like Sandler that universities were happy to award doctorates to women but then unwilling to hire them to teach.

But to the extent that academic hiring decisions were made at the departmental level, the report highlighted what would become a challenge to implementing affirmative action plans, namely that those decisions were very decentralized and made by small faculty committees made up mostly of men.

The internal memo from the personnel officials reflected the attitudes that prevailed in many quarters at the time. First, it contended that the underlying assumption of the numbers that HEW highlighted was that

> having a PhD degree in an academic area qualifies an individual as a potential faculty member. . . . Because this University is considered, and considers itself, one of the fine institutions in this country, it seeks to maintain its quality by a hiring policy which maximizes the influx of truly excellent and outstanding individuals in their respective disciplines.
>
> Because of this fact, departments in this institution do not seek faculty members who have only the generic distinction of being "qualified" for a teaching position, but instead define "qualification" in terms of the admitted excellence of the existing department. When viewed in this light, the applicant may not be in the realm of the truly excellent faculty member desired by a department in this institution. As such the pool of people considered for a faculty position here is much smaller than the pool of "qualified" individuals country wide.

The unstated but underlying assumption seemed to be that Michigan was a great university and well-recognized men were the only scholars who could sustain that reputation.

The internal memo then contended that evaluating hiring policies with such broad brushstrokes was "a foolhardy task" because departments might be seeking a "truly excellent faculty member" in a particular area, such as "a professor of national reputation who can supplement the department's activities in medieval English literature."

The officials argued that the chart "has inaccuracies according to any data the University was able to find." That observation telegraphed what became quickly apparent to those trying to address job discrimination: The university's computer systems could not readily generate accurate employment information.

Finally, the officials argued that the investigators should have reviewed the acceptance rates of men and women who actually *applied* for graduate school programs. They said their research had found that the History Department had admitted 73 percent of the women who had applied, compared with 79 percent of the men. (It was the only department they cited on this point.)

The personnel officials also challenged the notion that the university's hiring practices amounted to an old-boy's network and then described exactly the kind of process that concerned HEW. They said that because a department would decide it needed a particular kind of specialist, the "actual process of obtaining a new faculty member often does not follow the pattern of reviewing unsolicited applications of eligible people such as may be done with non-faculty positions, or in industry. Instead, a department chairman may poll the faculty for names of outstanding people in the area in which he is looking for faculty. He then will contact these individuals apprising them of the opening."

The officials also rejected the suggestion that screening potential candidates for positions at conferences and professional meetings was discriminatory because "any person, male, female, black, white or what have you, who has either an interest or academic credentials may attend most conferences." To support their argument, they attached an exhibit demonstrating job inquiries from persons, both men and women, who were interested in positions in the Germanic Language and Literature Department who indicated they would be available for interviews at the next conference of the Modern Language Association. Over the past two years, the officials reported, 80 percent of unsolicited job applicants had said they would be attending the conference. "That they were not interviewed or hired reflects only the low need for faculty in that department, not a membership in a 'grapevine.'" They attached a copy of the standard reply they said was sent to *all* persons who inquired about openings in the German Department.

(At the fall 1969 meeting of the American Psychological Association, women charged that that organization accepted listings for "male" job openings. Under Sandler, WEAL had cited that practice in filing complaints against that association and the American Personnel and Guidance Association. In the prepared statement she delivered to Rep. Green's subcommittee, Sandler noted that women in the Modern Language Association, the American Sociological Association, the American Historical Association, the American Political Science Association, the American Society for Microbiology, and the American Association for the Advancement of Science had begun organizing caucuses to address discriminatory practices within their professional groups.)

The U-M officials also pushed back on the argument that all-male hiring committees contributed to sex discrimination. They contended that the implication was "that men always discriminate" and that the burden should be on the HEW compliance office to demonstrate that discrimination had, in fact, occurred.

Hayes and Evans were willing to concede that some departmental chairmen might have been unaware of the compliance requirements but contended that HEW's comments "are such generalities that it is not possible to respond to them specifically." They agreed that Michigan could improve its communications about the executive order's requirements. But, they argued, since those rules had only been in effect since October 1968, the university's record should only be judged since that date. Reviewed through that lens, they said, the employment numbers would look different. For instance, they said, while only 7 percent of faculty in the English Department were women, that reflected hiring decisions made over many years. Of the five persons hired for the 1970–1971 academic year, one was "a special acquisition (a black professor in a tenured position.)" Of the remaining four hires, one was a woman, giving the department a 25 percent rate regarding hiring women. (Again, the observation about the African-American hire is notable, in retrospect, in how the university viewed race and sex discrimination very differently in the fall of 1970. Excluding that faculty member from the total count also served to boost the percentage of slots that were filled by women.) But again, they argued, not every department could hire faculty members every year, and departments were usually looking for persons with particular qualifications.

The HEW findings then turned to the issue of nepotism, reporting that Michigan did not have a policy regarding the hiring of spouses, and that as a result, department chairmen "interpreted nepotism in different ways."

Some departments—and academic couples—found ways to get around the unwritten rules. U-M's Residential College (RC), founded within LSA in 1967, provided a home for a number of women whose husbands held posts in the same academic discipline, including Kathryn Kish Sklar and Marilyn Young in history, Zelda Gamson in sociology, and Ann Larimore in geography. In 1971, James Robertson, an English professor who served as the RC's first director, observed that "the net result [of the college's early hiring practices] has been a gradual devolvement of teaching and administrative load upon a crew of dedicated faculty without regular LS&A appointments: advanced graduate students, research center appointees who would like to teach, and wives of faculty members excluded from other University teaching appointments." (Over the years, faculty who taught in the RC would continue to encounter problems regarding their salaries and tenure prospects, and scholars like Helen Tanner would have trouble getting hired at all.)

Other faculty spouses, like Gamson and Davis, took jobs in Michigan's research institutes. One of Davis's graduate students later suggested that the Zoology and Botany Departments might have solved their perceived problem by hiring Davis and Zoology Chairman Allen's wife, Sally, in each other's departments, even though that was not the women's true area of expertise.

HEW, however, focused on the kind of thing they reviewed in Larimore's file and those of other members of "tandem teams." In addition to Larimore (identified by her married name of Kolars) and her husband, John, it listed 10 other couples who worked in the same department or institute: Margo and Hugh Aller in the Astronomy Department; Thelma and W. Ellison Chalmers at the Institute of Labor and Industrial Relations; Rachel and Stephen Kaplan and Lois and Martin Hoffman in the Psychology Department; Marjorie and Henry Townes in the Forestry Department; and Joan and Mark Chesler, Dale and James Crowfoot, Judith and Alan Guskin, Anita and John Lohman, and Glorianne and Simon Wittes, all in the School of Education. In every case but the Lohmans', the wife held a lower position that paid less than her husband's. In the case of the Kolarses, HEW noted that both were listed as associate professors, but Ann did not have tenure and earned only 81 percent of what her husband did.

Larimore recalled nearly 20 years later that in that era, associate professorships "were almost never awarded without tenure. That was unheard of. People would be shocked when I would say, 'Yes, I am an associate professor, but I don't have tenure.' That was explained, of course, by the Nepotism Rule. When HEW came to campus and asked them to show them the Nepotism Rule, it didn't exist. Certainly all the people I talked to early on in the sixties really did believe it was a rule—chairmen, deans. Husbands and wives could not be employed by the same department."

In their internal memo, the personnel officials pushed back strongly on this point, arguing that the university did have a nepotism policy—and, they conceded, all of the examples cited by HEW were, in fact, exceptions to it. But, they said, the examples cited by HEW "certainly did not establish any clear evidence that this policy has worked to the disadvantage of women." They argued that "a very careful analysis of the duties, responsibilities, qualifications, and experience of these individuals needs to be made" before any conclusions were drawn. They contended that a review of university personnel files showed that in every case, the salary differential could be explained by the better-paid spouse's additional experience or higher degree.

They attached a narrative provided by Al Guskin, the director of the School of Education's project that employed five of the couples, including Guskin and his wife. When he dealt with the Lohmans, Guskin's review noted that Anita was, in fact, paid less than her husband, contradicting the one positive example on the HEW list. Guskin said that although the husbands had the title of *lecturer* and the wives, *research associates*, starting that month, they would all be described as *research associates*. He said that the main reason for the distinction in the past was that the husbands worked full time and the wives worked part-time; it was unclear, he said, that one title was higher than the other. (Earlier in the year, Guskin had been a candidate in the search for a vice president of student services.)

Regarding the case of the Kolarses, Hayes and Evans said that any nepotism policy is "by its very nature bound to work to the disadvantage of one member of a family unit when they both desire employment." The fact that it worked against Ann Kolars, they said, "hardly constitutes evidence that this policy or its application promotes discrimination against women." John Kolars, they noted, was hired first, "which would usually dictate a differential in salary purely on a longevity basis." In this case, they added, "there also exists . . . idiosyncrasies about the two individuals involved which, while not appropriate to outline here, can be determined by interviewing Ann Kolars and mitigates the allegation." (It is unclear what the "idiosyncrasies" were and Larimore never pointed to any in subsequent interviews. Interestingly, when the couple's engagement was announced in the *New York Times* in August 1958, Larimore had been teaching at the University of Chicago for a year and was about to earn her doctorate; her fiancé, meanwhile, was about to earn his master's degree after serving in the U.S. Army during the postwar occupation of Japan and then with the U.S. Geological Survey.)

The HEW investigators cited two unidentified women who, they said, earned less than their male peers despite similar qualifications. The personnel officials responded that without knowing the women's names, "it is impossible to determine the legitimacy of the allegation." In commenting on Davis's letter to Lardent, they grudgingly acknowledged that her case "appears to be basically accurate although it tends to be overstated." Interviews with the department chairman, they said, "showed that his reluctance to raise Professor Davis's salary was based in part on how low her salary actually was," a rationale that seems, in retrospect, to be nonsensical.

The personnel officials then turned to the findings regarding non-academic personnel, the area of university hiring over which they presumably had more control. The HEW investigators said they had reviewed 305 of the 1,008 non-academic job classifications that then existed at U-M. At the time, the non-academic staff consisted of 3,415 men and 6,226 women. The investigators noted that there were 20 classifications that were almost entirely made up of women, with an average salary of $595.49. (HEW didn't specify in this particular analysis, but the figures appear to be monthly salaries.) Twenty-five job classifications were almost entirely made up of men; their average salary was $1,049.52. These findings, Scott wrote, "confirms allegations made in interviews that (1) there are jobs at the University of Michigan that are segregated by sex and (2) the 'female jobs' are the lower paying secretarial and clerical jobs with little status, responsibility, or opportunity for advancement."

The report provided two examples, demonstrating that as the salary and job difficulty increased, the percentage of men in the job category also rose. In the Office Supervisor category, the percentage of men holding the job rose from 4.3 percent at the lowest of three ranks to 38.1 percent at the highest. For persons in the Assistants in Research category, the percentage of men rose from 20 percent in the lowest of three ranks to 27 percent in the highest.

The department looked more specifically at the Accounting and Purchasing Department. Again it found that the job classification with the highest average salary (purchasing agent) had five employees who were men and one woman, earning an average salary of $1,525.00. In the lowest paid job category (senior accounting clerks at an average salary of $513.18), women outnumbered men, 46 to 3. Reviewing personnel files more closely, it reported that several women in the lower administrative jobs held MBAs or business degrees with accounting and purchasing experience and would be "qualified for high level positions" in these two areas.

In a detailed exhibit, HEW looked more closely at the histories of 25 persons who were working at various levels of administrative and research assistant jobs. It found that women were paid less than men with the same job titles, responsibilities, and experience. "Equally alarming," the Scott letter said, "is the documented tendency toward giving men higher starting salaries" than women in the same jobs. It charged that "women are hired originally as secretaries regardless of their qualifications," and personnel records indicated that all of the women who were processed through the personnel department were given typing tests, "while there was no indication that men ever were required to take the typing tests."

The investigators blamed *underhiring* for most of the job segregation, wage differentials, and lack of promotion opportunities; women were hired as secretaries while men were channeled into higher-paying categories. HEW wrote, "The underhiring is particularly apparent when comparing women with bachelor degrees in non-marketable subjects (i.e., English, Music and History). Because pay raises were based on a percentage of the present salary, a woman hired at a lower salary than a man "may never make up the initial inequity despite many promotions and salary adjustments." (Although Davis was an academic employee, her case provided a good demonstration of that problem.)

HEW also informed Michigan administrators that "a related problem and a source of concern and much frustration to the non-academic females . . . was the absence of job descriptions." Further, it said, not only did the university's recruitment advertising fail to carry the required Equal Employment Opportunity tagline, it was also "discriminatory in its content" when ads were headlined "Attention—Student Wives." (It was not until 1973 that the U.S. Supreme Court upheld that position when the *Pittsburgh Press* challenged a local ordinance that prohibited sex-segregated employment classifieds; up until then, many newspapers accepted them.)

In its final finding, HEW observed that no woman sat on U-M's Grievance Committee for non-academic employees; in an apparent misstatement, it referenced that "women comprise approximately two-thirds of the University's academic workforce."

Again, the university's personnel officials disputed Scott's findings. They argued that for the 191 job classifications filled by both men and women, there were 102 in which men were paid more, on average, than women, and 89 in which women were paid more. Thus, they argued, the HEW findings were "the result of some selective picking of classifications."

When they did not have numbers on their side, the officials said the HEW findings proved nothing: "While it is a fact that in the higher positions of the [office supervisor and research assistant groups] there is a greater proportion of men there is certainly no evidence that this is the result of discrimination against women." Then they fell back on their argument regarding the effective date of the executive order: any discrepancy among men and women "is the end result of hiring decisions which have been made over a long period of time and the result of decisions made by individual employees as to their continued willingness to remain in their positions. . . and that the collective results of those decisions made over a long period of time does not constitute evidence of discrimination against women in our hiring practices during the last two years when we were subject to the sex discrimination provisions of the executive order."

Regarding the relatively small number of women who were hired as directors, managers, and supervisors, the personnel officials argued that assignment to those jobs "requires an interest in those particular classifications as well as proper training and preparation for those particular classifications. There is no evidence to suggest that the ratio of female employees in these classifications is not in keeping with the ratio of female employees in the workforce who have the necessary preparation and interest to be employed in these particular classifications." Put more simply, they seemed to argue that HEW could not prove that women actually *wanted* to be supervisors. Similarly, they contended that there were proportionately higher numbers of women working as secretaries and nurses because there were "very few men who have the necessary skills or have an interest in" those fields. They disputed what they described as Scott's suggestion "that the representation of women in each and every classification should be proportional to their representation in the total workforce."

In reviewing Scott's case studies, the memo writer wrote: "I believe we have identified the specific individuals referred to in most of the cases cited. . . both from the information which is shown. . . . and from other information which we received from the investigator who was reviewing the non-academic records." The authors contended that there were several factual errors in the material, as presented, and that "there is a very obvious bias evident in these relatively small number of people who were selected to be included. . . ." They described the charts as "obvious excellent examples of the presentation of a very limited number of facts to support a preconceived conclusion."

They strongly disputed the assertion that all women who applied through the Personnel Office were given typing tests while men were not. But they did acknowledge that "there are significant numbers of women who accept employment at The University of Michigan in secretarial positions who have qualifications for more responsible positions." One of the primary reasons, they said, was that there were too many applicants for professional and administrative posts, relative to the number of job openings: "Under these circumstances a significant number of women prefer to accept clerical openings which are available for which they are qualified rather than be rejected for any employment at The University of Michigan, which is generally the fate of their male counterparts."

Regarding the complaints about the lack of job descriptions, the personnel officials responded, "The quality of this particular aspect of our personnel program is of course a reflection of the amount of manpower which is available to work on all the various personnel tasks and the relative priority which is given to this task as opposed to other tasks. While ideally good well-written job descriptions are a high priority item they all too frequently end up taking a backseat to problems which must have an answer right now."

Regarding the advertising directed to student wives, the officials commented that the headline "was not intended to be discriminatory but merely to call attention to a large group of people which we have reason to believe were currently seeking employment that we had positions available which we felt they might be interested in. If such attempts to design and place your ad in such a way that it will be read by people who are interested in and qualified for the type of employment which you are offering is discriminatory, then one of the very basic ingredients of a well-written advertisement is lost."

They also asserted that HEW's finding about the Grievance Committee was not accurate. They said that women supervisors served on the committee when the grievance originated from their area of responsibility. (Of course, since women made up a smaller percentage of supervisors, they were much less likely to serve; there was also a concern about having supervisors resolve grievances in the first place.)

In conclusion, Michigan officials said that "since there is obviously strong and substantial disagreement" concerning what HEW had found, they said "it seems rather pointless" to examine HEW's compliance demands. They recommended that university representatives meet with Scott or someone else from HEW to critically review the findings and try to build greater consensus about what the facts of the situation were.

The university, they said, should "express its willingness to strengthen its existing affirmative action program," but they concluded, "we do not feel that there are any legitimate findings which would justify the remedial action which Mr. Scott has suggested." They said Scott's team should present "concrete examples of a woman, or women, who have been discriminated against" so that "the pertinent facts" could be reviewed and corrective action taken, "if it is appropriate."

Ever the negotiator, Fleming's initial response to HEW was more diplomatic than the language of the internal memo a few weeks later. But there was widespread agreement among male managers that HEW had turned up problems that didn't really exist and that the university couldn't possibly do all the things the agency wanted.

Barbara Newell proposed a faster, more targeted response to the agency. Within a week after the HEW letter arrived, she drafted a short memo to Fleming, outlining the form a response could take and avoiding any debate over whether the findings were accurate. Responding to Scott's specific demands, she suggested that Michigan could:

- promise to discontinue advertising aimed at student wives
- reconstitute the Grievance Committee for non-academic employees
- pledge that each unit would review its employment records regarding men and women, and guarantee "no reprisals," presumably against women who lodged a complaint
- call on departments, schools, and divisions to determine by May 1971 the number of applications they had received from women seeking academic appointments and then have them develop recruitment plans for formulating "realistic goals" and procedures to be put in place by September 1971
- write a "statement on nepotism" and ask chairmen to review the effects of "past nepotism discussions" as part of the procedures they developed
- ask employing officers to review the status and qualifications of non-academic employees, promise changes in entry procedures, provide watchdog committees to review the procedures, and guarantee no reprisals.

Newell observed that most appointments to university committees were made by faculty groups, but suggested the university could promise to raise HEW's concerns with SACUA.

She agreed that the question regarding graduate admissions could be "omitted on grounds that this agency has no power over admissions." But, she added, "I think we had better get some good statistics on practices, student turn-over, etc. They will be back."

Newell also suggested forming "a committee to aid in the determination of University policy and to guide the central staff in the collection and compilation of data." This may have been the first time the notion of a "Women's Commission" was floated. Newell said that the reports generated at the departmental level could be directed to such a committee.

But as Michigan's top human resources officers were scrambling to track down—and make the case against—"the facts," HEW was already losing patience.

Scott remains an elusive figure in reconstructing the history of the HEW complaint. The investigators were careful about talking to the press while negotiations were under way. But Scott's immediate supervisor did sit for an interview with *Daily* reporters 18 months later. John Hodgdon was a rumpled, bespectacled civil servant, who had started his career investigating racial discrimination in schools at the height of the civil rights movement. In the later interview, Hodgdon acknowledged that "we've had some problems dealing with the investigations, dealing with the data. But my own feeling is that if we get the facts—you know America is a country which goes for facts: football scores, baseball scores—I think when we can show the institutions what the facts are, they'll pay attention.... If we just come in there and say, 'You're discriminating,' they'll say, 'Not me!'"

9
The Centennial Celebration

For at least a week, from October 6 to 13, 1970, the fact that the federal government had concluded that the University of Michigan discriminated against its women employees was the best kept secret in Ann Arbor.

A review of *Michigan Daily* newspapers from that week suggests it was a relatively quiet time on campus. The major news came from out of town: President Nixon proposing a cease-fire in Vietnam, Cambodia, and Laos; race-related violence breaking out in Pontiac, Michigan; the bombing of ROTC offices on the University of Washington campus. In Ann Arbor, a committee was completing work on a new campus legal system. Thirty members of Students for a Democratic Society staged a protest, calling for Dow Chemical Company recruiters to be barred from campus. Among other things, the protestors said Dow discriminated against blacks and women and argued that Michigan regulations prohibited recruiting by companies that, in the words of the *Daily* reporter, "practice sexism or racism."

Even at a slow time of year, it likely would have taken top officials a few days to decide how they *did* want to respond to HEW. In early October, Fleming was out of town at the annual meeting of the American Council of Education. When U-M's executive officers met on October 14, the "HEW letter" was the sixth item listed in the "Action Minutes" prepared by then-university secretary Richard Kennedy with the instructions: "No release prior to development of our response."

But the timing may have also been impacted by an accident of the university's calendar: A few days after Don Scott's letter arrived, the university was scheduled to kick off several days of events celebrating the 100th anniversary of the admission of Madelon Stockwell, U-M's first woman student.

Planning for the centennial had begun more than a year before. As the event evolved, it became a focal point for those trying to gather more information about the status of women at the university. It became a way for grass-roots groups to publicize themselves and attract more members. And, ultimately, it demonstrated the range of views on campus over what it meant to be a feminist and the best way to achieve feminist goals.

In mid-1969, Alison Myers, then director of alumnae affairs, and CCEW staff members began planning the celebration. Louise Cain, the center's founder who had returned as a staff member, wrote in a document titled "Unedited and Erratic Motions About 1970": "Somehow, we should fund some vehicle in 1970 to give women's opportunities at the U of Mich. a *push forward* so that the U. doesn't rest on self-congratulation. How can we make use of new flexibilities in attitude toward student demands to further the legitimate needs of our ladies! We are their only influential spokesmen!" But Cain's notion of who should be involved in the event remained a traditional one, referencing "Student groups—From Mortar Board to sororities"; women faculty groups, of which there were few; the Alumnae Office and its clubs; CCEW; and the university's media outlets.

Myers took charge of planning a May luncheon, described as "a gala which will be gay, happy and traditionally nostalgic. . . ." Eventually, the event honored the university's two living women Regents and featured a fashion show of historic costumes. CCEW, meanwhile, began planning for "our usual substantive conference, this time in the fall, to be called 'Women on Campus' and emphasizing current performance, research and statistics."

The women decided, probably correctly, that the centennial would attract greater support if they asked Fleming to appoint a formal committee to plan the event. He responded by naming a 20-member committee, only half of whom were women. It was a commentary itself on the scarcity of women then in the university's leadership ranks—and another item on PROBE's growing checklist of complaints.

When PROBE wrote Smith, Newell, and Pierpont in August 1970, seeking their cooperation in obtaining salary and personnel data, it quoted from the UM News' story on the committee's formation: "President Fleming has appointed a committee—including the University's only female Regent, Gertrude V. Huebner, and its only female executive officer, Acting Vice-President Barbara Newell—to plan celebrations marking the anniversary." PROBE went on to write, "One is tempted to conclude from this report that the writer from the University Relations Office was adding a touch of satire in pointing out that after 100 years of 'progress,' there are no women in permanent executive positions and so few women in prestigious jobs from which President Fleming could choose a committee; yet we're planning a celebration. However, that is not the case—unfortunately, it simply points to the prevailing attitude that the position of women in the University is of little or no importance whatsoever."

As part of the celebration, CCEW itself sponsored the paperback publication of Dorothy McGuigan's history of women at Michigan, A Dangerous Experiment, when McGuigan could not find a commercial or academic publisher willing to distribute the book. The photographs of alumna Margaret Bourke-White were also featured in a month-long exhibit at the university's art museum.

But at some point, Newell assembled a committee to plan a bigger event, conceived as "at least one day and perhaps as many as three consecutive days of seminars, colloquia, workshops . . . in many areas of academic excellence." In February 1970, Newell reported back that her committee had "defined 21–22 topics appropriate for investigation in depth." Now "they must also decide whether to have [a] big name as a kick-off speaker or a debate which will stimulate interest and attendance through difference of opinion." Two months later, when she warned that the program might cost more than had been originally budgeted, she was assured that "quality in the programming must not be sacrificed" and that more funds could be found if necessary.

Thus the centerpiece of the celebrations—at least in the eyes of women students—became a two-day teach-in on "The Changing Roles of Women in the U.S.": a Saturday program of panel discussions and workshops followed by the main event, a panel discussion in Hill Auditorium, U-M's performing arts venue, on Sunday.

Michigan had pioneered the concept of the teach-in, beginning with one organized in March 1965, focused on the war in Vietnam. In March 1970, 50,000 people attended one on the environment that helped launch the first Earth Day celebration five weeks later.

Graduate student Gretchen Wilson, who served on the organizing committee, told the *Daily*, "We hope the teach-in will give women a chance to meet together and rap about their common problems and interests. Hopefully, it will provide the participants with a chance to learn about themselves and their position in society."

Jean King observed of that time: "There was not a lot of communication among women. They were not an organized group. Particularly in the university they are very much insulated from each other. . . . There weren't any women's groups, except for faculty wives. There was no mechanism for women faculty to get to know each other. . . . So, the organizing and meeting people in other parts of the university they just didn't do it, they just didn't know."

The Saturday morning panels explored alternatives for women in academia, the professions, and in marriage. By then, King and Shortridge had established reputations as campus leaders, and both of them appeared as panelists, Shortridge on the panel on academia and King on the panel on the professions.

The academic panel, ranging in status from a graduate student (Shortridge) to an associate professor, attracted 100 women. According to the *Daily's* story, the five women "agreed emphatically that women are consistently discriminated against in the academic world, and that even to gain some little recognition a woman must be far more outstanding than her male counterpart."

Mary Bromage, a former reporter who taught English in the School of Business, was a former associate dean of women and the business school's only woman faculty member. As she was about to turn 64, she described what the reporter recounted was her "special position as the 'doll' and 'female on the pedestal.'" Mary Alice Shulman, a lecturer who was the first woman to teach in U-M's Economics Department, said she faced little overt discrimination, but noted that, as tokens, women presented little threat. "As numbers grow past tokenism," she said, "discrimination becomes real." Shortridge shared the details of her reporting to emphasize how little progress women faculty members had made.

Forty women attended the panel on the professions and heard King describe the status of women in the legal profession. That year, she said only 35 of the 400 students in Michigan's Law School were women.

The panel that drew the biggest crowd discussed "family, marriage and oppression." It featured Robin Morgan, founder of the Women's International Terrorist Conspiracy from Hell (WITCH); Adrienne Tentler, then a lecturer in the Psychology Department; Nadine Miller and Ellen Post of Radical Lesbians; and Lois Addison, a lecturer in the Philosophy Department.

Morgan asserted, "We are not a panel of experts, though, for every woman is an expert on her own oppression." Before the discussion started, the audience asked that the men who were present to leave. Morgan contended that the men's presence "would restrict the feeling of intimacy we hope to create in this session."

During the gathering, the lobby area between Haven and Mason Halls then known as The Fishbowl was transformed into a bazaar, with women's groups distributing information about their activities and, in some cases, hawking protest buttons. One of CCEW's contributions was a compilation of women's rights groups in the area. "Women who are seeking a path of action may find it helpful," the organization said. "But it is not a definitive list. Some groups have disbanded and information about others has not been available." CCEW itself said it welcomed all women to the center. Still, its mission remained narrowly defined. In the five-page handout, it said: "But we are here particularly to help the returning woman student complete her education; to help her with choosing a field and planning her course work, finding (or giving) her financial assistance, getting credits transferred, and in other ways running interference for her within the University."

Their compilation listed 16 groups, including both the Ann Arbor Women's Coalition Meeting (every Wednesday night at St. Andrew's Church) and the Women's Liberation Coalition (Ann Arbor), which held a mass meeting each month at the same church to review the decisions of its steering committee. They were separate from the Women's Liberation Coalition of Michigan, whose offices were in Detroit. Other groups included the Child Care Action Group and the Drop-In Day Care Center that had been started that summer at Markley Hall. There was an Abortion Counselling Group (abortion was not yet legal in Michigan) and a Life Styles Discussion Committee. The women who served as the contacts for Radical Lesbians and Sisters Rising were identified only by their first names, as were the contacts for the Michigan women's liberation coalition. Interestingly, NOW did not then have a formal chapter in Ann Arbor; the contact person who was listed lived in Chicago.

FOCUS was listed, along with King and Yourd's phone numbers, and Yourd was also listed as a contact for the Michigan Women's Commission. PROBE was also included but appeared to have been a late addition, tacked on to the end of the list. The compilation said, "PROBE is a coalition task force researching the condition of women at the University. This fall it is publishing a booklet which will cover the kinds of problems and discrimination women face, give advice to women new to the University and offer information on services for women. PROBE encourages any woman who encounters a problem to let them know about it and to join with them to solve the problems for themselves and all other women."

As part of its contribution to the centennial, CCEW distributed the best statistics it could come up with about women on campus. It wrote: "As background for discussing women on campus in this centennial year, the Center had anticipated the availability of a wide variety of data on enrollment and employment, both academic and non-academic. The University is still engaged in developing adequate systems and programs to make accurate information accessible. A complete report should be possible by the end of the year."

The center was able to distribute three charts analyzing the relative standing of women and men—in enrollment, faculty positions, and faculty salaries. But the charts presented raw numbers in an objective way, drawing no conclusions and making trends harder to discern. While the number of women students had increased since the 1969 fall term, their share of the total student population had actually dropped slightly, hovering around 38 or 39 percent, depending on how the student body was counted. Women represented 35 percent of the student body of the Rackham Graduate School.

The distribution of women across the university's colleges varied widely: With graduate students counted in the totals, women represented 44 percent of the students in LSA, a figure comparable to the freshman admissions quota. The population of the School of Music was evenly split. Not surprisingly, women students accounted for 99 percent of the School of Nursing and 62 percent of the Schools of Social Work and Education. But they represented only 11 percent of the School of Medicine, 7 percent of the Law School, 5 percent of the School of Business Administration, and a mere 2.5 percent of the School of Engineering.

CCEW then provided a chart of "active instructional staff" (excluding deans and department chairmen, which, if included, would have made the proportion of women faculty even worse). The chart showed that across the university, there were only 48 women who held the rank of professor; 10 were in the School of Nursing and 6 in the School of Social Work. Only 2.5 percent of LSA's 310 full professors were women. Across all the instructional ranks, the School of Engineering had two women, while Natural Resources, Law, and Business Administration each had one.

As for salary levels, CCEW showed that within LSA, women trailed the median salary at every instructional level; the median salary for women full professors was $16,900, $2,900 less than the median for the college overall. That was also less than the $17,418 median nine-month salary reported by a survey of 1,106 colleges published by the *Chronicle of Higher Education*. A closer look at the charts revealed the problems inherent in the university's reporting systems because different charts reported different faculty totals. (Unlike most of the university's colleges, LSA was large enough that an analysis of the median salaries of women would not reveal the salary of an individual.)

In the afternoon, 20 workshops were held on topics ranging from "Organizing Women as a Political Group" to "Social History of Women in the U.S." to "Black Women as a Doubly Oppressed Group." Libby Douvan led a discussion on the "Effects of Working Mothers on Young Children," providing a critical analysis of studies that had concluded there was a correlation between working mothers and juvenile delinquency. She also cited a study by her colleague Lois Hoffman that found that "women who enjoy their work feel that when they come home, they must be exceptional mothers. This makes them feel less guilty about liking their outside jobs."

About 100 men attended their own workshop on "Anti-Male Supremacy." The *Daily* article quoted one participant as saying, "Those of us who were kicked out of the meeting this morning with Robin

Morgan were disappointed, but we've got to understand that there are things that women want to talk about without men there."

The featured event was Sunday afternoon, when Newell was scheduled to moderate a panel at Hill Auditorium. The speakers included Rep. Griffiths, who had just succeeded in getting the Equal Rights Amendment (ERA) discharged from the House Judiciary Committee after years of debate; Catherine East, who had provided staff support to every presidentially appointed women's commission since John F. Kennedy's; and Jo-Ann Gardner, identified in advertisements for the event by her affiliation with the Association of Women Psychologists (likely the recently formed Association for Women in Psychology). But Gardner was also a founder of NOW, a leader of feminist groups in Pittsburgh, and, as a member of FOCUS, someone who had sought to testify against Carswell at his Senate hearings.

Those women were, to varying degrees, the faces of institutional feminism: older, professional women who were concerned about women's access to the levers of government, politics, jobs, and credit. The other panelists came from a more radical perspective.

Although advance publicity had touted Robin Morgan as a child actress on the television series based on *I Remember Mama*, she was also known as the organizer of the protests at the 1968 Miss America pageant and as the editor of *Sisterhood Is Powerful*, the ground-breaking anthology of feminist writings that was published that year. Marlene Dixon was touted as a "radical sociologist" in the display ad promoting the Sunday panel. In 1967, she had become the first woman in 19 years to hold a teaching position in the Sociology Department at the University of Chicago. But two years later the university did not renew her contract after she stepped out of a faculty procession to join a student protest during the inauguration of University President Edward Levi. Dixon's termination prompted a two-week sit-in of that university's Administration Building; she moved on to a short stint at McGill University in Toronto after that.

Nadine Miller was affiliated with Radical Lesbians, an organization that was included in CCEW's compilation of women's groups.

It was not reported until later, but after one of the late-afternoon workshops the previous day, a group of women lingered on to talk with Morgan, Dixon, and Miller. They decided they were unhappy with the structure of the Sunday panel and worked together to draft a statement explaining why.

When the Sunday event began, Morgan called on a woman to read the "coalition's" statement. The group contended that the program's structure was "anti-woman" and that "authoritarian forms," such as "panels of experts on stage, time limits and a moderator," served to "maintain the oppression of women." The coalition's representative went on to say, "We don't believe in experts on women's oppression. Every woman is an expert on her own oppression."

She then invited the women in the audience to join "the panel of experts" on the stage. Reports varied, but between one-fifth and one-fourth of the audience of 600 to 800 accepted the invitation. Gardner joined Morgan, Dixon, and Miller in sitting on the stage floor.

There was no plan after that, and when the group on the stage and those in the audience began breaking into small discussions, Newell tried to step back in to moderate. After what was described as "an emotional audience vote," the event proceeded as planned.

After Griffiths spoke, an audience member asked why some women opposed the ERA. Newell called on Griffiths to respond, but as she did, a woman on the stage grabbed her microphone to read a statement, upending a glass of water into Griffiths's lap. Eventually, the audience, on and off the stage, settled down and all the panelists were permitted to speak, with the understanding that no time limits would be imposed. Still, a political divide was on full display. As Dixon underscored it: "The businesswomen want to sit on the board of directors of United Fruit. We want to destroy United Fruit."

The session foreshadowed the divisions that would haunt the women's movement over the next decade, particularly as women wrestled over the best strategy to achieve ratification of the ERA. In an emotional moment, Gardner explained why she had joined the other three panelists on the floor: "I think all women are my sisters, whether or not I agree with their means and ends. . . . I reject the role of 'lady' because it is an exhibiting role. Women must be people, not ladies or sex objects. They must be what they define for themselves."

A half-century later, Newell recalled that "the thing that really makes me shudder" about the event "was that the member of Congress [was] booed."

Three days later women were still debating over what had transpired. In an opinion piece, *Daily* reporter Debra Thal disputed this author's editorial calling the event a "raucous circus." But Thal acknowledged that the women who took over the stage had failed to plan what would happen next.

In a letter to the *Daily*, a reader named Mary Ann Rodgers wrote: "Those feminists who were active in disrupting the Sunday afternoon meeting of the Women's teach-in at Hill Auditorium should know they were actively destroying leanings which some of us have had toward their movement....The amount of flack directed at professional women who are working within the system was surprising. The active feminists of Sunday might do well to realize that by their words and their behavior they have possibly directed women to the professional groups they despise rather than drawn women to themselves, as they say they wish to do."

CCEW's own symposium, "Women on Campus: 1970," followed three days later. Its publicity touted "a day which promises new insights from interesting and articulate speakers and spirited reactions from audience participants." Cain, who chaired the program, added a card to her speaking notes in case of an "emergency," presumably the disruption of her planned introduction of Libby Douvan. It read, "The tyranny of disruption of a University function is intolerable. I wish to ask this ~~courteous and civilized~~ group to demonstrate by voice if you wish the order of the day's proceedings to continue and this young woman to leave the platform" (strikethrough in original). (Before donating her papers to the Bentley Library, she added a note: "I never would have spoken in such a stiff and forced way, but writing the card prepared me adequately, I thought!")

But the symposium, with talks on "Toward a New Psychology of Women," "The Case of the Woman Graduate Student," and "The University and Women: What Directions?" proceeded without a disruption.

Still, a different kind of bombshell had landed in the headlines the day before: that federal investigators had concluded that Michigan discriminated against women and ordered it to take swift steps to correct the inequities.

In her remarks wrapping up the CCEW's symposium, Jean Campbell said, "The big job now is to think . . . what more the University can and should do right now for women. What does educating women mean at the University of Michigan? Who is thinking about it? Some students, a few faculty, a researcher here and there, The Center. Women want and need a higher priority of attention and they are getting it through the HEW investigation. It is important it seems to me, to translate the investigation from nuisance value to the record-keepers to creative concern. I will propose to Mr. Fleming that an all-University committee, including administrators, members of the faculty, staff, and students of varying ages, be appointed to assess the status of women and women's education at the University of Michigan and to recommend policies or action."

She wrote Fleming within the week to formally propose the committee. In a cover note, she acknowledged that her idea "has been complicated by the HEW investigation." But in the days since the symposium, she said, "It has become apparent that we are being forced to some administrative mechanism to respond to HEW. I would hope that working committee arrangements will serve the larger purpose as well as the immediate need." She said she had talked with Newell "at some length and she will, no doubt, convey what she feels is relevant."

In an interview a few years before he died, Fleming said he thought the commission was his idea, but the record suggests that Newell and Campbell both suggested it to him about the same time. In her later interview, Newell said, "In my eyes, Jean Campbell was so competent at running her own revolution—and it was a revolution. . . . If Fleming was going to get advice from anybody, he was going to get it from Jean."

Campbell was only two years younger than Fleming, and she knew how to be "lady like." She signed her cover note to him with "Jean," above the typewritten "Jean W. Campbell (Mrs. Angus)." In sending her memo, she used what was then the standard university routing slip. It had three blank lines, all of which were preprinted with the word "Mr."

10

The Response

Around Ann Arbor, the specific findings and demands of "the HEW Report" would remain confidential for nearly three months. But that was not the case within the executive suites of other major colleges.

When Michigan officials finally put out their press release a week after Scott's letter arrived, they tried to spin the situation as positively as they could:

> An existing affirmative action program to promote equal employment opportunities for members of minority groups is being revised by the University of Michigan to include women.
>
> But, according to U-M officials, the plan is not likely to be ready by the first week of November, to meet a 30-day deadline set by the Department of Health, Education and Welfare (HEW) regional Office of Civil Rights. And some differences are likely between the University and HEW both on what the situation is and what it ought to be.

To their credit, officials actually put out a press release, drawing more attention to their negotiations than many other colleges did. Joel Berger said the philosophy of Michigan's public relations officials at the time was that it was better to get bad news out early. Berger was fresh from a job at the University of Chicago, where he had been forced to vacate his office for two weeks because of the student sit-in over Marlene Dixon's dismissal. Fifty years later, Berger said his memories of responding to the HEW report were not as strong as those memories, but, he said, "I have no doubt that what was put out would have been drafted by Fleming."

HEW did not issue a press release of its own. But women activists were eager to learn what the investigation had found and had already waited longer for the findings than HEW had originally predicted. As Berger suggested, by putting out its own release, the university retained more control over the story.

PROBE cited the university's press release a month later in a long critique of how it believed officials were distorting news about the investigation. Referring to the release, it wrote, "To be expected, this is a clever bit of journalism geared to underplay the seriousness of the 'alleged sex discrimination.'"

The press release quoted only one sentence of Scott's letter, namely that an affirmative action program "must be submitted to this office within 30 days" to determine if it appears "acceptable and responsive to the problems we have identified."

Fleming, the press release said, had assured HEW "of an immediate analysis and the development of a revised affirmative action program. But, he said, 'It would seem unlikely that an affirmative program of the kind you envision could be generated within 30 days, even assuming we were in complete agreement.'"

The press release continued, "Fleming said, 'It is probable that there will be points of disagreement between us, some of which may be serious.'" (In its commentary, PROBE observed, "Perhaps HEW officials didn't know how to properly analyze the data they collected, but as for what the situation 'ought' to be, it ought to be clear to everyone that discrimination on the basis of sex must stop.")

At its conclusion, the university's press release noted that HEW called for "compensatory back pay to any female employee identified as having lost wages due to discriminatory treatment" since the executive order took effect. The press release said, "How such individuals are to be identified, and a judgment made as to whether there has been discrimination, may be matters of serious disagreement between HEW and the University, according to U-M officials." The press release did not emphasize this point, but it was issued exactly two years after the date the executive order took effect for federal contractors.

Fleming's response to HEW echoed the comments he had made to the *Ann Arbor News* six weeks earlier. Those quotations were highlighted by PROBE in a document it prepared before the teach-in entitled *The Feminine Mistake: Women at the University of Michigan*. (The organization displayed its sense of humor by dedicating the document "to all the men without whom it would never have been written.")

The press release continued, quoting Fleming: "We do not differ with respect to the principle of equal treatment for women." But Fleming added that "there are extraordinarily difficult problems in establishing criteria for what constitutes equal treatment, and we believe they are quite different from the now familiar problems in the field of race."

The press release said the examples of discrimination cited by the investigators "reveal an apparent lack of understanding of peculiar circumstances of a university work force." (On that point, PROBE chided Michigan for suggesting that the "peculiar circumstances" were "so complex that the HEW investigators can't understand it. We agree, the rationale for sex discrimination is difficult to understand—no matter who practices it.")

The HEW letter, the press release said, "noted women with college degrees in job classifications below some occupied by men without degrees." A university spokesman said, "We have wives of students who are working a year or two while their husbands are completing their graduate work. The result may be women in jobs for which they are over-qualified. First, we may not have openings to fit particular qualifications at the time employment is needed. Second, both the student wife and the University recognize that the employment is going to be for a limited time. We have to consider the longevity as well as qualifications in placing people."

That "rationalization" particularly infuriated PROBE when it published its analysis a month later. "Just how many of the full-time salaried personnel are actually wives of students, Mr. Fleming?" it asked. "What are the actual data? Is it not true that women applicants (wives of students or not), who say they plan to stay in Ann Arbor for a year or less, are sent to the part-time employment office where they are hired at low wages, no matter their qualifications, and this kind of appointment allows for no fringe benefits whatsoever?" The group also asked sarcastically, "Really, how many graduate students complete their degrees in 'a year or two?'"

The press release reported that 75 percent of the university's research volume was sponsored by federal agencies but did not suggest that any of it could be threatened. Indeed, it did not mention Scott's explicit warning of the steps Michigan needed to take "to continue its eligibility to receive government contracts."

After receiving the release, the *Daily* brought out the 60-point Tempo Heavy Condensed typeface it saved for its biggest stories to declare: "HEW DEMANDS 'U' INITIATE HIRING OF MORE WOMEN; SETS 30-DAY DEADLINE FOR FILING PROGRAM." The *Detroit Free Press* followed suit, putting Helen Fogel's story, headlined, "End Sex Bias, U-M Told; 30-Day Deadline Set," on its second front page. True to King's expectations, the *Ann Arbor News* ran the university's press release verbatim; Roy Reynolds, the reporter who covered the university beat, instead wrote a story about Fleming's "annoyance" over the Dow Chemical protest, which ended up outside his office.

Fogel noted that "it is theoretically possible for the government to withhold payments and other contracts from a non-complying contractor. In reality, the government rarely takes such a step." Both the HEW investigators and their superiors in Washington declined to comment further.

In hindsight, it may seem odd that HEW did not send a copy of its findings to King and Yourd. But, as noted in the Civil Rights Commission's report, most contract compliance officials thought their job was to bring contractors into compliance, and in the view of HEW, the investigation was "continuing." Also, the HEW letter did, in fact, include details about individual salaries, which the agency had pledged to keep confidential.

Two days after the stories appeared, King and Yourd hand-delivered a letter to Fleming, seeking a copy of Scott's letter. They also asked him to name the official to whom he had responded. (The women were probably concerned that he had written Scott's bosses.)

Three days later, Fleming replied, naming Scott as the recipient of his letter. Fleming then said, "I do not understand that Mr. Scott's letter was written for publication. We expect to release the substance of it at the time we respond more fully, and the substance of our reply will also be released." Inexplicably, Fleming addressed his letter to "Mrs. John C. King" and "Mrs. Kenneth L. Yourd," names the women didn't use when they wrote him and monikers that may have only annoyed them even more.

In fact, top officials sent many letters to HEW before they shared any of the findings with the Michigan community. However, even before Fleming told King and Yourd he wouldn't share the letter, he sent copies of at least parts of it to the presidents of other major universities, as well as the leaders of their lobbying organizations.

On October 14, 1970, the day the news stories appeared, Fleming wrote Edwin Young, the chancellor of the University of Wisconsin-Madison and a close friend:

> If you don't have enough trouble, here is the affirmative action part of an HEW letter which we just received on sex discrimination. The balance of the letter deals with alleged facts here.
>
> We are preparing an affirmative action program, and will have a draft ready in about three weeks, but we are not prepared to accept some of these conditions, and we are prepared to go all the way to the top in the battle.

Fleming told Young he would "keep you posted."

That day, he also mailed the same part of the letter to Ralph K. Huitt, executive director of the National Association of State Universities and Land-Grant Colleges. This time Fleming said the "balance of the letter simply sets forth alleged facts about our current operations." He then added, "We are much disturbed about some of the proposed actions, and believe other schools should be, too." Fleming also advised Huitt Young that he would have "a preliminary answer ready" for HEW in about three weeks.

Fleming also told Huitt he had already contacted Charles McCurdy, executive secretary of the Association of American Universities (AAU), which represented the top U.S. research universities, about putting the matter on the agenda of its upcoming meeting in Bloomington, Indiana. He asked Huitt to do the same for his organization's meeting in Washington in early November.

A. Geoffrey Norman, the university's vice president for research, advised Fleming a week later that the AAU's Council on Federal Relations had put the Campus Unrest Commission and White House science policy on the agenda (but there was no mention of HEW compliance investigations). By the end of the month, Fleming had decided to run for a seat on the council. Norman said he was pleased, "though this will add to the many claims on your time." Norman said one of the problems was "the short half-life of vice presidents" who represented their schools on the council.

Huitt wrote back before the end of the month after speaking to Chuck Kidd, the council's executive director, "about the problem you presented to me in your letter about the absurd application of The Fair Employment Act to the University of Michigan." (That was actually not the law that was the basis for HEW's action.) Huitt referenced a meeting Kidd and Fleming had had about "the matter" and said Kidd had sent his member institutions an inquiry about "experiences comparable to yours."

Huitt said he felt it would be best for the two organizations to coordinate their efforts. He wrote, "Chuck will turn over to me any replies he gets before the annual meeting of our Association. I do believe it is important for us to take these samples of our experiences as the basis for a presentation of the problem to the Executive Committee by yourself. When we are adequately prepared we ought to have a full discussion of it" with HEW Secretary Richardson.

Huitt, whose offices were in Washington, concluded by writing, "Perhaps ultimately we will have to take our problems to our representatives in Congress. They provide a peculiarly receptive audience to complaints about bureaucratic excess." (Huitt had previously served as assistant secretary of HEW for legislation in the Johnson administration, a job Richardson had held in Eisenhower's.)

Huitt's letter captures what seems to have been the prevailing attitude among the male leaders of America's major universities at the time: that the problem was not sex discrimination but rather overzealous federal bureaucrats, imposing aggressive remedies for "problems" that didn't really exist. (It would be another five years before one of the member colleges in Huitt's organization was headed by a woman when Lorene Rogers became president of the University of Texas at Austin.)

Fleming's papers reveal that over the coming weeks, he continued to strategize with his peers. On October 20, Harvard University President Nathan Pusey wrote: "You were good to remember to send me a copy of the affirmative action portion of Michigan's HEW letter. It is not unlike the recent letter we received from the Department although ours deals with minority groups rather than with the question of the status of women. Indeed the form and many of the sentences seem to be the same. I suspect it is only a matter of time before we get one like yours on the question of women's rights." Pusey agreed that the issue should be discussed at the AAU's upcoming meeting.

On Saturday, October 17, Michigan State University President Clifford Wharton was in Ann Arbor for the football game between the two rivals. The following Tuesday, Fleming referenced the brief talk they had had about the HEW order and sent Wharton "an extract" from the Scott letter. Fleming wrote: "The balance deals with facts peculiar to this University, but this section apparently represents the kind of affirmative order which they would expect to utilize in other cases. We believe it contains certain elements which would be very difficult to administer and I have therefore asked the various academic associations to place it on the agenda when the presidents meet within the next month or two."

D.B. "Woody" Varner, chancellor of the University of Nebraska, apparently heard Fleming speak about the issue and wrote on October 28: "I was intrigued with your report of the Affirmative Action auditing exercise. To the best of my knowledge and belief we have not yet had that pleasure, but I am now properly alerted." Varner asked Fleming if he would send him "a copy of their 13-page epistle dealing with your sins." Varner's reference suggests that Fleming was sharing the first 13 pages of Scott's letter but not the appendices. That section did include the salary details of husband and wife teams; it is not known whether he redacted the names before sending the document.

However, by the time Fleming responded to Varner on November 3, the university had heard back from HEW and the situation had grown tenser. In this letter to the Nebraska president, Fleming said university officials were meeting with "HEW people" in Chicago the following week; "I prefer not to have this [the document] spread around."

In follow-up reporting by Eileen Foley, a spokesman for Huitt insisted that Fleming was simply trying to "apprise [the organization's executive committee] of the situation," not trying to organize opposition. Jack Hamilton, Michigan's director of university relations, said, "It's going far out to say that he is trying to develop support to resist HEW's demands."

But around U-M, women didn't see it that way. In one of its regular communications, PROBE wrote that if the newspaper reports were true, "then our hopes for women on this campus are somewhat dimmed." If the organizations, "all housed in Washington with strong lobbying specialists, were to back University administrators in their attempts to resist the law, then we have big problems. University administrations have so many more resources than we do—private planes, low-cost secretarial services, money for lawyers, seven-figure budgets, etc. . . . PROBE is appalled that Mr. Fleming has chosen to apprise [Huitt's organization] with these facts when he has repeatedly refused to share the contents of the HEW demands with the thousands of people affected by it on his own campus."

King often made a point of how everything she did was on a shoestring. Twenty-five dollars for an event "was really hard to assemble. . . . We had no angels. Postage, long distance charges, and copying charges came out of our grocery money, mostly my family's. These were the years in which the Kings were way late in paying our pediatrician's bills. . . ."

Douvan, who retained a positive view of Fleming, remembered his initial response as "'I'm sure we can weather this and it will all go away.' Pretty soon, two weeks later, he was saying, 'Well, this is turning out to be a lot tougher than I ever expected. . . .'"

Newell recalled watching Fleming closely during the resolution of the BAM strike and how he worked to keep key university constituencies informed about his strategy. Reflecting on the HEW negotiations, she said, "There may have well been some questions about how seriously it was taken, but I also know that because of the sociology of academic departments...and the reticence to make any kind of change for anybody, he had a lot of work to do before he could make any commitments he could really live with."

In another context, Newell told a story that suggested Fleming was careful about picking his battles and assigned a lower priority to those involving women's concerns. She recalled that after she arrived at Michigan and learned that women were barred from the marching band, "I went straight to Fleming and said, 'What are you going to do about it?' And he said, 'Relax a minute. The guy who is the chair of the Music Department is retiring next year, and we'll get that changed at the time of his retirement. We don't need the fight now.' I must say I was a little discouraged by that response, but I think in retrospect it was a sensible way to go about it because there was so much intertwined with problems there—the music and the athletics and the sanctity of the football field." (As it turned out, longtime Michigan Band Director William D. Revelli, who chaired the Music School's Wind Instrument Department, retired in May 1971, and women were not admitted into the band until the fall of 1972.)

University presidents across the nation may have been confident they would find a sympathetic ear at the top of the HEW. But the Michigan investigation was moving forward at a complicated time for the huge agency, as a new secretary was taking over and the Nixon administration had mixed views about the direction the department should take. While there was a natural affinity between university administrators and an agency with "Education" in its name, there was also tension with the White House as more and more college presidents were unable to control unruly campus protests or, like Fleming, were actually speaking out publicly against the Vietnam War.

Richardson was happily serving as undersecretary of state when Nixon drafted him in June 1970 to replace Robert Finch at HEW, just a few weeks after King and Yourd sent their complaint to the Labor Department. Richardson's papers provide few details about the meetings he held with college presidents, but they do include transcripts of his often candid telephone calls. Soon after he was nominated, Richardson told a friend identified as "WBM," presumably his State Department colleague William B. Macomber Jr., that the president "reviewed what he thought he needed in HEW. Someone on the liberal side of the Republican party—someone basically sympathetic to the things that Department does. He needed someone with demonstrated interest, someone who had show [sic] to be a good administrator. He had been told I was. In terms of qualifications in the field, I have a lot more time in than [sic] I do in any other single area."

Patricia Reilly Hitt, who had been recruited by Finch to be assistant secretary for community and field services, recalled in a 1997 oral history that Finch "really had no prejudice against women, minorities, anything else. That was sort of—that presented difficulty for him. Because he was extraordinarily unprejudiced and supportive of women, minorities, everyone else. And he got into a little bit of difficulty with the White House. Not the President, but some of the staff over at the White House, because they all thought that . . . . [HEW] was a flaming liberal department [under Eisenhower]. It wasn't. It was more liberal, yes, than Treasury. But no more than Labor. No more than HUD."

Asked by her interviewer to define "flaming liberal," Hitt replied, "Flaming liberal[s] were supportive of minorities and women, and pro-minorities and pro-women, pro-minority programs. And some of them were pretty far out. But HEW had a reputation for being a very liberal department. But it really wasn't, because we accomplished some of the most conservative things that ever happened in that department."

A lot of Republicans, she said, "thought the [women's] place was in the home. . . . So that sometimes it's a little hard for them to grasp the fact that a woman could be president of IBM or whatever, But HEW was a— there was less prejudice in HEW than I think in any other department."

Over the summer months, as Rep. Green was holding her hearings and WEAL was filing complaints against more and more colleges, Richardson was scrambling to fill key vacancies and get up to speed on the issues his department faced a decade after he first served there. His new portfolio included initiatives to overhaul the welfare system and curb rising health care costs.

Addressing sex discrimination at universities, however, was not the same kind of domestic policy initiative. It was an enforcement task, assigned to the agency by the Labor Department. Now it was the responsibility of HEW's Office of Civil Rights, currently headed by Pottinger, a 30-year-old California lawyer recruited by Finch. His plate was already filled with challenging issues, not the least of which was how best to desegregate American schools when parents opposed busing their children across town. Another sensitive problem was the issue of the southern states whose public universities remained stubbornly segregated.

Louisiana and Mississippi would not even work with the department to develop a plan.

Pottinger had replaced Leon Panetta, then a Republican and a Finch aide, who had been forced out in February because of his too-aggressive stance on issues like busing. (Panetta went on, as a Democrat, to serve in Congress, as director of the Office of Management and Budget and as secretary of defense.) The same *Saturday Review* issue that publicized Sandler's home address carried an article on the facing page headlined "Crossroads for Desegregation":

> . . . [M]uch of what happens to the nation depends on the leadership of the administration. While most observers are still reluctant to believe that President Nixon intends to return the country to pre-1954, one man was willing to speak his mind without qualification. Leon E. Panetta, ousted as HEW's chief civil rights officer, angrily denounced the administration, charging, "The cause of equal justice is being destroyed, not by direct challenge, but by indirection, by confusion, by disunity, and by a lack of leadership and commitment to a truly equal society." Later, addressing the Women's National Press Club, he declared, "It has become more and more clear that the administration is going to cater to the voters of the Deep South states. . . . As long as they think they can get votes—rather than take the tough stand and not divide the country but bring us together—I expect this will continue."

Thus, HEW and the Office of Civil Rights were engaged in a difficult balancing act within the Nixon administration, and the staffs of the regional offices were often preoccupied with issues other than sex discrimination at universities.

What is also striking in a review of Richardson's papers a half century later is the absence of women in the discussions, particularly for an agency dealing with issues such as education, health care, and welfare that were traditionally considered to be of concern to women. In her job, Hitt was in charge of managing the regional offices, but it appears she had little involvement in their handling of the sex discrimination complaints.

In an oral history, Hitt later recalled of her job, "It was the place for me, because it had to do a lot of volunteer programs." Her office "was a conglomeration of programs and interests around the department that some time or another had been all gathered up and put together in with the field operation." Hitt said she visited all ten of the regional offices twice a year, talking with the regional directors and meeting with women staff members. Her visits, she recalled, often attracted media attention because of her status as the administration's top-ranked woman and the fact that cabinet members rarely visited second-tier cities like Kansas City and Seattle.

Just as King got to know women reporters in Michigan, Hitt cultivated relationships with a cadre of Washington-based reporters—Helen Thomas, Vera Glaser, Isabelle Shelton, and Frances Lewine—who were starting to ask tougher questions about the Nixon administration's record on appointing women. Hitt said she thought that most of the leading militant women "were kind of an embarrassment." But she came to realize that "getting there to any equality at all required some people, some extremism along the line."

Ironically, one of Richardson's early headaches was resolving a political fight over who would serve as director of HEW's Chicago regional office, where the Michigan investigation would be managed. Illinois Gov. George Ogilvie had lobbied aggressively for a state legislator, arguing in a phone call to Richardson that his guy deserved the appointment because Illinois's Electoral College votes had made the difference in Nixon's 1968 presidential victory.

But Richardson preferred Nebraskan Harold Booth, who ultimately got the job. ". . . We are in the process of decentralizing management of HEW programs to the field and the fellow who is the regional director is the representative of the Secretary and the coordinator and manager of this whole range of programs," Richardson told Ogilvie. "Booth has a record of performance capability as an administrator. He is in roles where he has organized large offices. He also has a law degree. In his job with State Farm, his function was to develop the diversive [sic] program and, in effect, to work on the kinds of things which we think are involved in the implementation of our decentralization process."

There is no "smoking gun" in the Richardson or Pottinger papers suggesting that the lobbying efforts of university presidents succeeded in blocking HEW's investigations of sex discrimination. (Rather the top officials sought compromises and backed down on some threats to withhold federal contracts.) But in the first of the four cabinet posts he would ultimately hold, Richardson appeared to focus more on Congress's active agenda and strengthening his own network of political connections. Still, as time went on, Pottinger seemed to grow more sensitive to the complaints of women academics and more frustrated by the opposition of university officials to making changes.

Their papers do, however, provide a window on the clubbiness of the "old boys' network" that prevailed at the time and the ways in which the academic and government worlds melded and interacted.

Richardson and Pottinger were both graduates of Harvard and earned their law degrees there; both were also involved with fundraising for their alma mater. Richardson had been a member of Harvard College's Board of Overseers when he was nominated as HEW secretary; he resigned to avoid a conflict of interest. His name was also among those floated in the summer of 1970 as Harvard was choosing a new president, something Richardson denied he had ever encouraged. (Fleming's name appeared on some of the same lists, but he wrote a friend that he never took it seriously because he did not attend Harvard and thus was "outside of the 'anointed' ranks.") HEW's investigation of discrimination at Harvard began a few months before Richardson took charge of the department.

In his first days on the job, Richardson was quick to respond when Michigan State President Wharton sought his help on a personnel matter. Wharton wanted to name Dr. Murray Goldstein, an assistant surgeon general, as the dean of MSU's new College of Osteopathic Medicine and hoped to find a way for the doctor to retain his commission in the U.S. Public Health Service. In their phone call, Richardson said, "If you are around or come in town, I would be pleased to hear how you find university life. I am going to develop a means of keeping in contact with the campuses." Wharton, who was near the end of his first year in office, responded, "I think that is important. The situation has changed very dramatically. There are areas where persons like yourself need to be kept informed. It is quite a different situation. There are certain aspects which are heartening and there are other aspects which are disheartening. I am new at it, but I find it very challenging." In a follow-up phone call to Dr. Roger Egeberg, the department's top health official and himself a former dean of the University of Southern California's School of Medicine, Richardson pointed out that "Wharton is the first Negro to head a University. His father was a Foreign Service officer." Technically, Richardson would have been correct if he had modified "University" by adding "large, predominately white."

At the time, the Office of Education had not yet been spun off into a separate cabinet department, and HEW was viewed as a huge, difficult-to-manage bureaucracy. Political cartoonist Pat Oliphant drew a cartoon showing Richardson arriving at the department and being welcomed by a large group of maniacal men, with the caption: "Come In, Sir! We Represent the Thousands on Your Staff. You'll Find Us Petty, Uncooperative, Devious, Unreliable and Thoroughly Bureaucratic. Welcome!"

It took Richardson six months to get Sidney P. Marland, Pittsburgh's former superintendent of schools, confirmed as commissioner of education. But Richardson's plans to bring in University of Connecticut President Homer Babbidge to work on higher education issues fell apart when Babbidge's board of trustees would not approve the leave of absence he had been counting on. Fred Harrington, the president of the University of Wisconsin system, who announced his resignation during the student protests of May 1970, was later approached about the job but declined. Marland told Richardson in a January 1971 phone call: "We are not going to find many people in higher education who have the leadership and enthusiasm for the [Nixon] administration. It isn't there." The job went vacant until 1972.

Richardson appeared interested in meeting with higher education officials, if not necessarily tackling their problems with sex discrimination. His appointment books show that he did, in fact, meet with many of them in his early months on the job, but there were a wide range of topics to be discussed.

On September 1970, a few weeks before the Chicago regional office presented its findings to Michigan, an hour-long slot on his calendar was scheduled with representatives of six key higher education organizations: the state universities' association, the AAU, the ACE, the American Association of Junior Colleges, the National Catholic Education Association, and the Association of American Colleges. That fall, the calendar showed a number of meetings in the building labeled "re Higher Education" as well as a meeting with leaders of the Association of American Medical Colleges and deans of "Vet. Med Colleges." He also stopped in at the Shoreham Hotel when Huitt's organization met there in mid-November.

During the fall, monthly meetings were scheduled with a group that included Macalester College President Arthur Flemming; Joseph Cosand, who had been a member of the Carnegie Commission on Higher Education and had served in leadership roles with the ACE and the Association of Junior Colleges; and ACE President Logan Wilson. Others who attended from time to time were Illinois President David Henry and Allan Ostar, president of the American Association of Colleges and State Universities. Various high-level HEW staff members also participated, as did Daniel Patrick Moynihan, then a Harvard professor serving as counselor to President Nixon, and "Ed Morgan," presumably the deputy to John Ehrlichman, Nixon's top domestic policy adviser. Richardson told Ehrlichman that Flemming had "picked up the challenge" Moynihan had made in a recent speech to the ACE and had set up the first meeting with the presidents on October 16, the same week Robben Fleming was sending the HEW letter to other presidents. (Cosand actually joined Michigan's School of Education in 1971 and then took a leave of absence the following year to fill the higher education vacancy at HEW.)

In his own dealings with Richardson a few months later, Robben Fleming seemed to rely heavily on what he called "the Flemming group" to make the universities' case to the HEW secretary. What the Michigan president probably didn't know was that Arthur Flemming had been quietly lobbying Richardson for a job.

Flemming had actually served as HEW secretary from 1958 to 1961, before becoming president of the University of Oregon and then moving on to Macalester College. He was about to chair the 1971 White House Conference on Aging. In one letter, he wrote Richardson:

> If you feel that I could play a role, either full-time or part-time in the Department in the field of education, I would be happy to think out loud with you about possibilities.
>
> It is great to have the opportunity of working at the grass roots of higher education during this period and I continue to obtain great satisfaction out of the work. And yet at this critical period in education I wanted you to know that I am willing to explore the question of whether it would be possible to render further service on the national scene.

No one knows anything about this letter. There is not even a carbon in existence. I just feel better that I have written it. I can think of a dozen and one reasons why if I were in your position I would dismiss the idea. If you do, you don't have to take time to give me any of the reasons. I will understand.

Richardson's personal papers and transcripts of his phone calls reveal his growing awkwardness over Flemming's job inquiries. Richardson had served as an assistant secretary under Flemming and was puzzled why his former boss was so eager to return to a subordinate position. In November, Richardson learned from Finch that Nixon would oppose Flemming's appointment because of a political disagreement dating back to 1960; Finch also said it was rumored that the Macalester trustees were not going to renew Flemming's contract in the coming year because of disappointment over his fundraising. (In her own oral history, Hitt recalled that the White House had viewed Flemming as "a flaming liberal.")

Richardson told Finch that Flemming had been helpful in representing the views of higher education, noting that he had just brought in "representatives of the [ACE] for a meeting to cover our whole student assistance package." If HEW's sex discrimination investigations were discussed at the same meeting, Richardson did not mention them.

HEW itself was wrestling with its own sorry record of promoting women. In February 1971, Richardson launched a Women's Action Plan, and on June 4, about a year after he became secretary, HEW produced its own plans for recruiting more women. An introduction said: "The policy premise of these plans is that every position in the Department of Health, Education, and Welfare can be performed by a qualified woman."

In 1972, the department issued a progress report, which included an eloquent message from Richardson. It read:

The second half of the twentieth century has seen Americans begin the attempt to identify and sever the bonds of discrimination that have constrained so many of our citizens. Momentum is gathering to redeem our national commitment to the significance of the individual, a commitment that, for too long, Indians, Blacks, Chicanos and other minorities found hollow and lacking. This drive to honor our commitment to the individual has now reached, and is eroding, perhaps the most ironic of our national injustices—the traditional discrimination America has practiced against its largest single majority group—women.

Indeed, never before has there been so widespread a need for changes in the status of women. Some believe that these changes ought to be desired by all our citizens. One need not subscribe to this view to agree that changes are necessary for and desired by some. For certainly it is important to the welfare of our society that women should be free to pursue their interests and apply their abilities without the impediment of discriminatory barriers.

The chief obstacle to overcoming discrimination against women may be that it has deep psychological roots in sincere and positive concerns for women. It is now widely agreed that however logical these concerns may once have appeared, they were at least exaggerated if not entirely mistaken. They are no longer acceptable—not, at least—if America is to keep faith with its commitment to the value of individual opportunity.

Richardson's secretary had transcribed phone calls in which senators and her boss had referred to secretaries and college-age women as "girls." But 18 months after becoming head of HEW, Richardson seemed to "get" the role the department needed to play in the larger societal changes. The premises that underlay the creation of the department's Women's Action Program at the start of 1971, he said, "were (1) that many changes are needed in the status of women both within the Department and in American society, and (2) that this Department has a unique responsibility and opportunity to bring about those changes."

Since HEW's "flaws" as a workplace were, he said, "in large measure reflections of institutionalized activities and practices of American society," the program's second objective was to "translate the concerns of Department employees into actions that could lead to the elimination not only of the Department's but of the larger society's sex discrimination practices."

11
The Contract

Why the University of Michigan?

There is no definitive answer to the question of why, among the 100 or so complaints that women brought against American universities that year, HEW took its toughest stance on this one. Certainly, King and Yourd's lobbying and publicity efforts probably played a role. HEW officials may have been feeling the heat after their grilling by Edith Green. Perhaps Esther Lardent and her youthful colleague made the case to sympathetic bosses that something had to be done about what they had turned up in the personnel files. Perhaps Don Scott had a wife or daughter who had been thwarted in her own professional aspirations. Or perhaps he and his colleagues were irked by the tenor of Robben Fleming's responses.

But others thought that it made strategic sense for the federal government to target Michigan. As Ann Larimore put it: "This was a very large, public university of high standing, so that if HEW could make a case against the University of Michigan, and make it stick, that would send reverberations through higher education." Library Science Professor Rose Vainstein, a former federal employee, echoed that view. The national pressure, she recalled, "was coming particularly, I think, on prestigious universities like Michigan because I think they had a feeling that if they could show discriminatory practices at a place like Michigan, then everybody else would fall in line."

At the time, Michigan was the public university that had attracted the most federal contracting dollars, and Fleming had emerged as a leading spokesman for higher education.

Reviewing the dozens of complaints that Sandler had already filed on behalf of WEAL, government officials may have preferred to make a test case of one that she hadn't handled. By investigating Harvard and Michigan, Sandler observed years later, "They went after one of the most prestigious private and public universities." *Science* magazine also supported that view (perhaps after interviewing Sandler). In 1971, it reported, that HEW had chosen Michigan "as a testing ground for programs ending sex discrimination against women."

Late in his life, Fleming himself agreed, saying that he was "neither surprised nor uneasy" about HEW's focus on Michigan. "When any major cause like this comes up, what the government tends to do is to pick some of the universities with the big names, on the theory that if they can whip them into line, they can pull the others faster," recalled Fleming. "So we were a good one to study in that sense. We were known to be willing to talk about almost anything."

Observers also said that by playing a prominent role nationally, Fleming sought to work out a solution that would suit Michigan, rather than letting another college accept precedents he couldn't live with. Gerhard L. Weinberg, the professor of German history who then headed the faculty senate, captured the prevailing mindset in a letter to Fleming that fall:

> It seems to me that in spite of the publicistic [sic] and other disadvantages that we may have as a result of being first in line on this one, there is an enormous advantage in being able to try to work out a settlement in accordance with our best judgment rather than being stuck, to all intents and purposes, with whatever has been decided at other universities. Surely if any other institution makes an agreement with HEW that we would consider improper, it would be terribly difficult for us to avoid being shoved into the same corner. Since I am confident that our own judgment of what is proper in this area is likely to be sounder than that of most other universities, it seems to me much pref-

erable that we should be first in line rather than third, fourth or last. This thought should make you feel better about those alert ladies—if they will excuse the expression—who have been responsible for getting us to the head of the line.

But, unlike many of the complaints that Sandler had guided at dozens of other colleges, the "alert ladies" at Michigan ensured that the FOCUS complaint and its resolution would continue to be followed closely by local media and women activists.

Still, there was widespread confusion (among both government officials and federal contractors) about the compliance requirements. Sandler later observed: "What is sanctioned by one regional office may be viewed as a violation by investigators in another region." University presidents concluded the same thing as they began to compare notes. In a February 1971 memo to members of the AAU's Council on Federal Relations, Charles Kidd said that Richardson and Pottinger "realize that the Regional Offices are not staffed with people who understand universities, their hiring procedures, their governance, etc. They both realize that knowledge of these matters is required if the rules relating to discrimination and their administration are to be reasonable. Given the admitted deficiencies of the Regional staff in this area, university officials need not accept without protest rulings, requests for information, etc., which seem unreasonable."

Fleming recalled many years later: "I was disappointed very often in the people who they had doing things because I so often had the impression they didn't know very much about what they were doing. And that too was understandable because there hadn't been much precedent for it." Fleming chuckled repeatedly over his memory of an unidentified HEW investigator who, he said, challenged the fact Michigan sponsored separate men's and women's glee clubs.

Stan Pottinger's papers show that on November 4, 1970, a few weeks after Michigan received its letter, the Office of Civil Rights he directed was still drafting its manual on how to enforce the executive order and had not yet disseminated it to the regional offices. Four of the manual's seven chapters had been completed, but the ones on "higher education" and "contract compliance" had not. A month later,

John Hodgdon and a colleague, Kenneth Mines, attended a meeting of the regional civil rights officials in California. Among the topics Pottinger was scheduled to discuss was "the priorities for allocating [the Office of Civil Rights's] time and manpower to higher education compliance."

For some reason, the Chicago regional office moved more aggressively than most of its nine other counterparts. Perhaps like Macaluso, the civil servants who worked there were gunning for a fight. On October 11, 1970, within days of Scott's letter, the Chicago *Sun-Times* published a scoop on a 1,155-page report by the U.S. Commission on Civil Rights that was highly critical of federal enforcement of the nation's civil rights laws, including the Kennedy and Johnson-era executive orders. While the report focused primarily on racial discrimination, it touched briefly on sex discrimination and the laws that impacted higher education.

In its review, the commission pointed to a "lack of funds, outright hostility of bureaucrats toward civil rights and timid use of federal sanctions." Reviewing 16 agencies that were responsible for monitoring contract compliance, the report found, that "no contract has ever been terminated nor any company disbarred" for failure to meet civil rights requirements. The newspaper said it received a copy of the report "from non-commission sources" and published it a day ahead of the formal release date. The leak might have come from the Chicago office of one of the agencies that was reviewed.

On October 23, Fleming wrote a former colleague at Illinois, "Things have been calm this fall. It is even conceivable that it will remain that way." What he didn't know was that the Chicago officials had already decided U-M's response was unacceptable and were not going to wait 30 days to tell it so.

In an October 22 letter, Don Scott wrote Fleming: "Our office does not consider your [October 7] letter responsive to our findings of deficiencies at your institution. The regulations provide that when deficiencies are found in a contractor's Equal Employment Opportunity Program, a written letter of commitment for overcoming the specific deficiencies is required before an institution can be certified as eligible to compete for Federal contracts."

Then Scott threw down the gauntlet:

Our Washington office has a recent request for clearance of a proposed contract between the A.I.D. [the U.S. Agency for International Development] and the University of Michigan. The proposed contract is in the amount of $400,000 to provide advice and assistance to the Government of Nepal in establishing and providing family planning services. In that your letter does not constitute a commitment for overcoming the deficiencies pointed out as a result of our recent review we are not in a position to recommend clearance of the contract until we have specific commitments for overcoming the deficiencies pointed out in our letter of October 6.

If you are unable to respond with an Affirmative Action Plan within 30 days, please give us your estimate as to the earliest date you can complete the program with its necessary analysis and evaluations. Also point out in your letter those areas in which you believe there is disagreement. We also need to know your intentions in those areas where you feel there is no agreement.

This time, Scott's letter was apparently delivered by traditional mail, as it was time-stamped by Fleming's office on October 26. Four more days had ticked by.

Scott, King recalled, "was very persistent. He had an independence that Fleming was not used to. And he was a government official. He didn't have to kowtow as a faculty member would have had to. He had the right to those records and the University wouldn't give them to him."

For their part, university officials continued to argue that they *were* doing a good job of hiring and promoting women. In a closed-door session of the October 15–16 Regents' meeting, they briefed the board on "HEW comments on alleged discrimination against women." In what seems today like an oddly parallel universe, Robert Knauss, in his first report as vice president for student affairs, noted that the University Placement Office "has been a logical focus for efforts to equalize women's pay scales with men's, to eliminate sex discrimination in hiring practices, and to get rid of the notion of 'women's work' fields. 'Women's Liberation' entered many of the discussions during the Midwest College Placement Association's annual meeting a few weeks ago. The Office has become more active in its campaign against job discrimination of all types."

On October 15, the administration's employee publication, the *UM News*, said, "Significant increases in top employment classifications are evident, while correspondingly significant decreases in the lowest category" had been achieved for women. On October 26, the *University Record* ran a chart under the headline, "Report Shows Gains in Hiring Minorities." It stated:

> A report filed with HEW last summer, based on a survey of the racial/ethnic composition of the staff begun last winter, shows that the University of Michigan is making progress in the hiring of women and members of minority groups. It indicates further that persons in these categories more and more are occupying top positions, that there is clear evidence of upward mobility of female minority group staff members.

The article went on: "Sex bias is a fairly recent challenge, however. For years, universities as well as most other large institutions have worked to improve the lot of their minority group work forces and to plan affirmative action programs for equal employment practices." It reported that HEW had identified "certain 'problems,'" the quote marks suggesting they were "problems" only in the eyes of the agency. It also said that 50 colleges had been charged with sex discrimination, "a fairly recent challenge."

But as the weeks went by, more and more people, both women and men, joined in wondering: What *had* HEW found? And if the university refused to share the agency's findings, were they actually much worse than anyone thought?

The queries came from persons across the breadth of the political spectrum.

As Halloween approached, the women of "the Sunday Night Group," likely a small consciousness-raising group affiliated with the Ann Arbor Women's Liberation Coalition, tacked a handwritten letter on the front door of the president's house on South University Street. It told Fleming, "In keeping with the spirit of Halloween, we. . . are hereby demanding of you the following political treat:

1. the release to the public, by Wednesday, October 28, at noon of the *complete and unaltered* HEW report on discrimination against women at the university.
2. a statement about your intentions to comply with the HEW demand that the university state, by November 6, its plans to end discrimination against women.

We know that we are not making undue demands on you, as they but support those already made by HEW, S.G.C. [Student Government Council] and Focus-Probe.

If our demands for these treats are not met by the Wednesday noon deadline, we will, as is traditional for Halloween, respond with a trick.

Fleming was not amused. He sent a copy of what he described as the "charming document" to James Brinkerhoff, who was in charge of campus security. Fleming detailed his family's plans for the coming week, suggesting that because no one would be home over Halloween weekend, the security staff should be alerted. There is no evidence that the women actually followed through on their threatened "trick."

The manifesto came at the end of a month in which the Regents had held an open session where representatives of several campus groups, including the Child Care Action Group, the Gay Liberation Front, and the Radical Lesbians, had been able to present proposals directly to the Regents. The sessions had not gone well, with some Regents decrying the exercise as a waste of time or expressing their view that the activists didn't represent the vast majority of students.

Thus, Fleming was likely surprised when he received a thoughtful letter from a member of that "silent majority." On October 31, engineering student Gloria E. Gladman wrote him, saying, "It has taken me this long to write to you in response to your statements regarding the HEW report of the University's discriminatory practices toward women. I don't usually get that angry: I'm an older student, a conservative and an engineer. . . . As a rule I have gone along with the University on most of its issues." She then went on:

As a woman on campus for five years, I've been aware of the discriminatory practices and attitudes of the University directed unknowingly and knowingly toward women. I've always kept my cool; feeling things would become better, especially with the movement toward elimination of racial discrimination. Unfortunately I am finding your attitude and statements with regard to sex discrimination on campus exactly paralleling the administration's unenlightened stand years ago when the University was labeled by a government investigation as a white, racist university. It took rabble-rousing, sit-ins, and ugly headlines to get a semblance of justice for blacks. . . and even now there are accusations by the blacks that the University merely put a bandage over the wound for public appearance reasons only.

Don't underestimate the feelings of women on this campus and the capabilities of current University policy and attitudes radicalizing a lot of "ordinary" women on campus. When one wakes up and discovers the shackles on her own wrists and ankles it is a very frightening experience. I still believe things can be worked out rationally and through the proper channels but public stands such as the one you took on the HEW report and the "Dream of a young woman" plaque on the front of the L.S.A. building make me wonder whether maybe I'm wrong on that, too. Don't radicalize me and for heaven's sake DON'T INSULT MY INTELLIGENCE with paternalizing attitudes. The best thing you can do is to take an open, honest, positively-constructive attitude and not try to "put one over" on me just to deflect unfavorable publicity. Don't be quick to say, "Things can't be done!" because I know they can be done quietly if the right attitude is taken.

She signed off her letter, "Hopefully."

Gladman did not detail the discriminatory practices and attitudes that she had observed on campus. But it *was* a very challenging time to be a woman in the Engineering School. It was not until 1895, a quarter-century after women were first admitted to Michigan, that the engineering program admitted its first woman student. According to the statistics CCEW compiled for the teach-in, the number of women in the school had increased from 89 in 1969 to 106 in 1970, but women still represented only about 2.5 percent of the total, a smaller percentage than in the medical, law, or business schools. Nevertheless, Michigan's record was better than the nation as a whole; across the country, women were awarded less than 1 percent of the bachelor's degrees in engineering during the 1969–70 academic year.

Before responding to Gladman, Fleming apparently double-checked her background: a handwritten note in the margin of the letter said she was a 1969 graduate of LSA, who was from Leland, Michigan, a rural town in the northern part of the Lower Peninsula. In her senior year, she had lived in Martha Cook dormitory, the women-only residence with the most traditional, restrictive rules.

After confirming that Gladman was not a campus activist, Fleming struck a different tone than in his earlier response to King and Yourd. He expressed puzzlement over what he had said that had so aggravated her "since I have said very little on the subject pending conclusion of the discussions with HEW. Perhaps it is the fact that I have said little that concerns you."

He then provided a more expansive answer than he had to the FOCUS leaders about why the university had not shared the HEW findings. He said that the agency's letter was "filled with names and alleged facts. As a matter of policy, I am told, they do not release such letters. We do not think it is proper to do so, and we are frequently criticized where there is a chance that someone's name or facts pertaining to his job will be released."

Privacy concerns were becoming a new defense for top university officials. Anti-war activism and other kinds of political advocacy could still jeopardize the careers of untenured faculty members. The HEW report itself did not telegraph those kinds of details, but, university officials seemed to warn, if an aggressive government agency came digging through its personnel files, that kind of information might easily fall into the wrong hands.

The privacy issue was highlighted in a front-page *New York Times* story on November 8. Under the headline "Women Forcing Colleges to Give Job Data to U.S.," the reporter wrote, "Women's liberation activities are forcing more than 2,000 colleges and universities to make their personnel records available for inspection by Federal investigators looking into job discrimination." The story quoted "one high Federal civil rights official" as saying, "Most colleges are very jealous of opening their personnel records because they may reveal that a person is a drunk, a homosexual or a Communist." But he assured the reporter that HEW's investigators weren't interested in that. Another official said investigators knew they were "bound in confidence."

Sandler, too, asserted that opening the records would not "damage academic freedom." The investigators were "only interested in the qualifications of people, not their political beliefs." Further, she said bluntly, "Nobody has to take a Government contract and if they want the Government money they will have to follow the Federal rules."

The *Times* article reflected the widening nature of the complaints. Sandler and Ann Scott, the NOW leader, were now traveling more widely to speak about them. Scott developed an "Academic Discrimination Kit" to help faculty women understand their rights and how to pursue a complaint. One version, retained by King in her papers, was distributed at the meeting of the Modern Language Association on December 27, 1970. The previous May, Scott had written an article entitled "The Half-Eaten Apple: A Look at Sex Discrimination at the University" for the biweekly news magazine *The Reporter*. It focused on discrimination in the State University of New York system, and Sandler included it in the transcripts of the Green hearings. Scott later pointed to the article as the reason she was never granted tenure. She eventually left the University of Buffalo to lobby for NOW on a full-time basis.

When Fleming responded to Gladman about the situation at Michigan, he revealed that university officials would be meeting with HEW officials the following week, and said, "I am hopeful that some kind of an agreement can be worked out which can then be publicized." (It would actually be another month before that information was released.) In the meantime, he told the student that if she had "specific allegations of discrimination I will be glad to know of them and to see that they are investigated."

In fact, Don Scott's report had highlighted the particulars of Margaret Davis's case, at least 10 cases in which wives earned less than their husbands, and 15 unidentified examples of non-academic women who appeared to have suffered discrimination in their placements or salaries. There were, in fact, "specific allegations" that could be reviewed.

Late in October, King received a phone call from someone in the office of U.S. Rep. Garry E. Brown, a Republican from Kalamazoo, Michigan, telling her that HEW *had* held up a U-M contract, but that the caller didn't know which one. "This was a sample of what women in Congressional staffs were doing for us," King recalled. It also, she said, "demonstrated an alertness in Brown's office at least to our work and to how to get hold of us." She tipped off the *Daily* staff, and reporters went to work to try to confirm the details.

On October 30, Michigan's executive officers met to discuss the HEW situation, and on November 3, Fleming responded to Scott's letter, an exchange that was not made public at the time. Fleming enclosed two exhibits. One, labeled Exhibit A, was an edited version of the memo Hayes and Burns had written, challenging virtually every one of HEW's findings. Fleming said, "In general, it is our position that the evidence does not support the suggestion that there has been discrimination."

Fleming said the university's "most serious objections" remained HEW's assertion of jurisdiction over graduate admissions, its requirement that back-pay settlements would extend back before a woman actually filed a complaint, and that the proportion of women faculty members was expected to reflect their relative proportion of job applicants. That requirement, he argued, "totally misconceives the nature of academic employment. It also lends itself to immediate abuse by artificial stimulation of applications."

But Fleming went on: "Although we do not believe that the kind of proposals you have made for an affirmative action program are warranted, we have prepared amendments to our current program which we believe will adequately and constructively meet whatever problems there may be and tend to minimize and ferret out cases of real or imagined discrimination." The three-page plan included establishing a Commission on Women, adding women to university committees that "do not presently contain satisfactory female representation," and centralizing grievance procedures and requiring that women be included. Fleming also said the university would begin a process "to review existing policies and procedures and to seek out cases of possible sex discrimination." The plan, however, included no dates by which any of the items would be accomplished.

Fleming's closing paragraph telegraphed his mood: "One final comment. In your letter of October 22, 1970, you indicated that certain contracts between the government and the University were being held up pending clearance of the matter of female discrimination. We find this a capricious act since not even the thirty days which your letter of October 6 indicated had elapsed. It is particularly offensive because in the past we have dealt with one another on a basis of mutual respect and confidence. In any case, we suggest that the opportunity for a hearing, established in Subpart D of the Executive Order and the Rules and Regulations of the Department of Labor, be utilized to at least afford us some semblance of due process." Fleming noted that a university delegation would be meeting with the Chicago staff the following week. "We look forward to a frank airing of our mutual problems at that time," he wrote.

By November 6, the *Daily* had confirmed which contract had been delayed: HEW had held up the renewal of a contract between the Agency for International Development (AID) and U-M's Center for Population Planning to provide family-planning guidance to the government of Nepal. (The male reporter can no longer remember who served as the source for his scoop.) Owen Kiely, director of HEW's Contract Compliance Division, said that all new and renewed contracts would be subject to the same treatment. At the time, Michigan held $66 million worth of federal contracts.

Fleming continued to project calm: "At the present time, the matter is of no concern to us. We are concentrating on the broader question of arriving at an agreement with HEW." He added that this was "normal procedure," and that the university could request a hearing on the contract if it chose. So far it had not. However, Fleming had privately told HEW that it was violating due process and cited the pertinent federal regulations in requesting a hearing on the thrust of its findings.

King recalled that when she and her fellow activists heard that a family-planning contract had been held up, "It was not a happy discovery. We were very glad that the Feds were acting but sad that the contract was for birth control services in Nepal. I am sure the choice was not deliberate (but in our bad moments we were afraid it was). The positive view was that it was probably the first U-M contract that came past after Chicago concluded that Fleming was not going to cooperate with the investigation."

In another interview, she said, "The irony of that choice of contract was not lost on us and in our more paranoiac moments we thought it was deliberately chosen. I am sure it wasn't though—when HEW decided they had found sex discrimination—or at least that the U-M was stonewalling them—they just grabbed the first contract to fly by."

The *Detroit News'* coverage of the story reflected why that paper was not the FOCUS leaders' natural media ally. Underneath the headline "U-M Bows to Women's Power," the story continued:

> A dozen Ann Arbor women, fighting the University of Michigan's hiring policies, have won a victory for American women—and lost one for the ladies of Nepal.
>
> Because of their complaint, the U.S. Health, Education and Welfare Department (HEW) has withheld a $400,000 study contract which was to be awarded to the University.
>
> That was the victory for American women.
>
> But the Ann Arbor women are blushing. They just found out that what they blocked was a family planning study in Nepal.
>
> And that was the loss for the ladies of Nepal.

Republican Mary Yourd may have been the one to reach out to the more conservative *Detroit News* because this was a rare newspaper article that quoted her. She said that at first she thought the contract choice was "incredible." Then, the male reporter wrote, "She laughed and said, 'Poor Nepal.'"

Yourd said the women had had no idea what kind of contract would be held up. "Really," she said, "this was just happenstance. It was just the contract that happened to be under negotiation when we made our complaint."

Libby Douvan later recounted her memories of how the FOCUS members responded. ". . . it was a terrible irony that the first contract held up was in the public health school and it was something that women *really* supported. But in the long haul, that had to be yielded temporarily in order to make the point that we really wanted to make."

The news that a contract had actually been withheld had a galvaniz-ing effect. The next day, Jim Neubacher, the *Daily's* editorial page editor, declared that it was "time for some answers":

> The Department of Health, Education and Welfare has demon-strated that it is serious in demanding that the University end its discriminatory practices against women by hitting the Universi-ty where it hurts most—in the pocketbook.
>
> If past precedent holds true, the administration will now move faster, and we may see some affirmative action in promot-ing equal employment and treatment of women soon after next Tuesday's University-HEW meeting in Chicago. . . .
>
> The University has done nothing. Fleming has not moved one inch. He claims that he has disagreements with the HEW report, and hopes to be able to convince them Tuesday that they are wrong. Since Fleming has refused to divulge the HEW report, or state publicly his specific objections to it, we can only wait until Tuesday before judging the substance of Fleming's procras-tination—assuming, of course, that Fleming will then share his thoughts with his "many constituencies."
>
> They had better be good objections. Women at this Univer-sity have demonstrated that they will no longer tolerate being treated as accessories and pleasantries in the academic setting. The HEW department has demonstrated that it is going to en-force the law, and cut off federal funds unless there is action.
>
> Fleming has kept his objections, and the report, secret. In this way, there can be no dialogue, no debate; Fleming's argu-ments to HEW officials will see no rebuttal from women. That leads one to suspect that Fleming is hesitant to debate.
>
> They had better be good arguments. Otherwise, when they do become public, as eventually they will, Fleming will find him-self looking like a Southern school board official trying to per-suade civil rights officials to lay off.

Over that weekend, news reports offered varying numbers on the state of investigations nationwide. The stories suggest that university spokesmen were pushing the story line that Michigan wasn't the only college HEW was going after. In a curiously unbylined story, the *Daily* reported that HEW had investigated 25 schools and imposed "temporary financial sanctions" against 11 of them in addition to the university. The Harvard case was referenced again, as were three other unidentified schools. The story also provided reactions from staff members of the Center for Population Planning, whose contract was at stake. Stuart Baggaley, a senior administrative assistant, said, "There isn't even a contract yet." Although the center had accepted the contract, he said no formal agreement between AID and the university had been arranged. John Takeshita, a professor of public health, said the contract delay would not undermine the center's programs. The center is "extremely busy in other activities," and if the program is blocked, "we won't suffer that much."

Minutes of meetings that fall of the center's governing body project no sense of alarm. On September 1, the minutes reported, "The AID Nepal Contract has not been signed yet. AID officials will be here this week for a site visit." On October 5, responding to the minority admissions goal the university had set during the BAM strike, the minutes noted that an interracial faculty-student committee would be organized to develop procedures for recruiting minority students. On December 7, the minutes read: "Mr. Baggaley reported that the Nepal AID contract is presently hung up on the HEW 'discrimination against women' case at the U of M. A hold was placed on contract negotiations (not on grants). CPP has requested AID continue progress on the contract so things can move promptly when the HEW hold is lifted." The center was also closely monitoring negotiations over a $1 million grant from AID to support programmatic services.

The *New York Times* story about privacy concerns said that in addition to Michigan, investigations were "under way" at Harvard; Loyola of Chicago; George Washington University; and the Universities of Maryland, Pittsburgh, and Southern Illinois. Agency officials were quoted as saying discussions were under way "with about 25" colleges about the sex discrimination complaints. The official estimated that funds had been denied to about a dozen institutions, but that all but three had subsequently complied with orders to open their records.

Michigan's AID contract was the only one the article specifically cited, and the reporter distinguished it by saying that it was "in jeopardy because the Federal investigators found the university guilty of sex discrimination and it did not agree to compliance procedures."

The newspaper story's lead referencing 2,000 colleges being forced to produce their records was simply an estimate of the number of schools that held federal contracts; Hodgdon acknowledged in one interview that HEW didn't even know which colleges *were* federal contractors.

Michigan provided its version of the story on Monday, as officials prepared to head for Chicago. The November 9 *University Record* said, "U-M joins a growing list of universities and colleges which have been asked by HEW to implement affirmative action programs for women. The Universities of Pittsburgh, Illinois, Wisconsin, Georgia and Brown are other recent additions to a list of about 25 institutions or systems HEW says are not meeting its current definitions of fair employment." It said the Chicago regional office "has indicated" that an AID contract "is being held up."

The *Detroit News'* story on the AID contract quoted Owen Kiely as saying that HEW had withheld "34 contracts on the basis of civil rights complaints of this kind," although those numbers may have included complaints based on race or religion and other kinds of federal contractors. As time went on, HEW struggled to provide accurate numbers on how many complaints had actually been filed and the status of their investigations.

On November 8, the *Daily* reported that Fleming had asked the Ann Arbor Women's Coalition to come up with a program to address the HEW concerns. One must speculate that if Fleming *had* asked the group to produce a plan, it was likely an offhanded comment in a moment of frustration, since he did not seem to be seeking input from anyone beyond his inner circle or certainly not from the women who had actually filed the complaint. Nevertheless, the women's group seized the opportunity to respond, refusing, in a formal letter, to offer a plan. Because "they had no access to the HEW report to which the University is trying to respond, it is inconsistent for the University to suggest that the women of this University write their own program." The group said that although they had demanded to be involved in the planning of the program, "the burden of responsibility is on the University, not the women subject to that discrimination." Two days later, their letter appeared in the *Daily,* this time co-signed by leaders of Students for a Democratic Society, Students to Support the Auto Workers, and the Ann Arbor Tenants Union.

All around campus, both men and women were becoming more sensitized to sexism, and it could be found wherever people looked. That same weekend, the Wolverines trounced Illinois at Michigan Stadium, 42-0, and the "Marching Men of Michigan" provided a halftime salute to the centennial of women's admission. (Centennial planners had not suggested that the band produce a show, and it was probably not until the teach-in that the band's leaders realized there was a centennial that might be celebrated.) Sports reporters covering the game did not make note of the band's show, but some spectators did. The next week, the *Daily* ran two critical letters to the editor:

> If whoever was responsible for the halftime band program last Saturday could not think of anything better than "There Is Nothing Like a Dame," or "Spinnin' Wheel" and the strip tease theme to commemorate one hundred years of academic activity by women at the University, it is time for him, or her, to retire. I can't believe that HEW was impressed either.

The letter was written by an unidentified reader named Virginia Davis Nordin, a law school instructor who, within a year, would become the second chair of the Commission on Women. Neither Nordin nor the *Daily's* editors felt the need to explain the reference to "HEW."

Three men and three women, at least some of whom were staff members of the Survey Research Center, wrote a second letter, imagining the choices the band might have made for a halftime show celebrating minorities, including "twirlers in white gloves and black face." It noted, "How unfortunate it is that while the society changes around us and roles for women and men are being redefined, the Michigan Band cannot match its unquestioned musical excellence with an appreciation of the social realities of the day."

Michigan's male-only bastions continued to be challenged. A few weeks earlier, Pat Atkins, the *Daily's* executive sports editor, had filed a complaint with the Office of Student Services when she discovered she had never been invited to the Athletic Department's traditional pregame "smokers" for out-of-town press and football coaches. Nor had Newell or Regent Huebner ever been invited to join their male peers at the gatherings.

The smokers were paid for by the "M" Graduate Club, the organization of alumni varsity letter winners, and held at a motel off campus. The club's president, William Mazer, said the group's executive committee had recently voted not to invite women. He probably did not help university officials' negotiating position with HEW when he added, "We didn't invite women for their own protection. When a group of men get together and drink, the language gets a bit rough. Women should feel honored not to be invited." Huebner, then 55, told the *Daily* she did not feel excluded.

PROBE, meanwhile, was continuing to gather momentum. Early on, the group began reaching out to campus women by posting signs on the inside of the doors of campus toilet stalls. "It was a purely female method of communication," King recalled in 1994. "No man would ever see it—which was important in our strategy many times in that era. The reason we used the doors on toilet stalls was mainly to avoid having the literature torn off of bulletin boards. . . . If we posted in every women's room in the U, it was likely that almost every female student and staff member would read it especially if the posting stayed up for several days." The woman in the booth "would be sitting down and might have time to read it (not as likely if it was posted on a mirror—many of us during that period didn't use mirrors much. I remember my instructions to the distributors to post them two-thirds of the way down on the inside of the stall door.) It was also a very cheap way to reach U-M women (both students and staff) that we would have difficulty reaching with any other method."

The PROBE women clearly viewed King as their general. "Jean was kind of like our Mother Superior," one member remembered. "She was older than the rest of us, and a lawyer, so she had a certain amount of ability and experience that the rest of us didn't have. . . . I'm sure she said, 'Well, look at this, they didn't mention it, here's what you gotta do.' And I'm sure we obeyed. Because she, in a lot of ways, she was the brains behind the whole HEW thing, and she just did so much of that piece of it."

Now PROBE became even bolder. Still frustrated in its efforts to get university employment data, it drafted a lengthy report, detailing what it called "the misleading news" that the university was distributing. PROBE said the university's stories were "designed to minimize HEW's report on sex discrimination" and that "if the campaign succeeds, the University may not have to take effective affirmative action."

The group's November 6 memo analyzed Michigan's first press release and challenged the attitudes Fleming had displayed when he had talked about "the preference of the market" in his earlier *Ann Arbor News* interview. "What we resent most," the group wrote, "is the hypocrisy of persons like Mr. Fleming, who view themselves as informed and reasonable people, yet consistently refuse to avail themselves of the knowledge that might upset their values and basic assumptions. It is imperative that administrators in positions of power take the initiative to first educate themselves to the fact and then to see to it that lower level administrators and staff be made aware and mandated to change their behavior to more constructive patterns."

PROBE also referenced recent articles in university publications about employment trends, faulting one for not even mentioning the HEW investigation and the other for publishing a chart that excluded two pertinent footnotes. (Michigan subsequently published a story about PROBE's complaints as well as a corrected chart.) PROBE also taunted university officials for waiting until now to publicize statistics on women employees, when the executive order had taken effect two years earlier. The group also contended that some recent promotions of women did not include raises and were made to remove the women from potential union bargaining units.

In addition, PROBE asked campus women to share which issues were the most important to them, offering a choice of better, more targeted communications; the posting of job openings; tuition-free courses; university-sponsored child care; or a grievance committee that included women. It also solicited members, donations, and additional ideas.

PROBE decided to try to use U-M's interdepartmental mail system to deliver its document. Two dozen members culled names from the staff directory and then stuffed and addressed about 6,000 envelopes. Between 1,500 and 2,000 were distributed before Gilbert Lutz, the system's manager, held up the rest, saying that the letters were "illegal" because the mail system was supposed to be used only for "inter-departmental communications." Lutz said "my men" knew the normal volume of mail and recognized a surge when they saw it. PROBE contended it had the right to use the system because its memo dealt with "University business."

The group said it was gratified that within a few days, it had received about 75 responses, although it noted that many were unsigned because women were afraid of reprisals. The mailing, a PROBE member later recalled, "brought more attention and more involvement, plus it was a lot of fun. In a sense, it was using the University systems to tweak them a little bit. . . . We were a very witty group. We were always enjoying ourselves."

They were different, another member recalled, from other protest groups of the time: "It was much more in a sort of women's model of things, which is to be very sort of optimistic and 'Well, if we just show them the data, they'll understand.'"

On November 10, university officials had their next formal interaction with HEW as Vice President Fedele Fauri, Newell, Allmand, Cash, Hayes, and General Counsel William Lemmer traveled to Chicago to meet with the regional officials. Allan Smith, a lawyer by training who was now in charge of the academic side of the university and its budgets, often played a major role in negotiations with HEW. But on this occasion, Fauri was the designated team leader. Fauri, also a lawyer by training, had served as dean of the School of Social Work for 19 years before he was named vice president for state relations and planning that summer, following the suicide of Arthur Ross. Fauri's background included experience in Michigan state government and with Congress at a time when the university was wrestling over what kind of government engagement it needed. After he became responsible for managing the university's affirmative action plans, he was quoted as saying, "I don't know why I have anything to do with sex."

In a November 5 memo designating Fauri as team leader, Fleming cautioned the others: "In general, we should be careful to keep the conversation within the confines of their letter and ours. This will naturally involve answering questions about their original analysis, etc. Will you all please check with Mr. Fauri on the general nature and conduct of the meeting." (In another demonstration of Fleming's national prominence, he was on his way to Houston to speak to a meeting of the Broadcasters Promotion Association.)

Before the Chicago meeting, Fauri told a reporter, "We are going to ascertain whether HEW's position is their original position and whether the filing of new material by the University has changed anything." Fauri would not comment on what "new material" had been submitted, because it was in response to the HEW letter that still had not been disclosed. "After we return," he said, "I'm sure a statement will be released."

The morning the team headed to Chicago, it was reported that Allan Smith would ask departments to make 3 percent cuts in their salary budgets for the 1971–72 academic year. University officials said they were anticipating decreased financial support from the State Legislature because the United Auto Workers strike against General Motors was headed into its eighth week. Still, some thought it odd that Smith was anticipating state cuts before they had actually been imposed. Michigan was, in fact, entering a period of fiscal austerity. A few weeks before, Fleming had warned top officials that the university was "facing increasingly severe financial pressure at a time when the effects of inflation are still being keenly felt." But a cynic could have easily concluded that Smith's directive was timed to start making the case that the university could not afford to add staff, raise salaries, or make generous back-pay adjustments.

When the team returned from Chicago, Fauri described the session to the *Daily* as "a chance for a meeting of the minds. They interpreted the statements in the original report to us and we tried to interpret our position to them."

Fauri's handwritten notes from the meeting provide additional clues on how the meeting with Hodgdon and Scott played out and the points that each side tried to make: "We stated that we were in the [hand-written word is not clear, but likely "evaluation"] stage. They said no—that was the meeting with Fleming—1 hr. I ridiculed this—and that you couldn't be expected to just give commitment of U—merely on glancing at their findings."

At another point, he wrote: "Hodgdon—women afraid to be identified—Known as kooks."

The meeting recessed for 45 minutes so that the Chicago officials had time to read "Exhibit B," the proposed amendments to Michigan's affirmative action plan. Upon returning, they "agreed" that it was "helpful." Fauri made notes that the officials felt points 11 and 12, appointing more women to university committees and creating a Commission on Women, were "responsive to their letter of Oct. 6." But points 1 through 4 were reportedly judged as "inadequate—do not include timetables and goals—do not assign specific responsibility and accountability." Fauri also wrote, "Letter of Commitment—must include 'provision for submission of the program and date of completion.' Show detailed plans and target dates for correction of discrepancies." Fauri also noted: "We hammered the due process—no hearing—unilateral action." Graduate admissions remained a big sticking point.

Don Scott's view of the meeting was communicated in a telegram he sent Fleming a month later. The conference, he wrote, "included a frank airing of the view of both sides in this matter." But he said that neither Fleming's November 3 letter nor the subsequent discussion with officials "were considered an adequate response to our letter of findings."

Scott also wrote, "We are confused by the contradiction in tone" between Exhibit A, which was based on the Hayes-Burns memo that had disputed every HEW finding, and Exhibit B, the proposed affirmative action plan. "Among many other things we believe Exhibit 'A' overlooks the intent of our letter of findings. We pointed out areas and instances which were problems and barriers to Equal Employment Opportunity for women in your institution," he wrote. "Exhibit 'A' would indicate that the University finds that no evidence of discrimination against women exists or that slight improvement in practices and procedures is necessary. We have already indicated that we do not share this view." While there were undoubtedly facts that Michigan could have successfully challenged in HEW's initial findings, sharing the very combative arguments from the personnel officials was, in hindsight, probably a strategic mistake.

Following the meeting, a U-M spokesman told Helen Fogel it would not issue a statement until Fauri's team had had a chance to meet with Fleming. But he did demonstrate some new anxiety on the part of the administration: While no other contract but the AID one was said to be "pending," if the difficulty was not worked out in "a couple or several more weeks we'll be in trouble." He also raised the privacy concern in a new way: "We could have real problems with students for instance if we were turning our personnel files over to the government." He said the university only opened individual files if HEW demanded it.

Fogel observed that "some legal theorists maintain that such opening of records to government agencies is a betrayal of confidence and an invasion of privacy. 'It is,' said the University of Michigan spokesman, 'a can of worms no one wanted to open.'" But the reporter asserted that HEW intended to protect employee confidentiality and it was, in fact, one reason "all their investigations and conversations are shrouded in secrecy, which leads many of those who file charges with investigators to believe that they neither want nor are trying to enforce law." Though not attributed to King or Sandler, the last statement likely reflected their frustration that they still did not know what HEW had actually found.

A few days later, HEW said it would complete its review of the university's response within a week of the visit. But John Hodgdon told the reporter, "Discrimination against women is not an easy problem to correct. There will be a lot of work ahead before this problem is resolved."

As Michigan officials waited, Newell did some reporting on the status of HEW investigations at other colleges. On November 9, she wrote a memo, saying she "took the liberty" of phoning the University of Pittsburgh, where women had staged a sit-in the previous April to force changes in hiring policies. (Newell had ties to Pittsburgh and before the start of the 1971–72 school year, would take a new job there.) In response to HEW, she said, the president had created a President's Advisory Committee on Women's Opportunity, and recently added more black women to the group. Over the summer, Pittsburgh had submitted an affirmative action plan with "general goals," and HEW had rejected it. On October 8, Pittsburgh, she reported, had been told to produce an acceptable plan or otherwise contracts "would be withdrawn."

Newell said that in the past few days, the president had produced a plan "which shows existing employment by rank, sex, race, by school and department unit for the faculty, and by classification level and department unit for non-academic. Each department chairman was asked to analyze the market and to outline the nature of his recruitment efforts and to establish goals for blacks and women that were achievable by September 1971. No formal criteria were established and no definition of sufficiency. The chairmens' results have been summarized by school and Pittsburgh is promising to make the school quotas, not the specific department quotas." Newell said that HEW would have the report shortly.

It is noteworthy that Newell used both the terms *goals* and *quotas* in her memo, a distinction that would become more controversial as the months went on.

A few days later, Newell reported that she had also spoken with a "Dr. Bert Phillip" at the University of Maryland, the university that was the focus of Sandler's first complaint. Newell noted that Maryland had submitted an affirmative action plan for minorities in fall of 1969 and that the following spring, after Sandler had filed her complaint, HEW asked the university to modify the plan to include women. "This fall such an amended program was filed," she said. "They are presently waiting a response to their program."

The *Daily* kept checking with HEW, and a week after the Chicago visit, Hodgdon told a reporter that Michigan's response still didn't pass muster: "The University has not given HEW the commitment that is required in order for our department to advise federal agencies that the University is now awardable for federal contracts." Hodgon said that the negotiations were ongoing, but that HEW and the university were "just a little way down the road towards settlement."

Then, like a mantra—or a statement his superiors had authorized him to make—he repeated the words he had used just a few days before: "Discrimination against women in our society is not an easy problem to correct and there will be a lot of work ahead before this matter can be resolved."

But the university's financial pressures continued to mount. That same day, legislative negotiators announced that the budgets for state-supported colleges would be cut 1 percent in the current academic year—$735,048 in Michigan's case—to help make up a budget shortfall.

As the Regents gathered for their monthly meeting, Michael Radock, vice president for university relations, described Michigan's recent public relations strategy, confirming that it was trying to keep a low profile:

> HEW's Chicago regional civil rights office wrote a lengthy letter on Oct. 6, detailing its survey of the University's practices in employment of females, and making recommendations for changes. . . little detail released by University, but considerable

attention and investigation by the media. . . other sources made public failure of the HEW contract compliance office to recommend approval of an AID-UM contract for family planning assistance in Nepal. . . Information services, except for a brief description of the differences with HEW and the plan for a meeting with HEW for discussion, only confirmed or tried to correct information developed elsewhere.

In October, Fleming had told Nebraska President Varner that he preferred not to have the HEW letter "spread around." But it did get spread around, possibly by secretaries opening up their male bosses' mail at other universities. On November 20, the day of the Regents meeting, *Science* magazine, the publication of the American Association for the Advancement of Science, wrote about the growing number of investigations and became the first news outlet to publish the nine requirements that HEW had stipulated must be included in Michigan's affirmative action plan. (The *Daily* reprinted the full story from *Science*, but the university and HEW still would not confirm the article's details, and the HEW investigation was not discussed during the open portion of the Regents' meeting.)

Science reported that WEAL had now filed more than 200 complaints against universities and that HEW had held up contracts at three other unidentified universities, in addition to Michigan. It also reported that Michigan was trying to build support to resist HEW. "Calling the demands 'totally unreasonable,'" the article said, "Michigan officials circulated copies to several other university administrations in an attempt to gain support." It reported that Michigan had argued that "the bookwork involved in determining who had suffered discrimination would be monumental."

It then quoted Roy McKinney, deputy director of HEW's Contract Compliance Division: "The requirement for supplying such information is clearly spelled out in each federal contract signed by the universities. HEW will allow extra time for bookkeeping work, but will not grant a reprieve from the regulations."

The article attributed HEW's eagerness to go after the colleges to the fact that "feminism is currently a popular cause with several members of Congress." It also said certain schools, notably the University of Illinois, are "quietly working toward an affirmative action plan."

That perception may have been more a matter of the extent to which WEAL's complaint against Illinois was actively publicized, monitored, and supported on that campus. In a mid-December letter to Fleming, the college's president, David Henry, wrote, "At the moment, Illinois is getting somewhat 'softer' treatment but I predict that very soon we will be in the same lineup on the same issues." Illinois would have been investigated by the same regional office as Michigan, but the Chicago staff likely had its hands full dealing with Ann Arbor.

Henry told Fleming he had asked a staff member to forward Illinois's response to "our 'thirty-day letter' so that we may continue to work closely on this vexing matter." He promised to "keep my ear to the ground for any sound out of the Washington contacts," then closed by wishing his old friend, "Season's greetings and a happier New Year!"

As the holidays approached, the waiting game continued, as discussions went on behind closed doors in Ann Arbor, Chicago, and Washington. There were other concerns on campus. On November 21, the Wolverines' football season came to a disappointing end when they lost to Ohio State, 20-9, in Columbus. The following Monday, Fleming spoke with SACUA about the proposed budget cuts, and Athletic Director Don Canham defended the raises his department had recently received, citing unionization and increased overtime. He could have chanted "We're Number Nine," when he pointed out how his department's salaries then ranked among what were then the ten schools in the Big Ten.

The same day of the Ohio State game, the United States launched new bombing raids into North Vietnam, putting the war back on the *Daily's* front page, along with a rare editorial. But the *Daily* itself was not immune from the debates about gender discrimination. Members of the Radical Lesbians showed up at the paper the next Monday to object to an ad for Little Caesar's pizza that had appeared in the paper over the weekend. It featured a cartoon of two young men walking by a buxom blonde in fishnet stockings. "Pickups are cheaper at Little Caesar's," one of the men muses.

The Radical Lesbians learned that two women on the *Daily's* business staff had also objected to the ad but were overruled by their male superiors. Arguments over the *Daily's* advertising policy and whether the ad should have been accepted continued for several days. Andrew Thorburn, who had sold the ad, said it had run several times at Michigan State without causing a furor. "Although several women on the business staff had voiced their objections before the insertion, it was felt that these people did not necessarily represent the community at large," he wrote.

"Any advertiser who is not an active part of the University community has a hard time evaluating the strength of feelings over any particular issue," he continued. "Perhaps this has happened with Little Caesar's. If so, we both apologize despite the fact that we do not consider the ad to be either sexist or in bad taste."

Students went home for Thanksgiving break, but the debate continued when they returned.

12

The Deadline

As calendar year 1970 drew to a close, Jean King could regard the unfolding drama from the perspective of a former departmental secretary: "Knowing what I do about the inside of the university," she recalled years later, "I realize that between October 27 and the Christmas holiday... the faculty member who was applying for a grant would be notified when his grant was not going to come through and he'd complain to his dean and the dean would call Fleming. So I'm sure he sat there with Deans on his neck for weeks. And he had to give in. That was a force he just couldn't deal with."

The "grants" King referenced weren't actually at stake but contracts were. At the time, 34 percent of Michigan's research dollars were directed to life sciences; followed by engineering with 27 percent; physical sciences, 20 percent; social sciences, 14 percent; and humanities, 1 percent. In the previous academic year, HEW had been the contracting agency for $17.6 million worth of research at Michigan. In fiscal 1970, Michigan was second only to the Massachusetts Institute of Technology (MIT) in the total federal research dollars it received; MIT topped the list in those years because it was the home to several federal laboratories.

Robert E. Burroughs, director of research administration, told the *Daily* earlier that year that as of March 1970, 1,500 projects received federal research support. Another 1,001 proposals were seeking government sponsors; he estimated that only half would be accepted. Research projects provided jobs for 2,100 graduate students and 1,500 undergrads, and supported the work behind an estimated 300 doctoral dissertations.

A detail that no one seemed to acknowledge or emphasize during the HEW episode was that some of the university's biggest contracts were with the U.S. Department of Defense (DOD), and that DOD was the source of almost a quarter of the university's research dollars. Since 1967, classified military research in support of the Vietnam War had become a particular concern on campus, but by 1969, that had dropped to 42 classified contracts worth a total of $5.6 million. National security concerns might have been invoked if HEW had withheld or cancelled DOD contracts, but the reality was that the Pentagon's share of the research budget was declining while HEW's share was growing.

For public consumption, top university officials remained calm about HEW's compliance efforts. A few days after the Thanksgiving break, Roy Reynolds of the *Ann Arbor News* quoted Burroughs and wrote, "Recent reports that federal research contracts with the University are being stopped by the compliance division of the U.S. Department of Health, Education and Welfare, because of alleged U-M discrimination against women, are not true."

Burroughs told the paper that six contracts had recently been signed and three others were awaiting signatures: "HEW hasn't issued any official notice to stop negotiations or payments to the U-M as far as we know. If this really were official, every federal agency would have it."

But Burroughs was careful to add, "Of course, we don't expect it to continue this way. Don't minimize the importance we put on successful negotiations with HEW." Burroughs and Geoffrey Norman, vice president of research, acknowledged that "the period after Jan. 1 will be critical, because several federal research contracts are due to take effect then."

Later that week *Daily* Editor Martin Hirschman reviewed the situation and concluded that the university had "continued to receive a near-normal flow of contracts, grants and renewals." The article detailed some of the loopholes that enabled federal money to keep moving. While agencies such as the National Aeronautics and Space Administration and the U.S. Atomic Energy Commission awarded research "contracts," the National Science Foundation awarded research "grants," which were not covered by the executive order. HEW's Contract Compliance Division was supposed to review most of the contracts HEW itself awarded, but other agencies were required to seek clearance only on contracts worth more than $1 million. Although agencies could seek HEW's advice on smaller contracts, in practice they rarely did.

"They're realistic," Norman told Hirschman. "They don't believe the University of Michigan is any more guilty of sex discrimination than their own agencies. Furthermore, they've got their missions to complete."

University officials continued to assert that they had not finished negotiations over the AID contract, but HEW's Kiely said his agency had told AID not to award it. In addition, he said, HEW had not awarded a new contract to the university since October 6, when Scott had formally reported that Michigan was not in compliance.

Kiely further threatened that if the university did not produce an acceptable plan, HEW would turn the matter over to the Labor Department, which, he said, was empowered to enforce the contract ban across agencies.

Norman, a soft-spoken English botanist, commented, "I don't minimize the problem, but, on the other hand, I'm not getting panicked or anything."

But once again, Fleming's presidential papers reveal a different story. A week earlier, on the day before Thanksgiving, Burroughs's colleague Kenneth P. Burns had sent him a memo with the subject line "Equal Opportunity Clause." It detailed discussions Burns had had with the Air Force Office of Scientific Research (AFOSR) about the "current situation" of five new contracts, totaling $233,589 (about $1.5 million in 2020 dollars) with start dates of December 15, 1970 or January 1, 1971. The projects were to be directed by persons in five U-M units: the nuclear, aeronautical, and electrical engineering departments; the mathematics department; and the Geophysics Laboratory at Willow Run, a manufacturing/research complex near Ann Arbor.

Burns noted that since November 4, his office had been using this language when asked to provide "Certification of Equal Compliance": "Except that the Chicago Regional Office of the Department of Health, Education, and Welfare is currently conducting an investigation at The University of Michigan into charges of discrimination on the basis of sex."

On November 25, the day he wrote his memo, Burns said that Capt. R.T. Ribbentrop of AFOSR had informed him that "his director of procurement had told him to hold off signing" a modification of one of the contracts "until further notice." Burns described the contract as a continuation of a nuclear engineering project amounting to $24,928 for the next calendar year.

Burns told Burroughs, "I informed Captain Ribbentrop that the investigation was not completed and that I needed specific information as to the reason for the order to not sign the modification for continuing research." He said he had been informed earlier by Captain Dale Gaston of AFOSR that he planned to write a new contract for the Geophysics Lab project that was scheduled to start on December 15. Burns's narrative continued with military precision:

> At approximately 11:00 a.m., November 24, [sic] 1970, Captain Ribbentrop called again and indicated the temporary hold on completing contracts is based on the two letters dated October 6 and October 22 from HEW to President Fleming. The contents of these letters apparently provide the reason for action being taken. . . . Captain Ribbentrop suggested we contact Mrs. Arkedie at Area Code 202, 962-0368, HEW Compliance Office, for further information.
>
> At 3:15 p.m., November 25, 1970, Captains Gaston and Ribbentrop called to discuss funding of [the Geophysics Lab contract]. Both stated they could not guarantee costs if contract were not awarded and could not recommend we proceed without a contract. They did agree that if the contract was subsequently approved for awarding, they could assist by using an effective date earlier than the signature date if it was needed.
>
> I was further informed that a representative of the Procurement Office, AFOSR, has contacted the HEW Certification Compliance Office and requested guidance in writing. We expect to be advised of the content of the guidance. At the present time, we should not issue authorization to proceed with research or purchases for this continuing grant or the new contract.

The memo would have thrilled Jean King if she had known about it. She might smile like an indulgent mother as PROBE activists plastered toilet stalls with their flyers or when women activists considered protesting the lack of a university day care center by bringing their children to a Regents meeting for a "child-in." But she knew that holding up contracts was the best way to get the attention of top university administrators.

PROBE, she said, "wanted to negotiate with Fleming, and Fleming certainly wasn't about to do that. . . . They didn't have any leverage against him. The only leverage we had was HEW from outside the University. From inside the University he was in total control."

King treated federal contracts like a World War II bomber pilot might have ticked off the enemy planes he had downed on the nose of his fuselage; they were the metric that told her she was winning the war. She obsessed over the figures more than any PROBE activist did. As administration officials were scrambling, King learned from Muriel Ferris that 12 contracts under $1 million each had been held up, as well as a contract for $1.62 million with the Atomic Energy Commission. Various news reports later placed the total at amounts ranging from $3.5 million to $15 million. When the *Wall Street Journal* reported that the total was $7.5 million, a university official challenged the story, saying that figure was "impossible to substantiate." A newsroom executive said the reporter had gotten the figure from HEW. The only contract that the university itself ever publicly acknowledged was the one with AID, and even so, it dismissed the actual impact of the agency's action.

Meanwhile, Michigan's intransigence was angering more and more women across the campus. On November 30, nine women wrote Fleming, urging him "to release the HEW findings so that women can begin writing a program which will not only be acceptable to HEW but will also speak to the real needs of women on campus."

On December 5, Marcia Federbush, the wife of a mathematics professor, sent a handwritten letter to Fleming's home. She began: "Not being a member of PROBE, I was distressed last night to learn of the University's refusal to release the results of the HEW investigation and University's subsequent response, later rejected by HEW. It is particularly distressing since some of the information about the University of Michigan has become available through the publication *Science* and through administrators of other universities."

Federbush continued, "This is a period when women are suddenly becoming aware of the enormity of their debasement in all sectors of society. What hurts most of all is the realization that they have been living with obvious and subtle, purposeful and unintentional discrimination all their lives and have somehow either failed to recognize it or have not tried to change it."

Federbush said that when her husband, who served on the Mathematics Department's executive committee, "tells me with complete seriousness that the Math Department does not discriminate against women, I feel frustratedly indignant." She noted that of the department's 89 faculty members, not a single one was a woman. "Surely," she wrote, "when 52 percent of the population is female, there are some notably capable women mathematicians." She said that thanks to "the recruiting efforts of Prof. Maxwell Reade during the last few years, about 17 percent of the math grad students" were women. "It does not make sense that the department considers girls qualified to become students but not faculty members. Clearly, the University must recruit able women as faculty people with the same enthusiasm that it recruits blacks."

She closed by writing:

I am sure that you can well understand the inflamed feelings of a great many women whose lives are intimately entwined in the fabric of the University. To deny them access of the contents of a governmental investigation which may well affect all present and future women at Michigan is again to have decisions concerning their welfare made for them, above them, behind their backs, and without their knowledge or consultation.

If it is a question of not wishing to divulge specific names of individuals singled out by the report, certainly these can be concealed without obscuring the intent of its contents or the nature of the University's response to it. I feel that it is clearly desirable for women to know how the University is proposing to remedy existing inequities.

If it is at all in your power to do so, before another unpleasant confrontation materializes, won't you please reconsider the decision to maintain secrecy concerning this issue. I think we will all be better off for it.

But the university's time was, in fact, running out. On December 5, a staff member of the President's Office phoned the Chicago office and a few hours later, Scott sent his telegram formally notifying Fleming that neither his letters nor the November meeting represented an adequate response: "Until the University of Michigan has committed itself to overcoming the deficiencies in the letter outlining our findings this office will not be in position to clear the award of further Federal contracts." Scott said that if the university did not respond within 15 days, the Chicago office would recommend that its Washington office initiate "formal enforcement proceedings."

At that point, Fleming decided he had to get personally involved and his presidential papers reflect his new sense of urgency. That afternoon, he phoned Peter Muirhead, then HEW's top official dealing with higher education, as opposed to civil rights. "I think someone from education is essential because the enforcement people obviously know nothing about a university," he wrote in a memo to the executive officers. It appears he typed the memo himself over the weekend before he headed out of town for a meeting of the Big Ten presidents in Chicago. He gave very specific instructions on what should be done next.

"I not only do not oppose an equal-treatment-for-women policy, I think it is desirable," he asserted. However, he continued to object strongly to some of HEW's demands. Consequently, he proposed a new strategy: The university would give the Chicago regional office more of what it had asked for, but he was still not willing to cave on four points: the review of all the files for instances of discrimination, graduate admissions, the standard for evaluating recruitment efforts, and the date that would apply to back-pay awards. Consequently, he would send a telegram to HEW Secretary Richardson about the continued points of disagreement. The goal was to get "a 30-day moratorium on their contract hold-ups while we negotiate."

Fleming was now ready to call in some new big guns. In this memo, he suggested asking Wilbur J. Cohen to phone Richardson. Cohen, one of the nation's leading experts on welfare and social security programs, had served as HEW secretary for the final eight months of the Johnson administration before becoming dean of U-M's School of Education. He had interacted repeatedly with Richardson since Richardson's arrival at the department. Fleming mused that perhaps his telegram to Richardson should be followed up by a phone call from Cohen "saying how urgent this was to us." (There is no record of such a call in the transcripts of Richardson's office phone calls.)

At some point, Fleming also enlisted the help of Rep. Marvin Esch, the Republican congressman who represented Ann Arbor. Ever mindful of "constituent services," Esch had written the Labor Department on behalf of King and Yourd and now would press the case of their opponents, whether he realized it or not.

Fleming concluded by telling the executive officers, "Since time is of the essence now, will you all please think about and discuss this on Monday." Fleming said he would talk with Illinois President Henry "to see what they are going to do. Then on Tuesday morning, this may have to be the principal item on the [Executive Officers] agenda." On Thursday, Fauri reported to Fleming that he and Cohen had discussed some recent educational policy laws; the memo and its timing suggests he may have been exploring whether the university could find language in another education law that would let it challenge the federal interference.

But on Monday, Fleming did write Scott, finally pledging that the university would amend its existing affirmative action plan within 90 days to set specific numeric goals and timetables for hiring women. In a draft he wrote on the weekend, Fleming left blanks to specify how long various tasks would take. But in his final version, the president fudged on every time commitment that involved a review of personnel files, pledging only to address the problems within 30 days of when the file reviews were finished.

Michigan continued to challenge whether HEW had any jurisdiction over graduate admissions. On that point, the letter included no specific commitment, asserting that "There are no PhD graduate programs at the University of Michigan to which admissions are connected with specific employment opportunities." The university insisted that all such opportunities "are open to all qualified students without discrimination and will continue to be so administered."

Although many women had suffered pay discrimination for years, HEW could demand that they be compensated only back to October 13, 1968, the date Executive Order 11375 took effect. However, the financially strapped university committed only to providing back pay to the date it signed its first contract after the executive order took effect. Officials told a reporter that they did not know what that date was, but it was probably only a difference of a few weeks. It was a legal distinction that could only serve to anger women who were paying attention to the details.

The letter also included Michigan's first formal commitment to create a Commission on Women, reporting through Fauri.

The same day, two months after Scott's first letter, the university finally released portions of HEW's initial findings so that it could, in fact, demonstrate that it was being responsive. It released the "Exhibit B" plan that HEW had rejected, as well as excerpts from Scott's telegram. (It did not release Scott's most sarcastic comments or Exhibit A, the university document that denied the existence of any discrimination.)

For a change, this generated some favorable stories. Helen Fogel, who had covered the complaint since its earliest days, wrote that the university "appeared to have the lead on all other universities in attempts to eliminate effects of discrimination against women staff. While spokesmen for major universities across the country emphasized a growing awareness of sex discrimination on the campus and work underway to correct discriminatory practices, only Michigan had publicly announced concrete steps it will take to correct such practices."

But the *Daily*, characteristically, remained skeptical, writing that Fleming "claim[ed]" the submission "should satisfy all but two of HEW's objections to the first plan." It noted that although HEW had called for hiring women in the same proportion that they had applied for jobs, Fleming had committed only to "'the vigorous recruitment of females for academic positions' so that those with comparable qualifications" were given equal consideration as males.

Fleming, it said, called HEW's proposal "unworkable" because "it ignores the quality of applicants and lends itself to artificially increasing the number of women who apply."

In a tactical advantage for Fleming, that issue of the *Daily* was the last that would be published before a month-long break for semester exams and the holidays. Thus, there was no opportunity for second-day stories, follow-up phone calls to Hodgdon, or a platform for critical letters to the editor from King or PROBE. The *University Record* also did not publish in the second half of December. Fleming, therefore, was in a better position to do the kind of behind-the-scenes negotiating his memoir makes clear he preferred.

As U-M released its documents, Fleming wired Richardson about his continued objections. He again described as "unworkable" the notion that the university's employment of women should match the ratio at which they were applying. He also continued to object to HEW's assertion of jurisdiction over graduate admissions: "There are serious internal educational policy questions affecting not only this institution but many others. We are confident that you do not wish to use the contract compliance device to coerce universities into signing agreements on matters of profound significance without providing an opportunity to review the matter with your top officials."

Fleming did not tell the Michigan community that he was appealing to Richardson, but he attached a copy of the telegram when he responded to Scott. The message was clear: "I'm going over your head to your boss."

From the perspective of 50 years, the resistance of Fleming and other university presidents on the admissions issue is somewhat puzzling. Even if one concedes their legal point that the executive order applied only to employment, rather than admissions, why not at least commit to reviewing admissions policies to ensure that they did not discriminate against women graduate students? Two years before passage of the groundbreaking legislation that became known as "Title IX," they appear to reject "fairness" because they were unwilling to accept how the government defined it or admit that there was any problem at all.

The next day Fleming sent Illinois President Henry copies of the latest correspondence and complained, "We have had great difficulty in dealing with the Chicago office of HEW. Its people are not well informed and have to keep going to Washington. Our original reply, submitted within the thirty-day period, which expired November 6, received no answer at all for a month. Then came the telegram which is enclosed."

Fleming told Henry that Peter Muirhead was "sympathetic to a meeting with the Arthur Flemming group." But, Fleming cautioned, "Whether the Secretary will feel likewise is another question to which we will not know the answer for a day or two."

Fleming closed by saying, "It does seem to me important that on such key items as faculty recruitment we keep a relatively common line."

But Fleming's biggest immediate concern were the university's contracts. In his telegram to Richardson, he declared, "Because HEW is currently withholding approval of new or continuing contracts, some research and service activities in support of federal programs will be impaired within the next few days if the current embargo is not lifted." Fleming proposed three alternatives "for resolving the problem":

1. Lift the "contract embargo" until Richardson could discuss the policy questions with "the Arthur Flemming group with which you have been meeting."
2. Schedule a meeting with university officials before the end of the week "so that a temporary suspension of the embargo can be arranged pending clarification of these points."
3. Ask a "select group of university representatives to meet with you to evolve a common policy for a common problem."

Fleming noted: "We would point out that HEW's position cannot be prejudiced by taking such a step since there is a steady flow of contracts with the University of Michigan should the Department determine later to reinstate the embargo."

The president then declared: "We are unqualifiedly opposed to discrimination on the basis of sex, but we do not believe you intend that Executive Order 11246 be administered in a manner which could imperil vital educational objectives." He closed, "We will be grateful for an early reply."

Bernice Sandler discovered that universities, as federal contractors, were prohibited from discriminating on the basis of sex and filed dozens of complaints against U.S. colleges in the name of the Women's Equity Action League. (Photo courtesy of the Schlesinger Library, Radcliffe Institute, Harvard University.)

Jean Ledwith King, circa 1960s. King drew on her experiences as a U-M student and employee when she filed the sex discrimination complaint against the University of Michigan in May 1970. (Photo courtesy of the Bentley Historical Library.)

Kathleen Shortridge discusses U-M's record on hiring women and minorities at a 1974 Board of Regents meeting. In spring 1970, Shortridge authored a key article on sex discrimination at U-M and became a leader in both FOCUS and PROBE. (Photo by U-M News and Information Services, courtesy of the Bentley Historical Library.)

Holding the rank of full professor as well as an endowed chair, Elizabeth Douvan (center) of the Psychology Department was one of the highest-ranking women in the College of Literature, Science & the Arts when the FOCUS complaint was filed in 1970. Behind the scenes, she provided her statistical expertise to the drafting of the complaint. (Photo by U-M News and Information Services, courtesy of the Bentley Historical Library.)

In July 1970, Mary Maples Dunn, then a visiting professor from Bryn Mawr, told President Fleming that after a year at the University of Michigan, she had "a claustrophobic sense of living in a man's world." Dunn went on to become president of Smith College. (Photo courtesy of Smith College.)

The bas-relief sculpture "Dream of the Young Girl and Dream of the Young Man" first elicited complaints from campus women in August 1970. It remained installed on the LSA building for 34 more years. (Photo courtesy of the U-M Center for the Education of Women.)

Allan Smith, vice president for academic affairs, (from left) Clifford Minton, head of the first HEW investigative team, President Robben Fleming, and William L. Cash Jr., Fleming's assistant for human relations affairs, in August 1970, during HEW's first visit to investigate the FOCUS complaint. (Photo by U-M News and Information Services, courtesy of the Bentley Historical Library.)

Women take over the stage of Hill Auditorium during the October 1970 teach-in marking the centennial of the admission of women to the University of Michigan. (Photo by Denny Gainer, the *Michigan Daily*, courtesy of the Bentley Historical Library.)

The Center for the Continuing Education of Women
helped organize the 1970 celebration of the centennial
of the admission of women to Michigan. At one of
the events, then-Director Jean Campbell (second from
right) called on President Fleming to create a women's
commission. Helen Tanner (far right) was one of the
handful of women faculty who complained directly to
HEW about the sex discrimination they had experienced.
They gathered with (from left) Carol Hollenshead, Jane
Likert, Louise Cain, and Marjorie Lansing at a 1989
celebration of the center's 25th anniversary. (Photo
courtesy of the U-M Center for the Education of Women.)

Elliot L. Richardson, who served
as HEW secretary from June
1970 to January 1973. (Photo by
Marion S. Trikoso, courtesy of the
Library of Congress Prints and
Photographs Division.)

The Commission on Women at an early meeting, under the leadership of Barbara Newell (far back right). (Photo by U-M News and Information Services, courtesy of the Bentley Historical Library.)

Barbara Newell, then Fleming's special assistant, (foreground) chairs an early meeting of the Commission on Women. To Newell's left is Harriet Mills, a professor of Chinese language and literature, who later said her service on the commission opened her eyes to the extent of sex discrimination at U-M. (Photo by Tom Gottlieb, the *Michigan Daily*, courtesy of the Bentley Historical Library.)

University administrators developed and submitted the first goals and timetables to promote the hiring of women without the input of the Commission on Women or the members of PROBE. The two groups met at that time to discuss the situation. (Photo by Tom Gottlieb, the *Michigan Daily*, courtesy of the Bentley Historical Library.)

The meeting between the Commission on Women and the members of PROBE was covered on the front page of the *Michigan Daily* on March 10, 1971. Among the commission members who participated was Barbara Murphy, an analyst at the Survey Research Center (at left). (Photo by Tom Gottlieb, the *Michigan Daily*, courtesy of the Bentley Historical Library.)

'U' submits goals to HEW on equal hiring of women

By TAMMY JACOBS

University administrators have filed with the Department of Health, Education, and Welfare goals and timetables for implementing the University's affirmative action program for equal employment of women.

The statement of specific proposals, made public yesterday, was filed with a nine-point program in accordance with a 90-day deadline set by HEW Dec. 8, 1970.

HEW will now review the proposals and accepts or reject them.

The University's Commission on Women, created in January to review the affirmative action program and make recommendations towards insuring equal opportunities for women, has not yet considered the University's statement.

According to Barbara Newell, chairwoman of the Commission, the goals and timetables were formulated by the University administration, and will be discussed at the commission's regular meeting Friday.

Members of the Commission met with members of PROBE, a woman's group concerned with the role of women in the University last night, but refused to comment on the goals and timetables, which most of the women had not yet seen.

Newell said the Commission worked on its affirmative action program statement and made suggestions as to its composition.

THE UNIVERSITY'S Commission on Women meet last night with PROBE, a local women's group, to discuss the role of the Commission.

LAOS DRIVE:

N. Viets pushed back. U.S. says

Fedele Fauri, U-M vice president for state relations and planning, was put in charge of implementing U-M's affirmative action plans in 1971. (Photo by U-M News and Information Services, courtesy of the Bentley Historical Library.)

In 1971, Geography Professor Ann Larimore became the first woman to be elected to a full term on the governing board of U-M's Rackham Graduate School. During its investigation the previous year, HEW reviewed Larimore's personnel file to compare her salary to her husband's. (Photo by U-M News and Information Services, courtesy of the Bentley Historical Library.)

Cheryl Clark, a research associate at U-M's Highway Safety Research Institute, at a January 1972 hearing of her complaint over salary discrimination. To Clark's left is her attorney, then-U-M Law Professor Harry Edwards. (Photo by Jim Judkis, the *Michigan Daily*, courtesy of the Bentley Historical Library.)

In the years immediately following the HEW investigation, women faculty began organizing the Women's Studies Program. Its founders included (from left) Psychology Professor Elizabeth Douvan, History Professor Kathryn Kish Sklar, English Professor Margaret Lourie (standing), Psychology Professor Lois Hoffman, and Anthropology Professor Norma Diamond, shown here at a 1973 Center for the Education of Women event. (Photo courtesy of Margaret Lourie.)

Before joining the U-M Board of Regents in 1981, Political Science Professor Nellie Varner served as U-M's first affirmative action director. (Photo by U-M News and Information Services, Regents Collection, Box B18, courtesy of the Bentley Historical Library.)

13
Happy Holidays

Robben Fleming had reassured his campus family that everything was going to be all right. The only question was, did HEW agree? After all, only two months before, Michigan had issued a confident press release, describing how it was going to resolve the issue by making a few changes in its affirmative action plan for minorities. But HEW had responded that it wasn't impressed.

The day after Fleming wired Richardson, Rep. Esch phoned the HEW secretary. Esch was well-suited to make the call. He had earned three degrees, including a doctorate, from Michigan, and had taught speech at Wayne State University, a college subject to another complaint. Esch had reclaimed the Ann Arbor area congressional seat for the Republicans in 1966. The transcript of his phone call is preserved in Richardson's papers.

> *Esch*: I am sorry to bother you. I thought I would call you direct. I have something that is of direct concern to me. It concerns the University of Michigan descrimination [sic] against women. And I talked to Bob Fleming. Have been keeping up on it. I thin [sic] you probably got a wire from Bob Fleming on it within the last 24 hours. I don't know who in uour [sic] shop was handling it. Are you familiar with the situation?

Richardson: Only in a general way. I got a memo that arrived on my desk today.

Esch: The real issue [is] we have so many contracts with HEW and others in Ann Arbor. I know we are moving through a test case period. I think they feel strongly there have been one or two cases in which suggestions have been made as to what they need to comply with. That really needs to be reviewed by your office. We have an embargo that is going to affect the condition of funding for that. In fact next week they will be without funds and in the meantime I am sure your office and staff is struggling with the concept of what is a reasonable request in terms of moving on that. I am just concerned that we don't penalize one or two institutions especially in my district at a time when the department itself isn't certain as to what is reasonable and the regulations have not been clearly imposed. I think what Bob Fleming suggested was hoping the embargo would be removed on a temporary basis, would be reviewed by someone there, a special group that you would sit down and review the situation.

Richardson: OK. Well, let me follow it up and get back to you tomorrow, either directly or through the head of the Civil Rights Division Stan Pottinger and I will try and find out more about where it stands.

Esch: I think there are one or two legalities. Again I think it is a question of whether you want to penalize them at the same time—I think some of the areas are subject to review. I am sure you know Bob Fleming, he is a reasonable guy, wants to cooperate in every way possible.

Richardson: I will follow it up and one of us will get back to you tomorrow.

Esch: I heard a rumor that Arthur Flem[m]ing will be coming down there.

Richardson: He has been a lot of help in many things, but I don't think it is going to work out for him to come on board on a full-time basis.

It is not clear how quickly Richardson spoke with Pottinger. But days passed, and the weekend came and went. And finally, eight days after Fleming sent his telegram, Richardson responded with his own telegram. He said he had told Pottinger to meet with Fleming. He sent copies of the telegram to Hodgdon and Harold Booth, HEW's Chicago regional director.

Vice President Norman, whose research budget was at stake, now became the point person to work with Pottinger. In a memo dated December 15 (the day before the Richardson telegram), Norman reported on a "telecon" he and Pottinger had held. They had agreed, Norman wrote, that the distinction between new and continuing contracts was a vague one and dependent on agency policy. "Even new contracts support the pay of people in continuing programs," Norman noted. (In other words, the job of a current employee could be threatened if a contract were held up.)

Pottinger had provided details of 14 contracts "that had come to his attention." There were two (for $150,000 and $5,000) with the Interior Department's U.S. Geological Survey; two (for $200,000 and $400,000) with AID; two for $500,000 each with the National Air and Space Administration's Goddard Space Center; two (for $1.62 million and $525,000) with the Atomic Energy Commission's Argonne National Laboratory; and five contracts with the Air Force's Office of Scientific Research, presumably the five that Burroughs had heard about before Thanksgiving. Pottinger's list seems to match the one Ferris provided King. The Goddard contract was due to renew on December 15; one of the cited AID contracts may have been the original one for family planning services in Nepal.

Fauri later observed, "After the first program was [r]ejected, with all its attendant publicity, and the Nepalese family planning contract was held up, no one knew whether HEW would let contracts or not. There was a lot of double talk—we never knew whether the University was in conformance or not. The net result was that some contracts were held up, although perhaps not officially. There was a whole new climate in the series of negotiations—starting with a premise of mistrust."

After interviewing university officials, the author of the Harvard case study wrote, "It was generally felt that had UM and HEW not reached agreement and had not those federal funds begun to flow once again, UM would have met its January payroll only with great difficulty."

If that was truly the case, university officials never disclosed it at the time.

In his memo to Fleming, Norman reported that Pottinger "wanted us to understand the regulations." When a contract was less than a minimum amount set by an agency (usually $1 million), it was "entirely within the discretion of the Contracting Officer whether he will release a contract." Equal Opportunity Officers in each agency could disregard a failure to certify and "issue a contract once." There is, however, "a strong policy between agencies on honoring each other's findings."

With that perspective, it is puzzling that the AID contract became the focus of HEW's compliance efforts since it involved less than a million dollars and was awarded by another agency. One wonders whether it was, in fact, an easier contract for mid-level bureaucrats to target rather than a multi-million-dollar military contract, or whether an AID contracting officer was sympathetic to the women's cause and decided to step in and help.

Following his conversation with Pottinger, Norman wrote: "In HEW, he will lift any suspensions and forward contracts. (None have been held.)"

"In talking with Contracting Officers," Norman said Pottinger had advised "we should tell them that they can lift any suspension and go ahead at their discretion. If they refuse, instruct them to call us (HEW) and ask for an opinion. It is in fact not proper to hold continuing contracts if there has been no hearing." He said the persons to call were "Kieley," presumably Owen Kiely, and Albert T. Hamlin, then Pottinger's deputy.

Pottinger then offered to meet with university officials "at an early date, even Saturday if President Fleming wished." He offered to clear his calendar for December 21 to 23, but said, as Norman related it, "Whoever comes should have the authority to bind the University." Pottinger would have the authority to settle on behalf of HEW.

Pottinger backed up Norman's recounting of their phone call with a telegram to Fleming, offering again to meet on Saturday, if necessary. Other civil rights staff would attend, and he would invite one of HEW's higher education officials if Fleming wished.

Discussing HEW's policies on blocking contracts, Pottinger wrote that "no present contracts with HEW are in question. As for other agencies, I confirmed that the suspending of continuing contracts is entirely within each agency's own discretion. I informed Dr. Norman that I have instructed our staff to remain neutral on this issue; not to initiate contacts with such other agencies and; in the event such agencies request our opinion on the matter to respond that it is our policy not to suspend continuing contracts without first granting the University a formal hearing."

Meanwhile, Fleming was moving forward on an easier item: creating a Commission on Women, the idea suggested by Newell and Campbell back in October that had now been promised to HEW.

Campus activists remained skeptical. After Newell met with several women's groups, PROBE wrote her on December 11 and sent a copy to Fleming: "The establishment of a Women's Commission might be an initial step in the struggle to upgrade the status of women on our campus, but PROBE cannot support a commission which would emerge, fully formed from the central administration, more than vaguely reminiscent of those used by traditional authoritarian, bureaucratic males." PROBE offered to use its skills and expertise to help Michigan reach out to campus women. "This," it said, "we could undertake with an enthusiasm we cannot bring to the presently forming women's commission."

But Fleming forged ahead. On December 16, he wrote the executive officers that he had concluded that the current "Human Relations Structure" could not manage the problems of both women and minorities. He proposed a separate commission for each, one chaired by Bill Cash, then chair of the Human Relations Council, and the other chaired by Newell. Each would serve as the principal staff person for his or her respective constituencies.

Fleming himself drafted the proposed charge for the Commission on Women, a statement that was close to what was eventually formalized. He then turned to the question of its membership: "I conclude that I might as well appoint it. There will be criticism, but there will be under any system, and we can leave the way open in the letter of appointment to make changes later."

Fleming said Newell had drawn up "a representative list of people," and Russ Reister, U-M's personnel director, had provided names of non-academic staff members. Fleming said he had also spoken with SACUA: "That body did not show any enthusiasm about being involved, but did agree that I might just as well name the body." (Considering that the faculty generally want to be involved with *everything* in those days, it is notable their governing body was willing to take a pass on this.) Fleming said he had shared Newell's suggested names and SACUA had proposed two more: History Professor William Freehling, "who is apparently chairman of a committee on the status of women with either the History Department or some larger history organization" and "the other female member of the Assembly, other than Rosemary Sairi." Fleming conceded that he could not remember the woman's name, except that she came from the Library Science Department. (It was Professor Helen Lloyd. He also did not spell Sarri's name correctly.) Sarri, he was told, was "very active in other things, including the newly appointed Commission on the Allocation of Resources." At the time, the two women, according to Fleming, were the only women in the 60-member assembly.

Fleming asked Fauri to take the ideas and "noting (but not necessarily following) the SACUA suggestions" work together to give him a list that could be appointed the following week.

But PROBE also didn't slow down over the holidays.

Back in early August, even before the HEW investigators first arrived, PROBE had asked top university officials for salary and personnel data. Although the centennial teach-in had come and gone, PROBE persisted. On December 14, members of its "Research Committee" finally got a face-to-face meeting with Bill Cash, Fleming's human relations assistant, and Chuck Allmand, the assistant to the vice president for academic affairs. Both had been part of the delegation that had gone to Chicago but were not necessarily the most knowledgeable persons about the finer points of U-M's personnel systems.

The PROBE members recorded their meeting with the officials, prepared a 12-page transcript, and preserved it. The participating members were not identified in the transcript, but the group's leaders included women who worked as researchers at places like the Institute for Social Research (ISR) and the conflict resolution center and who knew how to run programs on the university's mainframe computers.

After several months of ignoring PROBE's request, university officials were now bowing to the inevitable. In their questioning, the PROBE members demonstrated the toughness of the best prosecutors. Both sides came with their own agendas.

Cash arrived late, and at the outset, Allmand was wary, trying to clarify whether all of the women worked for the university. They said they did and then asked what difference did it make? He replied, "Someone said there was a group composed of University and non-University people. It's not true of PROBE, it's all University people?"

The women said he might be confusing them with FOCUS, which, it said, "may or may not be" women within the university. But when Allmand tried to paint FOCUS as a "community group," one woman asserted that both groups included alumnae and that "our feeling is that this is also a University person."

Allmand then suggested that these members were "sort of like a retiree or a previous employee," and a woman replied, "Some of us who are alumnae also work here."

"From time to time?" Allmand asked.

"No, constantly," one replied.

Allmand told the women that officials were talking to HEW about creating a Commission on Women and that "we definitely are in need of individuals who would represent women on this commission, and we are interested in obtaining names from this group" of women who might be interested in serving. That was likely double-speak, because Fleming did not solicit names from PROBE or other women's organizations and none of PROBE's leaders was appointed.

Allmand said it was anticipated that the commission would be reviewing the same kinds of information that PROBE wanted. He said, "We would appreciate it if you or any of your members are interested in giving me your names," and then asked hopefully, "Can I assume you would all be interested?"

A woman replied, "I don't think you should assume that." She then asked, "Whose idea was the commission?"

Allmand first replied, "It was a recommendation of HEW" and then, when challenged, said, "It was mentioned during discussions with HEW; we asked them about. . ." (the transcription notes that something was lost). He then said Fleming would probably select the members from a list of names presented to him.

To that, a PROBE representative replied, "I think we have very grave concerns about the makeup of this Commission and whose appointees they would be." The women then raised other issues: To whom would the commission report and would it have a budget to support the antici-pated studies? Allmand said it would probably function like the Human Relations Council, with "blacks, some women and some administra-tors." When the women observed that there was only one woman on that council and that she was on leave, Allmand retorted, "Your infor-mation is wrong."

The women continued to pepper Allmand with questions about how the council operated and whether it ever produced a report, causing him to muse, "Wish Dr. Cash was here."

They then asked Allmand how long it would take to get the Wom-en's Commission organized; he replied "as quickly as possible between 30 and 60 days." A PROBE member responded, "I think in that sense PROBE is a step ahead of you. Since August, actually last spring, we have had a representative group that represents women from all areas of the University. We could start next week."

Allmand acknowledged that they could be helpful. "Because you have a head start on this, you could get it started faster instead of its starting cold. Inputs that you make could be helpful—as you say you have several months head start," he said. "Surely information and con-cerns you have and thinking you have done up to this point could start the commission going quickly."

But the PROBE members contended that they had "the woman-power to start the studies and to interpret the data." They urged All-mand to simply turn the information over to PROBE and let it run the studies.

Allmand immediately responded that Michigan didn't "want to be in a position to answer requests from various groups." When PROBE pressed him on how many requests he had received and from whom, he responded, "Probably two, three or four who say they have a group of women." The dialogue demonstrates PROBE's steely persistence:

> *Allmand*: We've had data requests from FOCUS, individual
> requests, this type of thing.
>
> *PROBE*: Oh, well!
>
> *Allmand*: There was another one. Well, it was a woman's
> organization, supposedly tied to a national women's
> group.

PROBE: What national group?

Allmand: Whatever it is.

PROBE: There are a lot of national groups. You mean NOW?

Allmand: No, when they first started.

PROBE: No, NOW, a national women's group. Do you have anything written?

Allmand: No.

The PROBE members said they would be happy to coordinate with other groups. A woman observed that the women's commission "is a University group and will have its questions to answer for the University. PROBE is more a grass roots group of University people themselves." Anyway, she concluded, "We don't see why two things can't go on simultaneously." One of the women anticipated that the commission would not be able to produce a study before July.

Cash then arrived, and the discussion shifted to integrating women's issues into the existing procedures and structures for addressing discrimination against minorities. Cash acknowledged that "the HEW Report didn't ask for a commission to be established." He said the university "had to make a decision on minority groups. One has to wait on the other." The women disputed that.

Cash said the university had been submitting a compliance report to HEW every six months. When asked if the reports were made public, he replied, "We send them to HEW."

Most of the rest of the meeting dealt with PROBE's desire to get its hands on Michigan's data on women employees. Cash acknowledged that the university had only recently been able to organize its data by "name and sex and by race. . . . If you had asked me six months ago, I couldn't have given it to you." At another point, he said he wanted to have "first priority on the data." When PROBE pushed back that it was not "your personal property," Cash responded, "Because from 1968 to last summer, it took me that [long] to get it where we can use it."

Cash, like most of the university's top administrators, was close to Fleming in age. After earning degrees at Fisk and Oberlin, he had earned a doctorate in counseling from Michigan. An early member of the Commission on Women recalled that he was a member of the "black aristocracy," who "said some unfortunate things that wound up in *Daily* headlines. At the time he thought everyone was nuts."

Cash said PROBE's request would need to be reviewed because the data was considered confidential. PROBE responded that it should be given the same access to data that the American Association of University Professors was given for its nationwide studies of faculty salaries.

One of the women tried another tack. "If PROBE could get on," she asked, "don't you think the University would put itself in a better position in the eyes of HEW? Isn't that a strong possibility?" PROBE then observed that the university's data analysis had already been found to be misleading, pointing to the charts in the *University Record* that had to be corrected.

With rapid-fire comments, the PROBE members pounced on this point, one noting that Ed Hayes had commented "that he really did not know how to analyze the data." She then asserted, "They need a data study with people who are qualified to do it. . . . We have three faculty members very capable of doing this kind of work. All the people here have had experience with it. We could only do good. It will have to be done sooner or later; it might as well be sooner."

The women continued to insist that they wanted "the tape." They said if they got it, they could run it at ISR, the University Computer Center, or Bendix, a defense manufacturer whose Aerospace Division was then located in Ann Arbor. When asked who would pay for it, one replied, "Hopefully you, but if not we would." The women had already solicited donations to support PROBE's work; they could do it again if they had to.

Cash later said that because "the tape" had never been released, Fleming would have to review the decision. Cash asserted, "We just don't give out information to everybody." One of the women then tried another tack:

I am sure Fleming would see the sense of it; it will help establish the credibility of the commission on campus. If we come up with similar kinds of conclusions it would be a help to the University. Even if the commission were established they would probably like an independent group for credibility purposes. We are very eager for it to be an effective commission. The people hardest to convince will be the students. If PROBE is able to point to cooperation, it will convince people on campus more than any administrative statements.

By the end of the meeting, it appears that the women had impressed the administrators with their tenacity, their knowledge of computer analysis, and, probably, some willingness to cooperate. Allmand shared that "there were errors in the way [the data] was punched and errors in the way it was collected. We're still in the process of trying to get the bugs out of it. We're not certain of the accuracy. Some things are fairly close to being accomplished. There were lots of errors on the first run. It is a new file that has not been validated. Our target date is this coming April because the report has to go in in July." In response to more questions, he acknowledged that SACUA's payroll numbers were "obtained manually from the budget." When the PROBE members offered to use that book and create their own punch cards, Allman conceded, "The budget book is published in June and people come in after that that aren't even identified by the book."

Although the PROBE members were frustrated by the number of data requests they had already made, they agreed to prepare another formal request for the officials to review. PROBE had waited more than five months for its meeting, but Allmand now agreed to schedule another one by the end of the week. He promised that Ed Hayes would participate since he knew more about the data. Still, Allmand cautioned, "I don't want anyone to go out of the room saying that you have the file. Release of files has not been done in the past nor do I feel it will be done."

When PROBE detailed the things it would need and wanted to "talk about deadlines," Allmand replied, "We haven't had enough man power."

Displaying the group's characteristic wit, one of the members replied, "You should try a little woman power."

After the second meeting, "Gaye," presumably Gaye Crouch, a research assistant at the conflict resolution center who would soon be identified as PROBE's president, sent King "a package of material" on

December 22, with a note attached. She said, "I believe the administration was surprised [sic] and impressed with the 'legitimacy' of the people who are on the [PROBE Research] Committee." She promised to tell King more "when we can talk."

Crouch's note transmitted a cache of leaked materials. "Enclosed is a package of material some of which you will find interesting. The letter from HEW to Fleming is HEW's second communication to UM concerning UM's proposed affirmative action," she wrote. (Michigan had not included Scott's December telegram when it released its exchanges with HEW two weeks before.) "PROBE seems to have a secret friend somewhere in the administration building. The letter was sent anonymously to Jeanne T., and simply signed 'a friend,'" she noted. ("Jeanne T." was presumably Jeanne Tashian, an early PROBE leader who was a graduate student in the School of Education.) The note continued:

> We've decided it might be best to not talk publicly or in meetings, about having a copy of this, in order to protect whoever sent it—thinking that security over there might tighten up if it was discovered that we have this copy. I'm sorry the copy is not more legible, but it looks like whoever copied it was in a hurry, and that's the best they could do. The part about admissions and back pay is particularly interesting.

"Gaye" noted she would be in town during the holidays and suggested that she and King get together to talk "after you've had a chance to look this stuff over."

During the same time period, it appears that someone prepared an undated, point-by-point critique of Fleming's December 8 response to Scott that was preserved in King's papers. It is not clear who prepared the document, but it was probably not King because the title deferentially refers to "Mr. Fleming." The analysis pointed to potential loopholes in what the university had promised to do. The concerns included that women might have to come forward individually to pursue back-pay complaints; that women were not included on faculty search committees that recruited new hires; that the new nepotism policy would address husband-and-wife "tandem teams" but did not rectify situations where departments had already rejected spouses working in the same field; and that academic women would not get first crack at promotions the way clerical and non-academic employees would.

Finally, the memo objected that Fauri would be in charge of implementing the affirmative action plan:

> Why Fedele Fauri? Why not a woman? A new position could be created specifically for a woman who would have power equal to that of Mr. Fauri. Sex discrimination is so rampant in the University that a much greater effort must be made to correct present inequities. The University could do much more than "create a commission on women." The problems already identified call for greater imagination and much more commitment on the part of the University to ensure that women can begin to attain equal status with men.

But over the holidays, there was no forum available through which to raise those issues. The president's men were already on their way to Washington.

On December 21, Allan Smith, vice president for academic affairs, finally got his audience at HEW. Two days later, he reported to the executive officers that he had met for 2 ½ hours with Pottinger, Hamlin, Roy McKinney of the Contract Compliance Division, and two lawyers from the HEW general counsel's office. The meeting, he said, was "cordial," and he noted that Pottinger promised to call him back within a few days.

Smith had briefly served as a government lawyer before coming to Michigan to teach law and later serve as dean of the Law School. "My basic position," he wrote, "was that U of M is entitled to be declared in compliance, on the basis of

1. Our amended affirmative action program filed November 3, plus our letter of commitment of December 8; and
2. Our agreement that we would abide by the decision of the Secretary on the question of jurisdiction over admissions to graduate study."

HEW's concerns, Smith said, were basically that:

1. "There should be some objective standard for measuring the ratio of female academic employees." (Smith said he responded that "the conditions are so variable that no single standard is appropriate or feasible without major impact on internal management.")
2. "Jurisdiction over admissions was essential to open the pool of PhD candidates on a non-discriminatory basis." (Smith said he argued that "admissions are one thing, employment another." As before, he cited legal precedent that the IRS and Social Security Administration considered graduate students to be students and not employees.)

Smith closed by writing, "We shall see."

Pottinger met with Richardson at the end of the day on December 22. The "University of Michigan" was listed as an agenda item under "Miscellaneous Reports," along with two Louisiana school districts and Brigham Young University, where the Mormon Church's prohibition on black membership was then the issue. Handwritten next to Michigan's name were the words "possible release of suspension." Perhaps it was understandable that the day before, Richardson told a member of Congress, "I must say, I was enjoying that job [at the State Department]. I would have liked to stay a while longer."

The same day, his friend, Brandeis President Charles Schottland, phoned and told him: "It has been rought [sic], this business of being president of a university. . . . I think this year all the universities are going to have a better year." Brandeis had weathered its own sit-in to improve minority admissions, and Schottland had been named president in its wake.

Schottland observed that there was "a constant negotiation between faculty and students, in a sense the faculty is much worse than the students. That is true of whether it is Harvard, Brandeis or MIT." He described how he had encouraged a troublesome faculty member to retire and then added, "I learned to do that by getting rid of civil servants in Washington." (In another example of the movement between HEW and universities in that era, Schottland had served as commissioner of the Social Security Administration during the Eisenhower administration.)

As the calendar counted down to the end of the year, Pottinger gave Fleming an early Christmas present, when he wrote him on December 24, outlining his understanding of the agreement HEW and Michigan had reached:

- Pottinger acknowledged that Michigan objected to using the percentage of women applicants as the appropriate metric for evaluating faculty hiring practices: "We agree that other appropriate indices may be used by the University in establishing goals, and that additional factors such as quality of applicants, the institutions from which they apply and, geographic areas represented, may also be considered." Still, Pottinger asserted that "the University will proceed with the establishment of goals and timetables for female employment in faculty positions, will state how the goals were arrived at and HEW will, as with other goals and timetables, evaluate their propriety and acceptability."
- Pottinger agreed to let Richardson resolve the question about jurisdiction over graduate admissions and agreed that the resulting policy would be applied on a nationwide basis. But, he said, if the secretary agreed with the HEW officials, "we would expect this to mean that the University would proceed with the corrective action originally requested in our letter of October 6," namely that goals and timetables would be established to improve the percentage of women who were admitted to graduate programs.
- In its written commitment to review files to achieve salary equity between men and women employees with the same qualifications who were performing the same jobs, the university had to agree that it would continue to do the reviews until the secretary said it was no longer necessary; that the burden would be on the university, not individual complainants; and that if individual complaints were filed, the complaining parties would have "the basic right to discovery." This point addressed a weakness the women's analysis had also identified.

Pottinger said that when he received Fleming's written concurrence, HEW would consider Michigan to be in compliance with the executive orders. "However," he said, "we would not be precluded from reimposing controls upon contract clearances should the agreements above and those previously made not be faithfully kept or should other evidence of non-compliance come to our attention." Pottinger then expressed his appreciation for "the cooperation of you and your staff during our negotiations."

On the final day of 1970, Fleming gave Pottinger that assurance: "It is our understanding that you will now make it officially known that the University of Michigan is in compliance with Executive Orders 11246 and 11375 for purposes of contract clearance."

But Fleming was still serving as a point man for other college presidents. He sent David Henry of Illinois a copy of his letter to Pottinger by "air/special delivery." He also sent Frederick P. Thieme, president of the University of Colorado, "our HEW materials." He had held off, he explained, "because it seemed that we were about to settle our difficulties." He suspected that Thieme already had received most of the papers through the AAU. He added that the remaining issues would be discussed when "the Arthur Flemming group" met with Richardson on January 4.

But in the meantime, Fleming finally got the headline he had been waiting for. When the *Daily* returned from its holiday break, it reported on January 6: "HEW Accepts 'U' Proposals to End Sex Bias in Employment." Two weeks later, the *Detroit Free Press* moved the story out of its women's section to declare on its second front page: "U-M Sex Bias Plan 'Historic.'" Owen Kiely, HEW's contract compliance director, used that word to describe the agreement and said, "The University could be a model to the extent that other institutions have these kinds of problems."

In January, Radock, the vice president for university relations, told the Regents, "The University received a good press" on the materials it released at the beginning of December, and the press release on its "settlement" with HEW earlier that month. "The HEW story has been a difficult one to handle with the media, beginning last summer, because of the rumors and speculation which could not be effectively countered until the University and HEW had reached substantial agreement," wrote Radock.

Kiely told the *Free Press* that $7.5 million worth of Michigan contracts had been held up on HEW's advice and that 16 other colleges and the 13 schools in the Georgia state college system were currently "targets of

HEW investigations." The colleges that Kiely identified were Manhattan Community College, Brooklyn College, Brown, Georgia Tech, Georgia State, Harvard, Loyola of Los Angeles, New Mexico State, Pittsburgh, St. Johns University in New York, Tufts, University of Georgia, University of San Francisco, University of Vermont, University of Wisconsin, and the University of Texas Medical School at Dallas.

In her response, Sandler played off the advertising tagline of a Phillip Morris campaign that was then pitching the Virginia Slims cigarette brand to women: "It's a beginning. But we've got a long way to go yet, baby."

14
Getting Started

As much as campus women, or even Robben Fleming, might have wanted to wave a magic wand and make sex discrimination disappear from the Michigan campus, it was not going to happen overnight. They were up against a long male-dominated history—and, as *TIME* magazine described their progress over the next two years: "Despite their determined efforts, the U of M women seem to be engaged not so much in a war of the sexes as in a slow dance—two steps forward, one step back."

The immediate crisis over contracts had been averted. The January 11 minutes of the Center for Population Planning's governing board reported on the topic of "AID Nepal": "The Washington version should be at the Center this week." But top university officials still had to come up with goals and timetables for their affirmative action plan, and their 90-day window was rapidly closing.

On January 4, the "Flemming Group" met with Richardson; the group included Flemming and Henry of Illinois, Cosand and Logan Wilson of ACE, and other officials from HEW (but not its civil rights office).

The next day Robben Fleming wrote outgoing Harvard President Pusey that he had done some thinking over the holidays about the immediate challenges universities faced and the role that the AAU could play in addressing them. The second of the seven issues he listed were "outside control problems," including "federal programs against race and sex discrimination." He said:

Our recent bout with HEW over the discrimination against women issue has made me increasingly conscious of the enormous clout of the federal government through the contract and grant device if it is used to accomplish a purpose not immediately connected with educational programs. My personal view happens to be that both in the area of race and women, colleges and universities need to do a good deal more to right the wrongs of the past. But this does not deceive me into thinking that these problems lend themselves to a highly bureaucratic approach, particularly if those who are administering the program know little or nothing of how a university operates. Thus I believe there is a role for the AAU to play in connection with federal control programs.

Finally, all of us are trying desperately to make profound changes through minority programs. One of our most serious problems is financial. Without help from the federal government, I do not see how it is going to be possible for us to make the progress which we have all adopted as an objective.

A week later, Pusey phoned Richardson, his former Board of Overseers colleague, to express his concerns about the graduate admissions issue and affirmative action in general. According to a transcript made of their conversation, Richardson told him, "I gather we have worked out a satisfactory solution of our immediate problems with Michigan and I sympathize with general proportionment [sic] that in an area like this where we are moving into territory which didn't used to be considered the business of the Federal government at all and where ideas and attitudes are in the process of evolution that it ought to be possible to find ways of dealing with it—On the other hand, the investigations may have had some. . . in so far they helped you identify the problems in terms of underlying facts and with respect to the process of enforcement of the law itself versus other ways of dealing with the situation."

But in an early expression of concern about the prospect of "quotas," Pusey noted that if the Harvard Law School had at most three tenured openings in a year and thought that only "five or eight people in the

United States" were "suitable" to teach the course, "they would be upset if they had to establish a target and say a certain percentage had to be women. That is the kind of problem it poses."

"I can't imagine we would proceed by setting a percentage quota," Richardson replied.

Pusey persisted. "They call it a target quota. That is what they are doing and it makes us all very mad," he said.

"I will get into it," Richardson said.

Through mid-January, Richardson continued to explore bringing on former University of Wisconsin President Harrington but abandoned the idea after then-Wisconsin Rep. Melvin Laird advised him that Harrington "was about as anti-Nixon as you can get." Richardson dropped in on a visit from representatives of the Association of American Medical Colleges and met with deans of schools of social work, an appointment Schottland had set up.

He also was doing scouting reports on Raymond Tanter, an African American who was then an assistant political science professor at Michigan. Richardson told Lincoln Bloomfield, an MIT political scientist, that he was trying to recruit some "qualified black candidates" for top jobs at HEW but that Tanter wanted to be "an assistant secretary or nothing," and Richardson had few positions at that level. Throughout his long career, Tanter moved back and forth between high-ranking government positions (mostly dealing with foreign policy) and Michigan, but did not go to HEW at that time.

On January 20, 1971, Fleming finally got the face-to-face meeting he wanted with Richardson. On the secretary's appointment calendar, it was billed as representatives of the AAU and participants included Charles Kidd and three other college presidents, Kingman Brewster of Yale, Robert Goheen of Princeton, and William Friday of the University of North Carolina (UNC). (Friday and the UNC system were then fighting HEW over the speed with which they had to desegregate that state's colleges.) Pusey's name was listed for the meeting but then crossed off.

In a follow-up letter to Richardson on January 29, Fleming recalled how they had "talked briefly about the general relationships between universities and HEW with respect to discrimination against women." But Fleming said that after the meeting, he had realized that the issue of graduate school admissions had *not* been discussed—an interesting omission because that was the outstanding issue the secretary was supposed to resolve for Michigan. "This is a question which is not unique to our University, and we feel that before you make a ruling some opportunity should be provided to the universities to present their side of the issue to you," said Fleming. "The American Council on Education has a group working on general problems on this area and could, I am sure, see that adequate representations were made on the matter. In any event, we would be grateful for an opportunity to be heard before a final decision is made."

Despite Richardson's vow to Pusey that he would get right on the issue of graduate school admissions, he didn't. Michigan's concession to "let Richardson decide" the issue turned out to be a shrewd move because the secretary never did. Richardson had more important concerns on his plate, and although agency lawyers worked over the next year on drafts outlining his policy choices, the matter was allowed to languish.

Pottinger's papers include an undated memo prepared by HEW officials to frame the decision for Richardson's review. Titled "Policy Issues on Sex Discrimination and Employment at the University of Michigan and Potentially Other Universities—ACTION Memorandum," it confirms the role the university had assumed in setting the template for the rest of the nation's universities—and provides another glimpse of the mindset of its top officials at the time. In laying out the arguments in support of taking on graduate admissions, HEW's headquarters officials noted that Michigan budgeted various kinds of support for graduate students under the "academic salaries" line item. In the Botany Department, 26 percent of that budget was designated for teaching fellows. HEW further observed that graduate students taught more than 30 percent of Michigan's undergraduate courses. Michigan once again argued that admissions were beyond the jurisdiction of the executive order, that HEW's attempts to influence them amounted to an interference with educational policy, and that such a change would interfere with its special programs to attract minority students. The most jaw-dropping argument was this one: "The elimination of sex discrimination in admissions and the strict application of academic standards will result in a majority female enrollment because of the superior academic achievements of

women. The University fears being 'inundated' by female applicants."
In response, HEW's internal draft said that argument was "invalid"
for several reasons: "Currently the University is 'inundated' by white
male applicants, students, and staff and does not object to this situation,
although it does object to being 'inundated' by female applicants. This
attitude indicates that the University will not change its policy until it is
forced to do so."

As the new year began, Pottinger took charge of managing the university officials. On January 19, the civil rights office director, Kiely, and
two lawyers from HEW's general counsel's office met with a delegation
that included Allan Smith; Martha Peterson, the president of Barnard;
administrators from Illinois, Harvard, and Georgia Southern College, all
of which were then under investigation; Chuck Kidd of the AAU, and
three ACE staff members. The February 5 memo that Kidd sent to his
Council on Federal Relations describing the meeting eventually found
its way to Jean King, and became public.

"The primary outcome of the meeting," Kidd wrote, "was a tentative
agreement to undertake the preparation of a set of advisory notes to be
issued by ACE with the hope that they could be in principle agreed to by
HEW." Kidd said that in the meantime he was distributing preliminary
notes in hopes they would help colleges deal with the regional offices.
In several places, Pottinger's December 24 letter to Fleming was cited as
a statement of the department's current policy.

The memo contended that "the 'statistical equity' concept has been
carried to absurd extremes" by some regional offices and discussed
other ways colleges could try to demonstrate their "good faith" efforts
to recruit more women. It cautioned, "In connection with the credence
sometimes given by regional office staff to gossip, inexperienced and
verbose visitors have at times raised false expectations or supported
false accusations among campus activists and malcontents."

Pottinger had asked whether the university officials would agree
that the problem of discrimination was "essentially the same among all
universities?" The officials generally agreed but were still reluctant to
support the development of national rules and guidelines to which they
would all be subjected.

Kidd said that "the prevailing attitude at HEW" was that as federal contractors, the universities had certified they would not discriminate, so the burden of proof was on them. He said there was also an assumption that sex discrimination in employment, salaries, and promotion was "widespread and blatant" and that university presidents could "unilaterally establish and enforce rules relating to hiring" by university subdivisions, which was not the case on the academic side of most institutions.

Kidd said that Kiely had acknowledged that individual regional offices had approached sex and race discrimination differently. The difference, in Kidd's reporting, "is due in large part to the fact that universities took discrimination against blacks as a serious problem which they were prepared to resolve as a matter of conscience, whereas HEW sees many deans, department heads and faculty members as taking a rather cavalier, doctrinaire and supercilious approach toward employment of women." He concluded, "There is no doubt some ground for this view."

Kidd said that university officials could appeal to headquarters staff if they felt that the regional offices were being "unreasonable." But he cautioned that "this is a touchy area" and that appeals should be "carefully considered," because "the Washington people are constrained to back the regional staff as far as possible."

In closing, Kidd said that institutions that were subject to reviews by HEW "may wish to get in touch with people who have been through the mill." U-M's Allan Smith was one of the four names suggested, along with officials from Wisconsin, Harvard, and the University of Southern California.

Pottinger's papers include his own handwritten notes from the meeting. He referenced complaints about regional offices' lack of understanding, the tight deadlines they were setting, and the data universities were expected to produce. He wrote down: "Chic office did not read U. Mich response to findings," possibly a complaint, probably from Smith, that Chicago officials had to interrupt their November meeting with the Michigan officials so that they could review the revised plan that Fleming had sent them a few days before. There were also some notes about ways that HEW might be able to help promote the recruitment of women.

But this observation by Pottinger stands out among the others: "Admission policy: Marked difference of attitude and method in sex as opposed to race. Was able to identify mutual understandings. Aggressive and abrasive in this area. Not as much mutual assistance."

Interestingly, on this occasion there *was* a woman in the room. Martha Peterson was the new president of the ACE, serving at a time when HEW was battling Barnard's parent institution, Columbia University, over its record on race and sex discrimination. HEW had told U-M to put more women on its decision-making committees, and Pottinger seemed to recognize the difference it could make. After a similar meeting 17 months later, Peterson wrote Pottinger, "Your statements of HEW's position on affirmative action did not surprise me. I was glad to hear them from you directly and will do my best to make sure your positions have a fair hearing when I am present." Pottinger responded, "I was pleased to have the opportunity to talk about our program to the ACE group, and particularly pleased to see at least one woman in attendance. When we complete the draft of our guidelines, I would consider it of great assistance if you would personally look at them and comment candidly on their likely effectiveness."

Amid the ongoing talks with Pottinger and Richardson, Fleming had managed to escape to Hawaii for a week's vacation in mid-January. As he left town for another week-long trip to California on January 29, he wrote Newell and the executive officers, "We must be moving along with our women's program for submission to HEW by March 8."

Some things were relatively easy to do.

Back on December 11, David Heebink, one of Fauri's deputies, had convened a small group of managers to begin moving forward on the university's commitments to HEW. Checking back with the group on January 6, he said that the first screening of non-academic employees "is now complete," turning up 159 women employees whose records should be reviewed further. "Hopefully, HEW will see fit to approve the screening system," he wrote.

When HEW made its initial demands, Newell had targeted the nepotism policy as something that could be fixed quickly, and a new policy was issued before the end of January. A family member was still barred from supervising another family member, but the policy said a "relationship by family or marriage shall constitute neither an advantage nor a deterrent to appointment by the University provided the individual meets and fulfills the appropriate University appointment standards." However, the policy still barred relatives from working for the same immediate supervisor without the prior written approval of the organizational unit and the Office of the Vice President for Academic Affairs. A PROBE spokeswoman complained to the *Daily* that except for requiring preapproval, the policy really hadn't been changed.

On January 7, the first members of the Commission on Women were announced, and a week later, they held their first meeting. As planned, Newell was named chairman. The commission was filled out with nine other women and two men: William Freehling, SACUA's suggested nominee, and Ed Hayes, manager of compensation plans and personnel information systems. Hayes had co-authored the internal memo that had disputed every one of HEW's initial findings. Harriet Mills, an associate professor of Chinese and another of the commission's original members, remembered Hayes many years later as "the one that sticks in your mind [as] the most persistent in causing problems" for women seeking changes. "That was because he was protecting the turf of the official institution," recalled Mills. (Freehling resigned within a matter of weeks, saying his teaching load was too heavy for him to be able to serve.)

The other original members were Jean Campbell of CCEW; Emily W. Gardner, a statistician in the Office of Staff Benefits; Barbara G. Murphy, a procedures analyst at the Survey Research Center; Jean M. Robinson, assistant director of the University Hospital's department of social work; Jean Schultz, a research associate in the Human Genetics Department; Mary P. Scott, secretary to the director of the Population Studies Center (a different university unit than the one whose contract had been at stake); and Betty M. Ullman, an assistant professor of biostatistics.

When Murphy, who had previously tried to organize the staff at ISR and had done some analysis of its salaries, recalled years later that when she received an envelope addressed from the President's Office, she thought "I was going to be fired."

Mills remembered that "one day Barbara Newell turned up in my office and said, 'Mr. Fleming is organizing some group in response to the government's injunction against the University, in connection with the settlement in response to the PROBE suit. Would you serve?' I said, 'I don't know A from Z, but I'd be glad to serve.'"

Mills was the only woman professor in her department and because she had been granted tenure when she arrived, she said she knew nothing of the problems other women faculty members were encountering. Recalling the commission's first meetings 30 years later, she said, "We were sat down and told there was a complaint. . . . But we knew nothing. As I remember, there was no agenda. . . . We weren't given any documentation. We were given a summary that 'we are under the government's dah-dah' . . . . and we should look into this to see if there is any truth" to it. So, she said, "I think we began to feel, 'what do we have to know?'"

King was initially contemptuous of the commission, viewing it as simply window dressing to impress HEW. Twenty years later, she recalled, "We didn't ask for it, HEW didn't ask for it, and we didn't want it." A PROBE member later described it as "a sort of the classic, higher education response: [I] need to appoint a committee to study it, make sense of it, get it off my desk."

But most women had more positive views. Nearly a half-century later, Newell recalled the commission meetings fondly. "The fact that we had a body of people that represented all aspects of the University coming together to talk frankly was really one of the more interesting, educational conversations that I've had," she said. "There was amazing rapport between groups. The academics were truly backing up the clerical. There was an understanding of women as they faced some of the same problems but in different ways . . . ."

When the commission was formed, activist women again objected that Fleming had picked the members and that they would report through Fauri. "A commission selected by University administrators who have previously demonstrated an insensitivity and an unwillingness to deal fairly with problems of sex discrimination can only be expected to serve as a 'paper commission,'" PROBE said in a statement.

Fleming's papers suggest their fears were not unfounded. As he told Fauri to begin work on the affirmative action plan, he said, "the Commission on Women needs also to be kept informed and to have a chance to give advice on it." Still, he added, "In order that we meet the March 8 deadline we are going to have to concentrate on the immediate submission and let some of the other things go until later. That may not make some of the members of the Commission on Women happy at the moment, because they will doubtless want to get into broader areas immediately. The latter is fine, but it must not delay the immediate problem."

But many of Michigan's male administrators were still displaying the "cavalier" attitude that Charles Kidd had acknowledged persisted on American campuses. In mid-February, the *Daily* published "a special report," entitled "The 'U' Crusade for/against Women." Less than a year after he had edited Shortridge's initial exposé, Daniel Zwerdling again captured male officials in unguarded statements, possibly by appearing sympathetic when he interviewed them:

Pity the poor University: one of the great educational institutions in the nation, famed for liberal achievements, it is berated publicly by the U.S. Department of Health, Education and Welfare because it discriminates against—not blacks but—women. HEW ordered the leaders here, all of them men, to upgrade women: they must revamp hiring procedures, formulate employment goals and timetables, and scour their records, scrutinize every one, search their souls to discover women they have oppressed, and then pay back every penny which these women should have earned but didn't.

Think of the work! Allan Smith, vice president for academic affairs, calls this demand "an imposition." "Our objection is the godawful number of man hours it will take to do it," Smith complains. But University administrators are getting something out of the agreement; the national press has hailed the University's commitment as "historic," and even University officials trumpet their affirmative action plan as a nationwide first. It's true the University is the first college in the country to tackle the problem of sex discrimination. It sounds so glorious! One begins to forget the University started the discrimination in the first place. But behind administrative doors, the men of the University are grumbling.

In a highlighted quotation that did not actually appear in the text of the story, Fauri was quoted as saying, "We just want to get those bastards at HEW off our backs." In another highlighted section (again not in the story itself), Zwerdling wrote: "'Once you let women know they've got you over a barrel, they'll take everything they can get from you,' William Cash, the University's human relations director and member of the negotiating team with HEW, told me. 'Women just make life difficult.' I learned over his desk to squeeze a little horn that's mounted on wood and goes 'blaaht.' It's a 'Secretary Caller.'"

The article noted that Michigan had still not released all of what the article described as HEW's "scathing 20 page report, crammed with evidence of sex discrimination," presumably a reference to the appendices that accompanied Scott's first letter, although Zwerdling pegged this report to December. "There's confidential information in personnel files which we don't feel just anyone should be able to look at," one administrator said. Zwerdling wrote that the university claimed the report was full of "misinformation" that would cause more public harm than good.

He noted that Fleming had already told departments they couldn't hire any staff for at least three years, so "all new personnel must come from normal turnover, which means a woman's only hope is capturing positions vacated through resignations or retirement." Newell herself was raising that concern. "I'm afraid what we may be doing is just making sure that women aren't the first to be squeezed out," she said.

Zwerdling reported that the executive officers had considered suing HEW over the requirement that women receive back pay if they were victims of discrimination. Other reports said U-M counsel Lemmer had tried to organize attorneys from other colleges to challenge HEW in court. Smith complained to Zwerdling that "the normal procedure, overwhelmingly, in labor practice is to pay retroactive to the date of the complaint, not some arbitrary preplace in the past." Smith said the university objected to having to review 15,000 personnel files and wanted women to come forward with complaints. In the end, he said, "We finally decided, it's just work."

The Personnel Office, Zwerdling explained, had committed to reviewing job categories that included both men and women but that covered less than 25 percent of U-M's workforce. Personnel, Zwerdling wrote, had found only 160 women in a workforce of 10,000 whose salaries were inexplicably below "normal." Hayes said his department could explain all but 35 of the cases. He flatly declared, "As far as Personnel is concerned, discrimination against women does not exist."

PROBE complained that women were systematically hired for jobs that were below their training and abilities. Hayes bemoaned that it would take four hours to gather the facts on an individual's duties and responsibilities, and, multiplied across the university, that would amount to "24,000 man hours of effort." Smith continued to argue that the problem was that women were *accepting* jobs below their abilities. "We have hundreds of well qualified faculty wives who want to work to help support their husbands. Many of them have training to qualify them for jobs better than secretary," he said. "But we don't have many jobs available better than secretary. Do we tell them they can't work? They say they want to work, so we hire them as secretaries."

Smith continued, "We have a good many employees, knowing their tenure here is only three to five years because their husbands will leave, who don't seek a shift to a higher position. They don't want that additional responsibility." (A PROBE leader later told *TIME* magazine that "a lot of bright women are in dull, repetitive jobs here so they spend their time thinking up creative things" to spotlight sex discrimination on campus. Researcher Barbara Murphy recalled, "We could do our jobs with our eyes shut. All these women had an awful lot of extra energy for this stuff.")

Zwerdling's reporting reached a nationwide audience when he rewrote the article for *The New Republic*. When a woman physician from Adrian, Michigan, wrote Fauri to express her dismay over what he had said, he responded that if she was referring to the *Daily* article, his quotations had been "garbled." In the magazine's version of his quotation, he said, "In tight times like these we can't afford to have any contracts held up. We just want to get these bastards at HEW off our backs."

Echoing the complaints of activist women, Zwerdling observed in his *Daily* story that the Commission on Women itself was emblematic of the university's lack of commitment because it had no budget or real powers. Newell, he said, had already complained that it was "a floating crap game," until administrators agreed to grant its members time off with pay so they could attend the commission's Friday afternoon meetings.

As chairman, Newell emerged as a more public champion of campus women than she had been when her sole job was serving as Fleming's executive assistant. Fleming's papers suggest that Newell was bumping up against a glass ceiling of her own. Over the years, as Newell was twice widowed by the age of 35 and became a single parent to an adopted daughter, Fleming and colleagues at other universities had served as mentors and created or found openings for her as they moved to new campuses. But now there was nowhere for her to go at Michigan if she wanted to move up the ladder of university administration.

The year before, as the search for a permanent vice president for student affairs dragged on, Newell had begun looking for a new job. Over an 18-month period, she was considered for high-ranking posts at Vassar, Cornell, the University of Nevada, the University of Northern Iowa, the University of Wisconsin-Green Bay, the University of California at Riverside, the University of Hawaii, and New Jersey's Department of Higher Education. She was also considered for the presidencies of St. Cloud State College in Minnesota and Reed College in Oregon.

In a letter to Cornell, Fleming pointed to Newell's chairmanship of the commission and wrote: "Now that women's rights groups have become so active, she is naturally a prime object of attention around the country and is getting numerous job soundings." In an email, Newell recalled that this "was a time when search committees were looking to interview women candidates, even if there was an inside candidate. I indulged in a wearing number of wild goose chases."

A draft summary of the commission's history prepared a few years later read:

> On January 13, the Commission met for the first time in President Fleming's conference room to discuss the charge to the Commission, and to discuss procedures. The group made plans to meet in subcommittees to draft several letters, and the work of the Commission was underway.
>
> What was it that sparked this sudden flurry of activity on behalf of women? Where had the idea for the Commission originated? What was it really supposed to do? The answers to these questions are surprisingly difficult to obtain. Obviously, the plan for a Commission for Women did not suddenly strike the University's president in early January, 1971; and the fact that "speed (was) of the essence" did not derive solely from the innate merit of the idea. . . .

HEW approved the idea of a commission, and so it happened that the University found itself blessed or burdened, depending on one's point of view, with a group of individuals whose responsibility was to monitor, investigate and otherwise promote university efforts on behalf of campus women. . . .

From the outset, it was clear that the Commission's mandate included the interests of female secretaries, female professors, female technicians, female clerks, female administrators, female researchers—women throughout the University; and, indeed, as the Commission was to discover, women in every department of the University sorely needed such representation. The one exception to the universal representation on the Commission was an obvious one—the student population. There had been some disagreement between the University and HEW as to whether the latter had any jurisdiction in regard to graduate admissions, and perhaps this is why no women students were originally appointed. The Commission almost immediately arranged to have two students nominated, however, and today two students—one a graduate, one an undergraduate—sit on the Commission. . . .

But while the organizational work was being carried out, two activities demanded the immediate attention of the Commission—and launched it abruptly into the rapid stream of affirmative action plans flowing toward Washington—and HEW. These two efforts were the implementation of two key commitments to HEW, those of achieving. . . "salary equity between male and female employees having equivalent qualifications, responsibilities, and performance in the same job classification," and of preparing "numeric goals and timetables," which would set forth anticipated results by all university departments of their efforts to recruit and promote qualified women in both academic and non-academic staff positions.

HEW had repeatedly told the university it had to prepare goals and timetables for the hiring of women, and on February 1, deans, directors, department heads, and supervisors were instructed to produce them. They received instructions from the Commission on Women, sent out on the letterhead of the Office of the President. The memo was likely written by Newell:

> Increased numbers of women must be employed at all levels of the academic ladder and at the upper levels of non-academic employment. Additionally, the University must demonstrate a broadening of the range of jobs to which women are employed.
>
> Educationally, the University has a further responsibility. If women students are to be placed in an environment where they can develop to their fullest potential, if men students are to be prepared to work comfortably with women colleagues and supervisors, if future teachers and parents are to be prepared to develop fully the potential of their children of both sexes then our attitudes must be more enlightened and models must be available. These models will come from women employed in responsible positions in the University community.

The memo was accompanied by a chart showing the current breakdown of Michigan's colleges by gender. "You may be interested to know," the memo said, "that in the area of academic employment the active instructional staff is composed of 87% men and 13% women. The inclusion of women ranges from none in Pharmacy to 95% in Nursing. . . ."

"We are all just beginning to try to find appropriate guides for employment goals," the memo closed. "Little hard data are available about absenteeism, drop-out rates, and productivity. What little documentation we have indicates many fallacious assumptions abound. To dispel folklore and establish meaningful goals will require time, study, and cooperation." (The previous fall, Newell had written Fleming, critiquing a recent study of women's job performances, and noting there were few reliable statistics.) The commission's memo included its recommendations for ways that managers could address the promotion and recruitment of women.

Managers were given what the university understood to be a list of their unit's current employees, by rank and gender, and then asked to project what their numbers would be for the next three academic years. The assignment produced a range of responses:

From Sidney Fine, chairman of the History Department, the focal point of Helen Tanner's complaint to HEW:

I regard the attached form as completely unrealistic. The department of history is unqualifiedly opposed to any discrimination, formal or informal, based on sex. The letters that our search committee send out will henceforth state that the department welcomes the nomination of women and members of minority groups. All candidates for academic and non-academic positions in the department of history are being and will be evaluated without regard to sex, color or religion. The quality of the applicants is our only concern. Since, however, our department staff is likely to be smaller in size in the next few years than it now is and since it is absolutely impossible to predict who the candidates will be for such positions as may fall vacant because of the death, resignation, or dismissal of current staff members, any projection of the composition of our staff by six [sic] in the next few years is absolutely worthless. We are engaging in flights of fancy in filling out these forms, and I am complying with President Fleming's request only under protest.

John Allen, chairman of the Zoology Department, where Margaret Davis was battling over her salary, wrote:

I cannot in good conscience predict whether any new staff (i.e. replacements for persons who have retired or resigned) will be male or female.

The search procedures now utilized by this department are completely objective. They involve contacting departmental heads and well known scientists who are engaged in graduate training and requesting their recommendations of prospective staff members. . . . The question of sex, race or other extraneous matters never enters the decision-making process.

In the past, the number of qualified women candidates for our staff positions has been very small. However, on the basis of our present graduate student population, it is my judgement that this situation will change drastically within a few years.

Allen observed that women now represented half of his graduate students and that their "academic performance is outstanding. . . . Furthermore, they are seriously interested in careers as professional zoologists. Many of their predecessors seemed to be content with having achieved their academic goal of a doctoral degree without seriously seeking an appropriate position."

W.A. Hiltner was chairman of the Astronomy Department, where astronomer Anne Cowley worked alongside her professor husband and was growing increasingly frustrated over her own status. Hiltner referenced the university's tight budgets and said that "only one new appointment in the Professor to Assistant Professor categories can be anticipated and that a male would be replaced by a female. . . . The number of qualified female candidates in astronomy is disappointingly small. . . . Very often a female astronomer will have an astronomer for a husband!"

W.J. McKeachie used his report to make a pitch for more funding for the Psychology Department: "In identifying the goals of the Department, we assumed that there would be no increase in state funds for additional staffing, but that through the Department's own efforts in obtaining grants, we would have some opportunities to meet our desperate need for teaching staff. . . . If there were no increase in staff, our chart should simply be made out in terms of promotions, since we do not have any retirements in immediate prospect and we do not normally lose staff members through resignation."

Ronald Wardhaugh, director of the English Language Institute, responded tersely: "The enclosed data on staffing goals and timetables indicate that [the institute] already has an equitable distribution of male and female employees. Only negligible changes will occur between 1971 and 1974."

Charles C. Hucker, chairman of Far Eastern Languages & Literature, described his department's pride in having lured Mills, "one of the most esteemed Chinese teachers in the country," from Cornell. "I cannot believe that the department has discriminated against her in any way, and I anticipate she will be promoted to a full professorship in the near future, as soon as she has completed scholarly work (now in progress) of the scope that our department and our college consider prerequisite for such promotion." Hucker highlighted the oft-cited issue of academic specialization: "It is not enough that a candidate be in the appropriate language field, i.e., Chinese or Japanese. The needs of the program may dictate that the candidate be a specialist, for example, in Chinese poetry. Not only will a thoroughly qualified Japanese specialist not do; a number of thoroughly qualified Chinese specialists (in thought, or fiction and drama, or linguistics) will not do either."

William P. Barth, associate director of the Center for Research in Conflict Resolution, where several PROBE members worked and whose future was then in jeopardy, described the challenges faced by the staff of research units and his center's frustration with the Personnel Department:

> [The Center] is not a teaching unit and therefore does not offer tenure appointments to academic staff. . . . With possibly one or two exceptions, there have been no women with academic appointments associated with these programs. Concerning the future program, one woman will serve as full time co-principal investigator on one of our projects. In conclusion, the status of professional women at the Center is a stark reflection of their status in society. They have been discriminated against both by acts of commission and omission.
>
> The small non-academic staff at the Center is comprised of women. In effect, they are the support staff for our research programs and are responsible for the administrative, fiscal, etc., operations of the organization. They provide the above services and receive inadequate rewards both in pay and in career opportunities. . . .
>
> . . . [W]e have in the past attempted to promote and up-grade their status but our attempts have been blocked by the personnel department. This seems to be an appropriate time for the personnel department to begin, on its own initiative, a re-consideration of the above and similar cases where promotions and pay increases have been requested for women. Given the attitude of the personnel administrators—despite their affirmative action program—I am deeply skeptical of their intentions concerning the elimination of sex discrimination.

Fleming's papers reveal other problems that popped up during the process. Floyd Bond, the dean of the Graduate School of Business Administration, wrote the president: "Are you aware that your communication on the subject 'Affirmative Action for Women' contained a computer printout showing the complete salaries of all faculty and staff members, and that such information was distributed in a manner that disclosed confidential information to unauthorized individuals?" Bond then recounted how a computer printout with the salaries of the Bureau of Business Research's staff members was not labeled "confidential" and had been opened by "a secretary who not long ago was considering suing the University for failure to keep campus sidewalks in proper condition." Bond added, "Knowing the unhappiness that can be caused by careless or indiscriminate disclosure of confidential salary information, I am deeply concerned about the looseness with which such data are frequently handled in the University."

Fleming checked with Newell, who told him that none of the commission members had seen the computer runs. She wrote, "Ed Hayes tells me all communications were addressed to the deans, directors and chairmen, and although normally such mailings are marked confidential, in the rush it was forgotten this time." Fleming advised Bond that the information never got to the commission and that the "goof" had occurred in the Personnel Office. Bond replied that he could see "no valid reason for distributing the printout in the first place."

The university did submit its goals and timetables—without all the sarcastic comments—by HEW's March 8 deadline. On March 2, Newell advised the Commission on Women that "it appears that the numbers [in the goals] are sufficiently inaccurate to cause extreme confusion" and asked them not to distribute them. Publicly she said that the commission had not reviewed the numbers but that it *had* provided input on the statement that accompanied them.

In its plan, Michigan said it would seek to increase the number of women on the instructional staff from 411 in 1970–71 to 550 in 1973–74. It also pledged to try to increase the number of women professors from 47 in 1970–71 to 78 in 1973–74. Even so, women would still make up only 6.6 percent of the total faculty. Allan Smith had told Zwerdling: "We have a University policy that says to department heads: 'You will be active, you will be aggressive, you will set up a goal.' Then it's up to the individual units to achieve it."

Michigan also acknowledged that the goals were developed "with recognition of the fact that for most of the schools and colleges there will be no increase in instructional positions for the next three years and that open positions in such cases will be limited to turnover" in current staff. All but three schools and colleges projected their teaching staffs would grow; Dentistry and Nursing said there would be no change, Library Science anticipated its staff would decline by three persons, including one woman. Business Administration did not complete its report before the goals had to be submitted.

The statement to HEW also hedged about the plan's quality, saying that "the probable decline in the fiscal support for higher education in the future, the necessary action in minority recruitment and placement, the speed with which these data were collected all indicate that these goals and timetables are subject to periodic revision."

Early on, the Commission on Women reached out to Sandler for her input on how Michigan's goals compared with other schools. Sandler replied that if Michigan managed to increase the proportion of women professors to 6.6 percent by the 1973–74 academic year, it would still lag behind the rest of the nation at 8.7 percent. Similarly, the goal for the total instructional staff—16 percent in 1973–74—was below the current national level of 19 percent. As a result, there was speculation that HEW would reject the goals and that Michigan would have to revise them. Fauri said, "We would welcome the commission's recommendations," and that "a great deal" of such a review "would be up to them."

Indeed, two months later, on May 17, Lucille I. Matthews, HEW's deputy regional civil rights director, wrote Fleming that the university's plan was "incomplete," and "we are unable to determine its acceptability." She said that the university's proposed computer evaluation of the qualifications of women employees was not "sufficiently specific." HEW wanted the goals and timetables for LSA and the Medical School broken down by departments. It also wanted every non-academic job classification to be broken down by sex to show not only new hires but also the anticipated turnover, promotions, and transfers of women who were qualified for higher-level jobs. Finally, it asked how the university planned to distribute the new nepotism policy. "In our review," she wrote, "we found that each department head contacted interpreted nepotism to suit his particular needs."

Matthews concluded, "Until we receive the information requested in this letter we will be unable to evaluate your plan as to its acceptability."

When the thrust of Matthews's letter was revealed a week later, PROBE said HEW had rejected the university's plan; Fleming said the agency was just seeking more information. The commission was also actively trying to get the information so that its members could better understand the problems they were supposed to address.

In a 2019 interview, Newell noted wryly that "one of the joys of this difficulty" was that "we were in the central administration dealing without really central data. It was the life before the computer. To try to get answers, say, in the 30 days, which was the first demand, there was a real question of whether it could conceivably be done. Now if we had been at [the University of] Wisconsin, I think the answer might have been yes, because that was a much more centralized place."

In a 2001 joint interview, Murphy recalled that the commission asked top university officials to provide "data on men and women's salaries and how they compared." Mills interjected, "Worse than that, even on who the women in this University were!"

Mills recalled, "We wanted a list, for example, of professors. And without going through, page by page, line by line, the University would not provide them." Asked why, the professor replied, "Because it was not what they wanted to encourage. . . ." Then she quipped, "You have to put your mindset back before Adam and Eve."

Murphy observed that because theirs was a "presidential commission," the women *did* get access to some information. But, Mills said, "We had to fight and fight and fight."

Murphy recalled that Hayes told his fellow commission members that it would take them "two years of analysis" to produce the kind of information the commission wanted.

At the outset, Hayes told the commission that among non-academic employees, there were only 1,200 women in job categories where there were enough men and women to make meaningful salary comparisons. The Personnel Office calculated mean salaries and mean length of service, and picked 157 employees to be reviewed. Personnel reported that fewer than 20 needed to be checked for possible discrimination.

As the commission continued to meet, Murphy recalled that she told Hayes, in what she described as her "brash, twenty-something way," that if he gave *her* "the tape," she could produce the analysis of staff salaries "overnight." She said because the administrators didn't think she could do it, they gave her the tape, and working with a colleague, she was able to complete the analysis. "Data processing," she recalled, "was pretty primitive still, but ISR had the newest and the fanciest, and we were able to run some regression analyses and show that we couldn't get any explanation for why women's salaries were lower. Not only that, but very low." ISR, she said, was one of the few places at the time that could do regression analysis on computers instead of calculators. "So this," she recalled, "was hot stuff!" (In regression analysis, two variables are compared to determine whether there is a correlation between them. For example, the salary levels of men and women could be compared to determine if there was a correlation between their relative hiring dates, years of experience, or highest degree earned.)

To the author of the Harvard case study, Hayes disputed Murphy's "overnight" claim, saying that by late April he had not heard back from the women. The study said Hayes explained that "the Commission had no budget for the programming work, that the women who had volunteered to do the work had to work on it in their spare time, and that the women were unfamiliar with the programming languages used in the personnel office. . . . At any rate, there is not much pressure for results— we're not sure what to do with the information once we have it."

Newell acknowledged the same problem at the time: "To whom do you take the files once they're identified? Go to the employee's supervisor? That's the person who made the decision in the first place. Go to the potential complainant? Since the procedures and salaries are considered by the University as the Administration's domain, grievances are also within their bounds. . . . Finally, if the allegations about the persecutions of woman complainants are true (and I've seen enough cases to make me think there is some truth to them), how can we use an advocate procedure to correct potential salary inequities?"

In a September 16, 1971 "Computer File Review Report," Murphy detailed what she and her ISR colleagues had been able to do with $455.50 worth of ISR computer time and $1,300 worth of donated volunteer labor. She knew that a hand-sort would be prohibitively expensive but also recognized that there were limits to the so-called Multiple-Classification Analysis they had done. In the end, Murphy recommended that the university pay for a proper computer analysis and make changes in its personnel record-keeping. But she also felt that "an extensive hand sort. . . was the only fair way to find cases of individual discrimination." Otherwise, "the onus of bringing complaints still rests with the employee, with the University not fulfilling its obligations to find cases of discrimination and rectify them."

Within a few months, the commission got a staff member and $10,000 for a more substantial file review.

Rightly or wrongly, Michigan *was* gaining a reputation as a place where women had achieved a breakthrough in addressing sex discrimination on campus. Cheryl Fields, another reporter that Sandler and King cultivated, wrote a front-page article for the *Chronicle of Higher Education* in March 1971: "Sex discrimination—and government and university efforts to get rid of it—has emerged in the past year as one of the most controversial and sensitive issues on the nation's campuses. While not as well-publicized as student unrest, federal investigations of whether women have been discriminated against in hiring, pay, and promotions at colleges and universities have challenged many institutions' self images and long-established policies and operating procedures." She then detailed the commitments that Michigan had made.

PROBE also began arranging for nationally known activists, such as NOW's Ann Scott and Democratic Rep. Bella Abzug of New York, to speak on campus. PROBE told its membership that another visitor, Mary Jean Collins-Robson, NOW's Midwest regional director, "reported that as a result of the HEW investigation of the U of M, Ann Arbor is regarded as a Midwestern feminist mecca." "OK, women," PROBE urged its members, "let's live up to that reputation."

But for much of the campus, the cycles of academic life went on as usual. In his report on the 1970–71 year, Acting LSA Dean Sussman devoted one paragraph of his 27-page report to women's concerns, including it in the "Minorities" section. He wrote:

> An action against the University involving the Department of Health, Education and Welfare propelled the University, and the College, into a confrontation with a group of women who have

claimed that they have been discriminated against by reasons of sex. One form of the complaint alleges that their salaries are lower and promotions slower; another argues that women are not hired to the faculty in numbers proportional to their availability. I have seen evidence of disaffection among some of our women colleagues, but others have pointedly disagreed. The former have mounted appeals, five of which have been acted upon. In at least one case, the appeal is being carried beyond the University, a development that could be of considerable significance not only to women but to other appellants.

A few months later, Sussman's successor, Dean Frank H.T. Rhodes, summarized for Fleming and other administrators the topics that had arisen during the college's recent retreat. The list included "salary, promotion and recruitment priorities" but no mention of HEW or potential sex discrimination.

And at the start of the 1971–72 academic year, the Center for Population Planning was implementing its once-held-up contract with the government of Nepal. Professor Thomas Poffenberger and his wife, Shirley, were scheduled to leave on September 19 for two months in Katmandu where Thomas would work as "chief of party" for the family-planning contract. It would support the field work of four researchers, all of them men.

The minutes of the department's governing committee noted that Shirley Poffenberger had just been promoted as "a research assistant." The only woman then teaching under the center's auspices was part-timer Lois Hoffman, who held a joint appointment as a lecturer in the Department of Psychology. Her then-husband, Martin, was a professor in that department, earning, HEW had discovered in the course of its investigation, $3,300 a year more than she did.

15
Sticking Points

At the start of 1971, Michigan had pledged to HEW that it would "achieve salary equity" between men and women with the same qualifications who were doing the same job and that it would extend back pay to women who had experienced discrimination.

It did not take long for a woman to ask for her check.

On January 26, Cheryl Clark, a research assistant with Michigan's Highway Safety Research Institute (HSRI), filed a complaint, charging that she was a victim of sex discrimination because she earned less than a male colleague with comparable experience. Clark contended that "no difference in job responsibilities, expectations or quality of work has been explained to me."

Clark's colleague held a master's degree while she was still working toward one. But, unlike her colleague, she reported to the research project's director and supervised three employees. She had also worked for the institute's alcohol research program for three years; her colleague's experience was in the armed services, computer programming, and urban studies.

Within a week of Clark's complaint, her department head rejected it, concluding that the salary differential was "in fact within the range dictated by sound salary and wage" distinctions. Clark then pursued her complaint to the University Complaint Review Committee, where, in June 1971, it was also rejected. The committee concluded that "based on your performance, your salary growth has been appropriate."

Clark was represented by Professor Harry T. Edwards, who the year before had become the first African American to teach in the Michigan Law School. (Edwards later went on to serve as a judge on the U.S. Court of Appeals for the DC Circuit.) Following Clark's adverse decision, Edwards wrote the Commission on Women that the ruling was "so ineptly evolved, illogical and childishly naïve, both as to the applicable facts and law, that it is embarrassing to see it over the signature of an official of the University of Michigan."

HEW had called for the university to revise its grievance procedure. It found that women rarely, if ever, served on review committees and noted that the first round of a complaint was through an employee's supervisor. Now Jean Campbell was asked to represent the commission on the university's review committee. She issued a dissenting opinion when the committee voted, two to one, to reject Clark's complaint.

In her report, Campbell noted that all of the women with bachelor's degrees in Clark's employment classification were receiving less than seven of the eight similarly qualified men in that classification. But in rejecting Clark's claim, the committee's two male members said they had taken into consideration "the market value of the individual's professional qualifications."

As it made its way through Michigan's bureaucracy, Clark's complaint drew national attention: *Science* magazine said it "may set major precedents for women's rights at American universities." Elsewhere, the case was heralded as the first time a woman had sued a U.S. university seeking back pay for sex discrimination.

According to the *Science* report, "Clark herself is a soft-spoken master's candidate in sociology, whom one university official describes as 'a good test case—she's the stereotype of the sweet little research assistant.' She receives an annual salary, in the alcohol safety program of HSRI, of $9,100. Last winter, she learned accidentally, that a male research associate was being paid $12,500, and that the amount for her own salary in the project's budget is $13,200, or more than $4,100 than she receives."

The committee's rejection of Clark's complaint made the *New York Times* under the headline "Michigan U. Bars Raise for Woman." Edwards said that the committee's procedures were "outrageous" and told the paper, "Every fear that we raised in advance about the deficiencies in the complaint procedure proved to be well founded."

As the Commission on Women lobbied for changes in the grievance procedure, officials agreed to a one-year test of a new approach: Each side would get to pick a committee member, and then those two representatives would choose the third member from a list designated by Fleming. Around the same time, Sen. Hart pressed Secretary Richardson for his opinion on the matter. Richardson responded that if his understanding of the case was correct, "the [existing] procedure would not appear to be a viable process whereby the University can fulfill its obligations to affirmatively ensure the equal treatment of all employees regardless of their sex. . . ."

But faculty members did not have access to the grievance procedure. On March 15, 1971, Zoology Professor Margaret Davis wrote "John and Al"—department chair Allen and LSA Dean Sussman—"I have been waiting to receive word from you regarding payment of the back wages due me." She pointed to the HEW agreement and said, "The responsibility for locating those employees to whom wages are owed rests with the University, not the employees. However, because more than 90 days have passed without word from you, although I know you are aware of my case, I am writing this letter to remind you, and to ask specifically when I can expect to receive my back pay?" Davis said she would need access to the department's salary data for the past three years. "I remind you that the right of discovery has been guaranteed employees by the University in its agreement with HEW," she said. Davis copied her letter to PROBE, Hodgdon, Kiely, and attorney Carol M. Stadler, identified elsewhere as a lawyer for NOW.

Allen tossed the ball to Sussman, telling him, "This question is the prerogative of the Dean's office and I am pleased to leave it in your capable hands." Sussman then wrote Davis that "a review of files has been undertaken and a procedure is being developed to review alleged inequities which may have resulted from sex discrimination. Any inequity found will be corrected within thirty days of that finding." He said Davis could pursue a complaint through the college grievance procedure if she disagreed with the finding. (Sussman's draft was addressed "Dear Margie," using a nickname a former colleague recalled Davis hated, but in the final version that was changed to "Dr. Davis.")

Three days after Davis wrote her bosses, her zoology colleague Associate Professor Lois Lowenthal also wrote Sussman to "protest vigorously the financial discrimination against me" by the department, LSA, and the university. "The discrimination obviously stems from my being a woman," wrote Lowenthal.

Lowenthal acknowledged that her expectations regarding salary and promotions dated back to the tenure of Dugald Brown, who had stepped down as the department's chairman in 1965. She said she felt her contributions had at least equaled or surpassed those of her male colleagues. "With each passing year I have nurtured a fading hope that such inequities would be recognized and that I would achieve equality. Nothing has been obtained."

> "Why am I writing to you now? There is one obvious answer—the time is ripe; publicity is advantageous; The University has made a commitment to HEW. But there is another answer too. For many years I felt that my having an income above and beyond my salary made my chairman dole limited funds to our faculty lacking outside resources." She said Allen now claimed that her outside income was not a consideration. "If not, then why, after fourteen years of service in teaching, counseling and administration is my salary so far below the mean? Why have I not been promoted?
>
> To be sure, I have not participated in sit-ins, stand-ins, teach-ins and whatever other "ins" bring attention (notoriety?) to our faculty. To be sure, I have served on college committees and departmental committees to the extent that precious little time remained for anything beyond teaching."

Helen Tanner also renewed her battle with the History Department. By April, she had requested and received a copy of Sidney Fine's version of the department's review of her appointment. Now she wrote Hodgdon again, angry that neither the Office of Civil Rights nor top university officials had responded to the letters she had sent the previous fall:

> The newspapers have carried headlines announcing an "historic plan" for overcoming discrimination at The University of Michigan, but of course a plan has no concrete value unless it is carried into action. Since I am not acquainted with other individual complaints, I am not in a position to evaluate the overall results of your investigation. A powerless "study commission" has been appointed, but the only man on the commission with academ-

ic rank has already resigned. Certainly, if discrimination cannot be overcome at the academic level of an educational institution, then the civil rights of women are diminished throughout all levels of the university system.

Did your investigation of The University of Michigan reveal the basic fact that the University directory's list of 83 History faculty members includes only one woman holding a regular appointment? And she is on the faculty only because women alumnae raised the money to bring a woman professor into the History department. The special chair was established in 1961, and for several years thereafter, the annual salary was paid through alumnae contributions. [Sylvia L. Thrupp was the first Alice Freeman Palmer Professor of History.] No other woman is a regular member of the History faculty. During the current academic year, there is a woman "adjunct associate professor," who commutes from Maryland to teach part-time in the Black history program. Two other young women teach History classes on a part-time basis in the Residential College, but are not considered members of the History Department.

Tanner told Hodgdon she was renewing her complaint and requested he come back to the university and do "a proper investigation." She hoped to "have an opportunity to discuss my specific case with you." She sent copies of her letter to Pottinger, four members of Congress, Fleming, Newell, Fine, and four other university administrators. She may not have helped her case by misspelling Fine's name "Sydney."

But a review of letters written about women like Tanner and Lowenthal demonstrate that on the academic side, the considerations were much more subjective and harder to challenge. Davis's salary didn't match her rank, but Tanner and Lowenthal didn't even have the rank.

Newell recalled that it was very hard to change academic hiring practices—what she called "back of the envelope" hiring—and who controlled the decision. "The whole institution is very reticent to give up their power, both in hiring and for admissions. I think it's easier to get change and clean directives and all the other nice things that go with it for clerical and all the other positions at the University than it is for the academics," Newell explained.

When Allan Smith asked John Allen for more information about Lowenthal and another associate professor, Mary Catherine Hinchey, who had taught in the Zoology Department since 1958, Allen enclosed a copy of their most recent promotion reviews, two years before. He said subsequent reviews would have been "pointless" because of the "stagnation" in their "performance"; neither had published a scholarly paper since then. Lowenthal taught histology, and he said her performance was "competent but not outstanding." He acknowledged that she was in charge of undergraduate counseling and did that job "efficiently," but he said that work could be performed "quite as well by a non-academic secretary." In the same letter, he recommended promotions for Davis and a male professor but transmitted the Promotion Committee's recommendation that another man not be promoted, even though "there is little comparison between his performance" and that of the two women.

As for Tanner, the previous fall she had produced letters attesting to the quality of her scholarship and teaching, but in a letter to William Cash, Fine had simply cited the opinion of Professor Charles Gibson, then the department's only specialist in Latin American history. Tanner, Fine explained, had been considered as someone who could fill in during the 1969 semester when Gibson was on leave. But, Fine wrote, "Professor Gibson, who is one of the most eminent men in the world in the field of Latin American history, believed—and the department's Executive Committee, of which he was then a member, concurred—that Mrs. Tanner, although a capable historian, did not measure up to the very high quality that the department of history looks for in regular appointments to its staff." Fine also noted that Tanner's expertise duplicated Gibson's, namely the colonial era.

Fine added, "It is also relevant to note that the department of history had developed a strong prejudice against the hiring of its own PhD's for full-time teaching and, indeed, had not appointed a Michigan PhD to its regular staff for almost 20 years. Mrs. Tanner, as you know, received her PhD at the University of Michigan." Fine did not acknowledge that when he was hired in 1948—22 years earlier—he had just earned *his* PhD from Michigan.

In May, Sussman responded formally to Davis. He said her salary differential stemmed from the limited grant funds that were available when she was hired. While he told Davis that he and Allen both acknowledged that "there was some inequity in your salary," it was "not the type of situation which is covered by the University's agreement with HEW." And because "the unusual salary adjustment" she had received at the start of the academic year "resolved this inequity in a manner which is consistent with University and College practice over the years," there was no basis for approving back pay.

When the Davis and Lowenthal cases got kicked up to the Office of Academic Affairs, internal memos reveal some of the attitudes and practices campus women were up against. In a memo that the number-crunching Hayes sent Allman about Lowenthal's case, Hayes said that in his review, he had found that Lowenthal's salary had lagged behind her male peers. He said Allen had acknowledged that was true but that it was appropriate "in light of her performance." Hayes said that when he asked Allen to put that in writing, "he expressed an extreme reluctance to do so."

"Apparently like Doctors (M.D.) he is extremely reluctant to take a hard public position which is critical of the performance of a member of the teaching staff," Hayes wrote. "I assume this is a matter of tradition and principle, rather than the inability to do so, but it will be very difficult, if not impossible to defend salary treatment on merit, if we are not willing to substantiate and justify these decisions."

In a separate memo about Davis's complaint, Hayes wrote:

Assuming that Dr. Davis's salary was unreasonably low, the question of why it was low needs also to be explored. It may have been low for reasons beyond sex discrimination. If such a position can be substantiated, then we are outside of the conditions under which we have agreed to grant backpay.

My general impression at this point, is that Dr. Davis may for reasons unknown at this point have been slightly underpaid, however, I feel we overreacted to her threats this past spring, and probably are not overpaying her. If that conclusion proves to be true, it raises several interesting questions of discrimination against males in the Zoology Department.

In mid-year, Newell stepped down as commission chair, leaving to become associate provost at the University of Pittsburgh.

Newell later said she decided to leave Michigan because "if you really worked hard to change the way they're doing things, the department chair is not going to love you. I found that really trying to follow up on what we found was quickly burning all the bridges that I had spent my time from the very first day building. . . . Not only was I being put in a box as the women's coordinator, but I was also—as a personality—I pushed, and it was not a happy combination. I was really going to find myself in an uncomfortable spot in the long run."

Fleming's version of her decision was slightly different. In a revealing letter to St. Cloud State's presidential search committee in December 1970, he wrote of Newell: "Except for the turbulence of the time, and the feeling of the students that they must be consulted on everything in that Office [of Student Services], she could doubtless have survived since she was popular even with students. The permanent Search Committee nevertheless preferred a man, and when he was appointed, she came back to me." He used her, he explained, "on a variety of substantive problems."

In the few months before Law School instructor Virginia Davis Nordin was appointed to replace Newell as the commission's chair, the members kept plugging away. Mills recalled, "You have a period of trying to stake out your mandate. What kind of issues can you attack? How would you proceed? The big issues were trying to identify conditions we could improve." One of those was child care. Mills, who was single and childless, acknowledged that "at first I didn't think it was the responsibility of the work place, but my own thinking has changed very radically. However, I kept quiet on this because I didn't think I had any right to talk about this."

She added, "Some of us at first thought that we should have more representation of X, Y and Z group, but as we got to working, I think we realized there was really no way to go." Of the original membership, "some continued to be active, some did not."

Still, as the 1971–72 academic year started, people on all sides of the HEW investigation were growing frustrated. University officials felt beleaguered by HEW's demands for more data and reports. HEW's civil rights investigators were overwhelmed by the mounting pile of complaints about other universities. Sandler, Scott, and other activists were frustrated that nearly two years after the Labor Department had issued regulations to prohibit discrimination by federal contractors, the regulations still did not mention "sex." And in Ann Arbor, women activists were also growing impatient. The Office of Student Services had added a Women's Advocate and was taking on new issues, such as women's access to campus health services. But a year had passed since HEW had issued its findings, and little had changed in the meantime.

In late November, PROBE decided to act. Taking over from FOCUS, it filed another formal complaint with the Labor Department. It charged that Michigan was acting in bad faith regarding the goals and timetables but that they were "distorted, confused and deficient" to begin with. As evidence of the university's bad faith, it cited the grievance procedures, its failure to give any woman back pay, the halting steps it was taking to identify victims of sex discrimination, and the goals and timetables themselves. It also cited, in the words of the *Daily,* the "University's use of the media to bias the public and gain support for the allegations that sex discrimination is an insignificant problem."

What further incensed the PROBE members was the news that the ACE had named Fleming to a small group of university presidents who were going to advise HEW how to deal with sex discrimination. By then, of course, Fleming was arguably the president with the most experience in that area, but women activists across the nation were shocked that an official whom they viewed as one of the worst culprits was being asked to play that role. The committee also included Presidents Wharton of Michigan State, Peterson of Barnard, Derek Bok of Harvard, and Terry Sanford of Duke. Three of the colleges were then under investigation. Wesleyan University Provost Sheila Tobias, then chairing the Professional Women's Caucus, said the presidents' appointments "just stinks to high heaven." Tobias anticipated that the presidents would lobby to weaken HEW's guidelines. But the ACE's Wilson responded, "We wanted to get people who had already had experience with HEW, so that they would be familiar with some of the problems that come up."

Activists also took note of a report from HEW's own Women's Action Group that found that while women made up 64 percent of the department's workforce, they held only 14 percent of its top positions. Zena Zumeta, then serving as Michigan's new "women's representative," observed, "Everyone needs a Prince Charming sometimes. But what do you do when all you've got is a broken-down prince?" WEAL, meanwhile, complained about HEW's failure to communicate about the status of investigations, delays in developing guidelines, and "demeaning" statements that some employees had made about women.

In an undated summary that the Office of Civil Rights prepared of the status of the complaints it had received between February 1970 and May 1971, it reported that WEAL had filed complaints against 250 colleges and universities. "These allegations," the memo said, "are general in nature dealing with the gamut of patterns of discrimination against women." The office said it had received complaints "of a more specific nature" from one or more individuals against 29 colleges and universities. These, it said, were filed by 40 individual women, one labor union local, and five campus women's groups. In addition to FOCUS at Michigan, the latter included the Women's Caucus at the University of California at Berkeley and groups at the universities of Chicago and Wisconsin.

Of some 230 compliance reviews it conducted during that same time, the office said 149 were conducted at colleges and universities. "About 82 of these reviews included sex discrimination to some extent," the office reported, "although the degree of attention paid to sex discrimination apparently varied considerably" across the reviews. The office said that affirmative action plans, including "remedial steps for sex discrimination," were in effect or being developed at about ten schools, now identified as Harvard, Loyola, Northwestern, Tufts, Illinois, Maryland, Michigan, Pittsburgh, Texas, and Vanderbilt.

In July, Pottinger had told the Associated Press: "There is a tendency on the part of many people we deal with to believe all the women's movement consists of is a bra-burning display and rhetorical rantings against the existence of men. There is that element," he said in the interview, "but when you find five women in an English department who have published as much or more than their male colleagues, who have equal degrees and who have been at the university longer, yet are paid less, have less tenure and are promoted at a slower rate, you're talking of something with real substance to it."

Still Pottinger acknowledged that while the size of his 92-member staff had tripled in the past year, the volume of complaints had increased to the point where his division had more cases than it could handle.

HEW's inability to hold Michigan's feet to the fire frustrated PROBE, the Commission on Women, and the campus women who were challenging their individual situations.

In response to the complaint PROBE filed in November 1971, Fleming said, "It can't be fairly charged that we're not doing anything to eliminate sex discrimination." But from the vantage point of the Commission on Women, Nordin said, "I don't think we'd argue with anything PROBE has to say."

"The University has always been too grudging in helping women along," she noted. "Commission members have always been hamstrung, both by the fact that not enough top-level administrators come out in support of affirmative action and because sex discrimination is so pervasive."

And from Chicago, Hodgdon said HEW's enforcement prospects were "very depressing." Although the agency had received Michigan's goals and timetables eight months before, it did not have the capacity to review them. His office was now investigating sex bias at 20 universities, and, he acknowledged, "We're just not adequately staffed to do the job."

Late in his life, Fleming made the same complaint. The retired president recalled, "They really weren't any better prepared than we were to face the question. The thing that made it even worse was that we shortly learned that because they were understaffed" HEW wasn't even looking at most of the things they were receiving. "They were just storing them in a big warehouse somewhere. And therefore it was unrealistic because here we would work like mad to get together something and it would go over there and nobody would ever see it."

On December 4, the Labor Department finally dealt with sex discrimination by federal contractors in a set of rules known as Revised Order No. 4. The regulations set off another howl of opposition from Fleming, his academic allies, and more conservative academics. They objected that the government was ordering them to hire women and minorities—as long as they were more qualified than the least qualified person currently in a department. In a *Detroit News* article headlined, "HEW Cuts Faculty Quality, Colleges Fear," an unidentified Michigan official complained that the rule could not be applied "without seriously diluting the quality of teaching." Another administrator said, "If HEW is really serious about enforcing that requirement, it would be disas-

234   CONQUERING HEROINES

trous. You can imagine the havoc it would wreak in the Department of Surgery, for instance."

Sidney Hook, a professor of philosophy at New York University, John Bunzel, president of San Jose State College, and Paul Seabury, a political scientist at Berkeley, were among the conservative academics who began to publicly challenge HEW's statistical approach to identifying sex discrimination: "They have completely disregarded the all-important criterion of qualifications or requisite skills," Hook told the *Detroit News*, "and assumed that what may be a legitimate inference in considering the presence or absence of discrimination in hiring individuals for an assembly line... holds for all levels of university instruction."

But HEW continued to hold firm. "This has been necessary," Pottinger responded to the *News*, "because of years of neglect by the universities. But I don't think this constitutes a quota system."

While Michigan was one of the rare universities that disclosed details of its investigation and affirmative action plan, the Labor Department took the position that colleges did not have to. In June 1971, the agency's solicitor ruled that the plans could be kept confidential because the contents "would be useful to competitors with regard to contemplated changes in the contractor's processes, types of production and overall business planning." Women argued that it was unlikely Harvard would suffer a competitive disadvantage if it released its plan, and eventually the Labor Department changed its position. But, Sandler noted, "Since the letter of findings also is kept confidential, it is all but impossible for women to find out what deficiencies exist on their campus, and what steps their institution is taking to correct these deficiencies." Indeed, some portions of HEW's findings about Michigan did not become publicly available until Fleming's papers were opened up in the University Archives, at least 10 years after they were transmitted, under the policy then in place.

As the weeks went by, the issues of salaries, back pay, and grievances became intertwined. HEW had ordered Michigan to compensate victims of discrimination back to the effective date of the executive order; in a time of tight budgets, lawyers Fleming and Smith cited legal precedents to argue that payments were owed only back to the date a complaint was filed. As lawyers at HEW and the Labor Department reviewed that legal question, the university used the delay as the basis for doing nothing.

Fleming heard Pottinger speak at a gathering of college officials at a Washington hotel in April 1971 and followed up with him afterwards. Pottinger had told his audience that the back-pay question was still under review. Fleming wrote that while the university was "examining its files right now," it did not "want to be bound by a rule that applies to no one else." Fleming asked Pottinger to provide a letter stating that the issue was still under review. "I would probably then hold our back-pay situation in abeyance simply to avoid reaching a position which might bind us to a rule no one else was expected to follow," said Fleming. Six weeks later, Pottinger provided such a letter.

In its early days, the Commission on Women quickly recognized what a daunting task it was to identify women who deserved back-pay awards. Women activists knew the price that women like Clark and Davis were paying to challenge their salaries and insisted that the university had pledged to HEW that it would take the initiative. Still, knowing how long the review might take, the commission began encouraging women to step forward so that the commission itself could review their situations.

At the end of December 1971, the American Association for the Advancement of Science (AAAS) held a symposium in Philadelphia titled "Women in Academia: Evolving Policies Toward Equal Opportunities." The AAAS's interest in the topic was likely fueled by its new president, Mina Rees, a mathematician who had just become president of the Graduate School and University Center of City University of New York. Pottinger was invited to speak, and his text reflected a growing frustration with the universities:

> I am somewhat surprised by the reaction of much of the academic community to its awakening realization that there are federal prohibitions against sex discrimination on campus.
>
> I say "surprised" not because universities, like most other corporate bodies, are by nature somewhat resistant to internal change. Nor is it surprising to find their critics occasionally resorting to rhetorical "overkill" in order to have legitimate grievances heard. Still, one might have expected that institutions which pride themselves on thoughtful analysis might apply some of it to the mundane issue of employment policies as well as to the cosmic political and social issues of our time.

Instead, however, University "establishment" critics imply that academia is somehow exempt from the anti-discrimination demands placed on the rest of society today. They claim that the university as an institution is so fragile, so neurotic, so unique and so superior that to require any hiring, promotion, or employment to take place by any standards other than the present metaphysical criteria generally used by universities will surely wreck institutions of higher learning, at least as we know them today.

Similarly, some non-establishment critics claim that the university as we know it today stinks, that the best way to make up for the sins of the past is to cut off all Federal contracts immediately, that no tears will be shed if the Executive Order serves to destroy the university and allows everybody to start from scratch in rebuilding it. Executive Order 11246, which addresses itself in clear and simple terms to the issue of fair employment, has thus become the catalyst for further heated debate on the nature of the university—its purpose, justification, failure, success and prospects for the future.

Pottinger then cited some of the statistics presented at Rep. Green's hearings to demonstrate that the position of women in academia had declined in the 20th century. Because, he said, there was "no great body of law" that extended the protections of the 14th Amendment to women, "we in HEW therefore recognize a special responsibility to use the legal tools available to us to assure equal employment opportunity for women on campus." He said he hoped that one byproduct of the executive order would be "a realization on campus that universities and colleges are not only special places of learning, but also employers having many of the same employment responsibilities as General Motors, the local supermarket, or a sheet metal firm working under the Philadelphia Plan."

He also responded to the conservative critics of affirmative action, arguing that even if affirmative action was viewed as "preferential treatment" for specific groups, that was "no rarity in American political life." He pointed to land grants to railroads, subsidies for airlines and farmers, and the special tax treatment for the clergy and the disabled. Such treatment, he said, was provided because Congress or the Executive Branch "deemed it in the interest of all of American society to do so."

"Too many universities continue to hire by the 'old boy' fraternity system of word of mouth. They continue to look in the traditional places. They travel across the seas for good people but refuse to go down the street," Pottinger said. "They persist with often irrelevant and obsolete standards and requirements that do no more than continue to exclude minorities and women. It is this 'business as usual' that the Executive Order is designed to alter."

Pottinger concluded: "For people whose life work has been new ideas, innovation, research and scholarship, we genuinely believe that this is not an unreasonable task."

Richardson's papers reveal that after two years of negotiating with Columbia, HEW's contract compliance division finally got that university to agree to cooperate at the very end of 1971, much the way it had forced U-M to come to the table the year before. But again some political pressure was brought to bear on HEW. On December 22, 1971, Richardson got a phone call from C.D. Ward, an aide to Vice President Agnew who was then reaching out to Republican governors. Ward told Richardson that then-New York Governor Nelson Rockefeller had phoned and asked him to urge Richardson to "sit down with President [William J.] McGill" because the sex discrimination regulations were "giving the medical school at Columbia University unbelievable problems."

Richardson replied that he would be willing to do so but noted, "We haven't asked Columbia to do anything a lot of other people haven't already done. I think, what I have seen of it, they are trying to make a Federal case out of it. I am not aware we have asked anything unreasonable of them. We have entered into agreements with 40 or 50, started with Michigan, Harvard, Stanford, Columbia. They have choked. I don't know why."

Ward responded that "Columbia gets about 14 million dollars out of their total 120 million from Federal contracts, which makes them pretty sensitive." Richardson replied, "That isn't a [sic] undue ratio for a big university."

At 4:30 pm on December 30, 1971, Pottinger reported to Richardson that Columbia had turned in an affirmative action plan earlier that day. But he also provided the secretary with a memo detailing how Columbia officials had stalled the development of their affirmative action plans for both minorities and women since January 1969, and how contracts had been suspended as the end of the year approached. Pottinger said he wanted Richardson to have the information available if he chose to call McGill that day.

Pottinger reviewed several federal contracts that were thought to be affected but cited only two that actually were, both again involving AID, where "disbursement of funds has been withheld pending the resolution of their compliance problems." As was the case with Michigan officials, Pottinger said he had told McGill that the university president could call him directly if he felt "he is not receiving prompt and fair treatment by our Contract Compliance Division." But Pottinger added, "As a general matter, while we are told by University officials that they are making efforts to collect their data, analyze it, and prepare an affirmative action plan, we have been provided with no plan to date." He asked Richardson not to make any commitment to lift the contract suspension order until they had had a chance to talk further.

The pressure that HEW was applying to Columbia may have reignited some fear in the hearts of Michigan officials. In December—a full year after U-M promised to do so—Vice President Smith instructed each of the university's academic units to review the salaries of every woman on their staffs, both instructional and non-instructional, and gave them a month to do so. Respondents could simply note "No change recommended," if the salary was deemed to be acceptable. Where salaries were thought to be inequitable, supervisors were told to suggest an adjustment.

With a fresh complaint from PROBE in hand, and Hodgdon imposing new deadlines, HEW's civil rights staff returned to Ann Arbor in February 1972—for the first time in 18 months. The goals and timetables still had not been approved, and HEW was still trying to get detailed personnel data out of the university. Hodgdon told the *Daily*, "We decided it would be foolish to give approval after being out of contact almost a year. The requested information will tell us the current situation and if any progress is being made."

The photograph that accompanied the *University Record*'s story on the HEW visit was different from the "grip-and-grin" one that had marked Minton's 1970 visit; this time there were also women at the table—Nordin from the Commission for Women and Lardent from HEW. (A few months earlier, the commission's name was quietly changed when astute U-M public relations officials realized that the acronym of the original name was COW.)

In advance of the February 4 meeting with the Chicago officials, Fleming urged Fauri to highlight the president's sense that the university's Ann Arbor workforce was actually shrinking in size. Once again, the discussions focused on what figures the university officials were capable of producing—and how quickly they could do it.

Immediately after the meeting with HEW, Fauri's assistant Heebink wrote his boss, musing over how Michigan should proceed in responding to the latest agreement. It could, he noted, "do everything humanly possible to comply," or "comply with the letter as far as the Executive Officers feel it is reasonable to do so, but resist (via the courts, if necessary) complying with those parts of the [Hodgdon] letter that are felt to be unreasonable." Or, he said, the university could respond "with a counter proposal specifying what kinds of information we intend to supply and when we will be able to supply it." He preferred the third choice.

"It seems to me," he explained, "to have a certain amount of inherent appeal compared to the other two because it is not 'weak kneed' like the first, and it is not a negative step as the second would tend to be. Rather, it could probably be developed in a constructive way which would show that we want to put our house in order and that we intend to take responsibility for doing so. I hate to see us put in the position of being told unilaterally by an outside agency what we should do about problems for which this University's administration is basically responsible." He then added, from the vantage point of the university's lobbying staff, "In sum, it seems to me that the University's autonomy is at stake here in somewhat the same way it is in Lansing. End of lecture." (At the time, university officials were wrestling with whether the university needed a larger presence in the nation's capital; it did not open a Washington office until 1990, one of the first U.S. colleges to do so.)

It may have been simply a coincidence, or the length of time it took to move U-M's massive bureaucracy. But the record shows that things that the university had pledged to do more than a year before started happening around the time the HEW officials returned to campus.

This time, the context was set, not by FOCUS or PROBE, but by the Commission for Women. In February 1972, its Cluster Communications Committee issued a 200-page report that the *University Record* covered in a special issue a month later. After the first goals and timetables were sent to HEW the previous May, the commission organized "clusters" of women from different constituencies—faculty, professional and administrative, and clerical—to review the plans and make recommendations for promoting greater equity. The reports reflected input from three colleges—Education, Social Work, and Law—and seven departments within LSA. Noting the dearth of responses from some corners of the university, the women cited as causes departmental lethargy, fear of reprisals, and the fact that some units didn't have enough women employees to generate a valid response.

These recommendations were different because they were prepared by insiders—professors, secretaries, and administrators. They were the result of several months of work and involved a willingness, in some cases, to criticize male superiors.

Among other things, the women found that U-M secretaries in the lowest clerical pay grade were paid so little that those with one dependent could qualify for food stamps. They pointed out that departments had counted part-time employees as full-timers to make their hiring numbers look better. Women in the professional and academic sectors reported that they had seen "no intent by the University to place women in managerial positions."

The month before, an outside consulting firm began evaluating and revising job classifications for professional and administrative employees across the whole university. In the end, the firm proposed 21 salary grades for 544 job categories. In September 1972, its review concluded that 13 percent of the staff—478 persons—earned less than they deserved and that women represented 70 percent of that group (their share of the workforce was 61 percent). The consultants estimated it would cost $322,000 to make up that salary discrepancy. Two years after the initial HEW findings, the consultants confirmed that women's average salaries were consistently lower than their male counterparts and that women tended to be clustered in the lower salary grades.

In February 1972, the same month HEW returned, Michigan finally announced it was making $94,295 worth of salary adjustments for 100 women on the academic side of the university (about $600,000 in 2020 dollars). The awards were made to 37 members of the teaching staff, 15 clerical staff members in academic departments, 25 non-academic staff members identified by the Personnel Office, and 23 out of the 424 cases that the Commission for Women had flagged for the Personnel Office to review.

Smith said, "We have something over 900 women with academic appointments and we wanted a rapid review, to correct any salaries deemed inequitable in the unit. The recommendations of the deans or department heads have now been put into effect, and notices to all affected personnel will be mailed as fast as we can process the forms." Smith said the individual adjustments ranged from about $300 to $4,000 a year.

Smith said Michigan would review the cases of women who complained to the commission before April 15 "without going through the full grievance procedure." Nordin publicized her phone number and pledged that complaints would be "reviewed quite promptly and with a considerable degree of confidentiality."

King naturally saw the salary adjustments as a major victory, even if it had taken more than a year to get them. As with all university salary matters, the adjustments were cloaked in secrecy and a list of the women who received them never released. But the word got around more informally. King later recalled that Libby Douvan's salary as a full professor was more than doubled. (In 1999, Douvan remembered she had been earning "probably $14,500 as a full professor, and my salary went up into the $30,000 somewhere.") Others King identified as possible beneficiaries were Marion Marzolf in the Journalism Department, Ann Larimore in Geography, Mary Alice Shulman and Helen Crafton in Economics, and Lorraine Nadelman in Psychology. (Marzolf and Larimore both confirmed they got salary adjustments during this time period but not necessarily as part of this particular review.)

In interviews 30 years later, Douvan recalled that "the idea that people were going to double our salaries, really, was both wonderful and absurd." But, "it was really remarkable. I went from being like a high-level teaching assistant to a full professor." Douvan said her old friend, History Professor Charles Trinkaus, used to ask her, "Well, Libby, did Allan Smith offer to give you the money for all those years you worked for half pay?" She said she replied, "Charles. . . let's be real."

Douvan said that as she neared her retirement in 1995, she and King would joke about filing a lawsuit because her pension benefits were going to be "half of what all my male colleagues" were going to earn.

King, she recalled, had said, "We could make something really interesting. . . ." Douvan imagined that "Every morning, I could get up, go down to the court, see what was happening. . . . We laughed a lot."

Larimore's salary was spotlighted when HEW flagged discrepancies in the salaries paid married couples in the same department. "I happened to be one of the people that they found evidence for," she recalled in 1986. "I was away on leave, out of the room so to speak, and when I came back from overseas my department chair looked at me and said, 'We put you in for tenure.' I didn't know at all what this meant because I had been away from the whole scene. . . . I began to realize that something strange was going on. I really had my consciousness raised at the time."

In submitting the papers to approve tenure for "Mrs. Kolars (or Dr. Larimore, as she sometimes prefers to be called)," Dean Sussman wrote in May 1971: "During her five years. . . it has become clear that her full time services are absolutely essential on a continuing basis, and that her tenured relationship with the University of Michigan is entirely appropriate and, by any reasonable standard, entirely justified. We are confident that the fact that Professor John Kolars, Ann's husband, holds an appointment in the Geography Department will create no problem so far as this tenured relationship is concerned. Both of the Kolarses are astute, knowledgeable, professional people, and the sensitivities which might develop have already been very carefully tested. . . ."

In her 1986 interview, Larimore recalled, "I can remember coming back to my department chairman and saying, 'I've never asked you for a raise, but now I'm asking for a raise because I don't think my salary is equitable. I understand that the rules have changed.' . . . I had played by the old rules. If there were going to be new rules, they would probably do better by me. During this period, I really got sensitized."

Marzolf recalled that she contacted the Commission for Women without telling her bosses, but said she never received a response. In May 1972, she did get a small raise, retroactive to February. "So we'll never know what motivated the pay raise," she said. Later that year, she successfully battled her department when a promised promotion did not come through after she had earned her doctorate. The wife of then-Department Chairman William Porter later confided to her that "Bill had been quite angry when he had to approve that raise."

Over in the Theater Department, Zelma Weisfeld remembered that around that time "they started pumping my salary up because it was so out of line. They had started me so low that even when I started getting increments, I just couldn't match the new people that were coming in. They were being brought in at higher salaries at assistant professor, and so they started pumping me up."

In his last interview on the topic, Fleming repeatedly asserted that "some of the best paid women professors. . . came to me, sometimes individually . . . and talked to me, saying that they wanted to make sure that anybody who got to be a full professor was a genuine full professor. They didn't want this to be the sort of thing in which just pressure was put on and so some people were promoted." He positioned himself as a man beset between two opposing camps of women.

Asked about Fleming's comments, Newell responded, "There were so few tenured women faculty in fields that were not ghettoized that I cannot remember any faculty women saying this to me." But she added that it was known she would not be sympathetic to that point of view.

Rose Vainstein in Library Science, who had felt the HEW investigator had asked her leading questions, later recalled: "I think sometimes the discriminatory cases had cause and other times they didn't. It's hard to differentiate and to know for certain whether or not a particular woman was being discriminated against because she was a woman or because there were substantive reasons about which we were not informed. I found myself being very cautious about always supporting everybody, *carte blanche*, who was saying 'I was being discriminated against.' But there's no doubt when you looked at the overall numbers that there were so few female appointments at the University that there was a hidden agenda from way back when, when appointments were made."

Meanwhile, as some women began receiving bigger paychecks, Davis and Clark were still fighting more public battles to get their salaries adjusted.

In January 1972, LSA's Executive Committee finally rendered its decision on Davis's complaint. According to the *Ann Arbor News* account, "Although the executive committee didn't reject her complaint, neither did it accept it. In effect, the committee said it couldn't make a final determination without knowing where the burden of proof rested. Members did agree that unequal pay for equal work had been paid. If the burden of proof rested with the University, the committee said, then Dr. Davis's claim for back wages should be upheld."

On February 24, the same week that 100 women got adjustments, Vice President Smith advised Davis that "a salary adjustment" would be made in her case. But he said, "We are not prepared to concede that the record established discrimination against you on the basis of sex." He added that "'the mistaken belief' that grant funds limited salary 'adversely affected' Dr. Davis's wage scale. 'It is clearly inconsistent with University practice to let grant funds determine salary.'" Davis told the reporter she expected that her adjustment would be in the range of $7,500.

Smith said that the back-pay requirement was not yet resolved because HEW had not yet accepted the university's affirmative action plan; that the commitment would be retroactive only if the same obligation was imposed on all other universities; and that there were "serious doubts" about HEW's power to enforce a back-pay obligation.

"They have, in fact, lost a case," Davis told the reporter. "It's clear that they will pay back wages in sex discrimination cases if women are willing to press hard enough." Davis said she decided to pursue her case as aggressively as she did "partly for the sake of women graduate students."

"The market is tight now," David added. "If the tenured faculty don't fight these battles, the younger women don't have a chance. Black faculty are very supportive of black students. But women faculty haven't taken this role. This sort of token regress on the part of the University is psychologically very important," she asserted. "It does do something for the status of women. Next time they hire a woman they'll be careful about setting the salary right. I've seen it already."

Similarly, even though Fleming agreed in July 1971 to let Clark continue to appeal her case during the one-year trial of the new grievance procedure, he would not concede that the initial decision had been wrong. "Long-standing practices of any university in the administration of its personnel provide payment of different salaries to persons with different academic degree levels although they are doing what the 'industrial world' would call 'the same job,'" he said. He noted that while a professor and an assistant professor might do the same work, it was well accepted that the full professor would get paid more.

Commission member Barbara Murphy, who, like Clark, worked as a researcher for a university institute, observed to the *Daily* that there was a difference in "relevant job criteria" between academic and non-academic workforces: "If a person has a dental degree and is working as a secretary, he should not get paid more for having that degree, but rather get paid as a secretary. If he were working as a dentist, however, then education [would] be important."

During the course of Clark's review, Michigan argued that the problem was not that Clark was paid too little but rather that her male colleague had been paid too much. In July 1972, the university finally agreed to give her a minimum increase of $1,320 annually, retroactive to the day her complaint was filed in January 1971. "This is a terrific step forward," said Nordin. "It indicates that if women persist in their complaints they will be vindicated."

Clark said she was "very pleased," but conceded that after 18 months, "It was almost anti-climactic. I thought we would lose." Lost amid all the jubilation was the fact that at the outset, the HEW regional office had stipulated that back pay should be awarded retroactive to October 1969, the effective date of the executive order.

On July 18, the day Clark's decision made the headlines, Lardent wrote Fauri, asking him for an update on the Clark and Davis complaints, and two more that were not as widely publicized, one from Anne Cowley in the Astronomy Department and the other from Joan Peters in Physical Education. The former two, he said, "have been resolved in favor of the grievants." A decision had not yet been reached in Cowley's case, and "thus far, Ms. Peters has not carried her case beyond the departmental level." At another point, the university acknowledged that when Peters filed her complaint, her department did not have a grievance procedure in place.

Cowley's story was a familiar one but with a particularly nasty twist. According to the "Findings of Fact," recited in the decision of her Grievance Committee, after she and her husband earned doctorates from the University of Michigan in 1963, they returned in 1967. Charles Cowley received a faculty appointment, and Anne got a job in the department as a research associate; both thought Anne would get a faculty post when funds became available.

In the fall of 1969, as the department prepared to consider granting tenure to Charles Cowley and two other assistant professors, some members pushed to adopt an anti-nepotism policy specifying that only one member of a family could serve in its professorial ranks. The policy, in effect, barred Cowley and a few other departmental spouses from advancement. It was published on February 27, 1970—six months before HEW arrived on campus and concluded that anti-nepotism policies led to sex discrimination.

That same fall, a former colleague of Anne Cowley's arrived as department chairman from the University of Chicago and tried to secure a faculty appointment for her. "However," according to the Findings of Fact in Cowley's grievance decision, "after talking with members of the Department, he learned there was not very much enthusiasm for her appointment and that he could not have obtained a majority vote in her favor." Some also felt that the department's next appointment should be in a different specialty.

The department began a search for a new professor, and in June 1971, Dean Sussman suggested they should consider Anne Cowley. The matter was discussed at the end of a long meeting, and Charles Cowley reminded his colleagues that the university had a new nepotism policy so their marriage should no longer be an issue. Charles then was excused from the meeting, and "several members of the faculty made remarks indicating they did not favor appointment of faculty wives. . . . There was no specific discussion of Complainant's qualifications." The vote was 9-1 against appointing her; six of the nine persons who opposed her appointment had served on the committee that had adopted the earlier policy on nepotism. When Cowley complained that she had not received a fair hearing, a second vote was scheduled for April 1972. Allmand reminded the department of the new nepotism policy, and more information was provided about Cowley's background and references. This time, the result of the secret ballot was 7-2 against her appointment, with two abstentions. When LSA's Executive Committee supported the department's decision, Cowley pursued two lines of complaint, one regarding her appointment, the other regarding her salary, citing the commitments the university had made to HEW. It would take yet another year for the grievance procedure to run its course.

It was hard for a woman to determine if she was the victim of sex discrimination when she didn't know what her male colleagues earned. The same month that Clark achieved her victory, the Michigan Regents voted, 6-2, to reject a request from the *Daily* to release all staff salaries, along with corresponding names, sex, race, length of service, and title. The Regents did, however, agree to release a previously confidential booklet that reviewed aggregate data on the salaries of the teaching staff.

In May, another policy change was instituted when Smith told deans, directors, and department chairmen that they would have to begin advertising to fill traditional faculty positions. "The excellence of the University as a whole depends in large part upon the excellence of its faculty," he wrote. "The recruitment of faculty should therefore have as its goal the employment of the best available talent." In the future, he said, units would be required to demonstrate that openings were advertised in professional journals, give the central administration two months' notice before hiring someone, and retain for three years a list of the names and résumés of candidates who were considered. A few weeks later, the university began requiring that non-academic openings be posted, too.

In 1986, Mills said she believed that changing the job posting rules was "the shining accomplishment of the total women's movement on this campus." She recalled that when the commission began its work, "it was illegal to go out and interview for another job in some other unit if you didn't tell your boss first." It took "two or three years of constant effort" to get the policy changed because "every possible obstacle [was] thrown up."

Mills and others noted that the commission achieved its greatest successes when it sought changes that affected large numbers of university employees. But the commission also looked for ways to educate more men and women on campus. It created a bi-weekly newsletter called the "WIN (Women's Information Network) Bulletin"; began producing a regular show on women's issues for WUOM Radio, U-M's radio station; and created a slide presentation called "Turn-About" that depicted a reversal of traditional workplace roles for men and women.

Women faculty members were also discovering new fields to study. By January 1972, CCEW could compile a list of eight course offerings that explored subjects through the eyes of women, and nine more that partially addressed a woman's perspective. The following year, many of the same scholars succeeded in pushing through a proposal to create a Women's Studies Department within LSA.

PROBE also looked for creative ways to highlight the problems that women continued to face on campus. In April 1972, a sub-group, calling itself the Ad Hoc Committee Concerned that President Fleming Does Not Meet with Enough Women, organized what it called "The Fleming Follow," during which the women sat outside Fleming's office for a week, compiling details of who actually got to see him. They found that of 145 visitors, only 21 were women, and all but one of them—Virginia Nordin, who had a weekly meeting—were part of a group. Fleming, for his part, subsequently met with the members several times to discuss their concerns. In thanking him, coordinator Jeanne Tashian said the discussions "have been generally worthwhile, somewhat productive, basically non-adversarial, in fact friendly."

In May, Richardson came to Ann Arbor to speak at a fundraising lunch honoring Rep. Esch. King and other activists were always concerned that they did not have the same access to the secretary that college presidents did. (They did not know that Esch had also lobbied Richardson at Fleming's behest.)

A briefing document that Esch's staff prepared for Richardson said, "As you are undoubtedly aware, this event is being held to establish the credibility of Marvin Esch, particularly within the higher education community. . . . Primarily, our intent is to open up entrees to the university community as well as the business community through this select group for later follow-up." Vice President Norman was one of four persons on the organizing committee; Fleming and Eastern Michigan President Harold Sponberg were listed among a handful of "special people" that Richardson should look for at the event.

The FBI alerted Richardson that there would be an anti-war demonstration outside of the Ramada Inn in downtown Ann Arbor, and a couple dozen protestors did show up. The demonstration was first on a list of "highlights" prepared as background for the secretary, followed by the Ann Arbor City Council's recent moves to liberalize the city's marijuana laws. The list then noted: "A sex discrimination case has been pending for over two years. The University has responded positively and is currently expanding its affirmative action program at the request of the Regional Office." Finally, the summary noted that Michigan was one of the "largest grant-receiving institutions in the country," so large, in fact, that the regional office maintained three full-time resident auditors there.

King and a few of her friends hatched a plot to actually attend the luncheon and bring their cause to Richardson's attention. They pooled their resources to raise the $25 they needed for a ticket and then crafted a floral display—93 dandelions and seven tulips—arranged between the strings of a tennis racket fashioned to look like a gyno, the feminine symbol. The arrangement was intended to show the relative proportion of men and women tenured faculty members at Michigan.

King recalled that she enlisted "our daintiest, slightly built activist" to deliver the flowers to Richardson. "She was very non-threatening looking; that's why we chose her," King said. A news story said the woman was a U-M secretary, using the assumed name "Martha Harris."

The flowers were accompanied by a poem, "Elliott [sic] See!!" set to the meter of Edgar Allan Poe's "Annabel Lee." The final verse read:

> But our cause it is stronger by far than the one
> Of those better off than we—
> And neither the angels in heaven above
> Nor the demons down under the sea,
> Can ever dissever us from HEW
> And beautiful OFCC.
> . . . IF YOU DON'T LET THEM!!

After the woman urged Richardson to take up the issues of back pay and graduate admissions, he accepted the bouquet and said, "Of course, as you know, the University of Michigan was one of the first to come under fire from us, and we are closely watching the situation." His prepared speech praised Esch but made no mention of the complaint.

But behind the scenes, HEW's lower-level officials were still nagging Michigan. On October 27, 1972, Kenneth R. Mines, the new regional civil rights director, wrote Fleming that the university had failed once again to meet its commitments for improving its complaint procedures, pointing to problems with discovery, due process, and the time it took to resolve a complaint. He cited the experiences of Davis, Clark, and Peters of the Physical Education Department. This time, Fleming lost his characteristic cool. In the exchange of letters, which were kept in-house, he replied to Mines:

> Before your letter arrived, we were encouraged to think that a new era might be at hand in HEW-University relations. Your guidelines had finally been issued, and our people felt that they had been engaged in meaningful exchanges with your people over the course of the past year.
>
> As the result of your letter, I must tell you that there is now only profound discouragement that our relations are ever going to improve. We are aware that there are deficiencies in our program. We are making strenuous efforts to correct them. We thought we had made some progress in gaining understanding among your people that in universities, unlike industries, there is an immense amount of democratic input which goes into any decision and that this necessarily slows our progress.
>
> We had hoped. . . that we might in the future expect to get a letter from you which would say: "These are our tentative findings. There may have been developments since we reviewed your program, or we may not fully understand some of the materials which we have. . . ."
>
> Instead, from our standpoint, we are lectured about due process without this concept being seen as a two-way street and we are faced once again with a blunt ultimatum: "In order to comply. . . the University must amend these procedures so as to eliminate the deficiencies noted above within 30 days of the receipt of this letter."
>
> I would be less than frank if I did not tell you that we resent this kind of treatment. We have spent thousands of work-hours and dollars in trying to comply in good faith with HEW directives. We have done this at a time when you must know that universities all over the country are in serious financial difficulties. Whether or not you agree with our positions, they are neither frivolous nor capricious. We deserve more than abrupt "findings" and ultimata.

Fleming said that both the Commission for Women and LSA were working on improvements to the grievance procedures, but he did not know whether either would be completed within 30 days. "I would suppose it would be to your advantage to let us proceed without receiving orders from elsewhere," he noted. Four weeks later, Fleming followed that letter up with a more detailed response. He concluded, "Though we received no reply to my letter of November 3, we remain willing to discuss these matters with you."

By then, the Michigan women were widely credited as the most successful of those who had filed complaints across the country. Women at other colleges in the state were also seeking more direct help from King. On November 24, 1972, *Science* ran the first of two stories about sex discrimination at Michigan colleges. Under the headline, "Women in Michigan: Academic Sexism Under Siege," the story focused on what women were doing at the state's three major public universities but made clear which college had assumed the lead:

> Universities have been so busy worrying about undoing racial discrimination that they have not, until recently, concentrated on discrimination affecting women. All that began to change in 1970. . . . Michigan, whose star school, UM, was subsequently threatened with a hold on federal contracts, has turned into one of the busiest forums in the nation for women seeking to eradicate sex bias in higher education.
>
> Since then, with UM blazing the trail and threats of the federal ax curbing administrative complacency, affirmative action plans, women's commissions, contract compliance committees, salary studies, and organizational reshufflings have been cropping up around the state.
>
> Women in academe are divided over whether any significant changes are occurring. But most seem to agree that Michigan women are better organized and more politically savvy than their sisters in neighboring states and more united in their goals and strategies than women in other big universities, where fragmentation within academic departments tends to thwart their thrust.

Meanwhile, a *TIME* magazine article, "Battle of Ann Arbor," summarized the progress the women had achieved over the past three years: a women's commission had been established, a file review had led to raises for more than 100 women, a management consulting firm had found extensive discrimination, and new grievance and job posting procedures had been put in place. "Trouble is, say the women of U. of M., even those innovations are often sidestepped by a recalcitrant administration," the *TIME* writer noted.

The writer continued: "The biggest stumbling block, the women contend, is the sometimes unconscious discrimination evident in male attitudes."

At the turn of the year, those attitudes were on display in the *University Record*. In a letter to the editor, James Crump Jr., who taught alongside Harriet Mills in the Department of Far Eastern Languages and Literature, offered up a poem:

> *I think that I prefer to see*
> *A chairperson who is womanly*
> *And if the choice were up to me*
> *A freshperson who's a comely she.*

A woman decided to respond. She was Meryl Johnson, identified as a research curator at U-M's Kelsey Museum. Johnson was one of those under-appreciated women, toiling away in a non-teaching job. A few years earlier, she and Chemistry Professor Adon A. Gordus had won a grant to explore using radiation to study pigments as a way of establishing the origin, date, and authenticity of paintings.

The *University Record* and *TIME* did not explain why she might have been angry, but the first part of the *Science* series did: "Johnson, a chemist and art historian, recently produced a paper on Italian Renaissance paint which drew considerable attention in scholarly circles. When the news got around, she says, her boss 'went around for a week saying there were two Meryl Johnsons in the department'—one a woman, one the man who had made the scholarly coup. Johnson believes her appointment was rubber-stamped because of the ambiguous nature of her first name."

Her response to Crump:

> *Indeed we share*
> *Your appetite for golden hair*
> *And shapely figures slim and trim*
> *And do admire a comely him,*
> *But keep our minds upon our work*
> *And tolerate each shapeless jerk*
> *Outranking us in pay and powers*
> *Who would demand we all be flowers.*

16
The Turning Point

In March 1973, the director of HEW's Chicago civil rights office told Michigan that its amended affirmative action plan was still "deficient." The agency required "a detailed response to these findings, including specific actions to be taken and timetables for implementing each commitment." The cycle continued: a new deadline, more deficiencies, another visit, and another round of letters from King to members of Congress, this time to the growing number of women members from other states.

Four months later, U-M sent HEW a 500-page report, with hiring goals now detailed out to 1976. By now the report's compilation was under the direction of Nellie Varner, who had been appointed affirmative action director the year before. Private federal contractors were now required to have a point person for affirmative action, but it made sense for the university to have one too.

But the review of the past few years—made public later in October—still showed that little progress had been made. The time period reflected in the study, Varner said, "had an employment pattern which selected males almost exclusively." But she said she was optimistic that the university would eventually comply because "if people are bombarded with something long enough, they begin to change their behavior."

Asked how long he thought it would take, Allan Smith told a reporter, "We're going to be in this business for a long time. . . . How long does it take to change human nature?"

As the months went by, political tides shifted and the federal government retreated from the more aggressive role it had once played in addressing discrimination. While some longtime civil servants challenged the universities' practices, their priorities—and budgets—were ultimately set by the political superiors to whom they reported.

In January 1975, the U.S. Commission on Civil Rights assessed the sorry state of discrimination in education, finding much to criticize about HEW's enforcement of the executive order and the universities' level of cooperation. It reviewed the compliance files of four universities, including Michigan, and found "a pattern of inadequate compliance reviews, inordinate delays and unexcusable failures to take enforcement action where there were clear violations of the Executive order regulations."

HEW's investigation of Michigan, it recounted, had found "extreme underutilization of women in academic positions due to discriminatory hiring practices, salary inequities between women and men, and severe sex segregation in nonacademic jobs." It detailed four years' worth of back-and-forth arguments before noting that "as of September 1974, OCR had not issued a letter of findings approving or disapproving [Michigan's affirmative action] plan."

The report's detailed review of three other universities found similar delays:

- Nearly four years after HEW had first tried to conduct a compliance review at Harvard, it finally accepted that university's revised affirmative action plan, but with 13 qualifications. In November 1973, the Office of Civil Rights said the plan was still lacking "a review of salaries for inequities; an identification of selection standards; and an analysis of promotions, new hires, tenure acquisitions, and terminations for each category of employees," in the words of the Civil Rights Commission's report.
- Although a sex discrimination complaint was filed against the University of Washington in August 1969, the Office of Civil Rights' initial compliance review did not include sex discrimination. After four years of negotiations over the university's affirmative action plan, the regional civil rights officials in Seattle recommended that a show-cause order be issued against the university, threatening to

withhold its contracts. That order was not issued, but the office's headquarters officials said the university's plan was still deficient. In late 1974, a conciliation agreement was finally worked out, but the Civil Rights Commission said it still suffered from "fundamental deficiencies of vague language and noncompliance with OFCC regulations."

- At Berkeley, where WEAL had first filed a complaint in June 1970, HEW did not issue its findings of discrimination against both women and minorities until November 1972. Berkeley's contracts were not threatened until November 1973, and it subsequently reached a conciliation agreement with HEW in March 1974. But again, the Civil Rights Commission flagged numerous ways in which it said the agreement failed to meet current guidelines and regulations. "Particularly outrageous," it said, was that the plan included no commitment to "identify affected class members or to develop appropriate class relief."

But the Civil Rights Commission's report also had tough words for HEW. "The present slow, halting and ineffective approach to implementing the constitutional rights of women and minorities for equal employment opportunities in the field of higher education is due in no small part to HEW's failure to take action," the report said. The commission found that although 60 percent of the resources of HEW's Higher Education Division had been devoted to its contract compliance program, it had approved affirmative action plans for only 20 colleges, or 2.2 percent of the total. In fiscal 1974, it had conducted onsite compliance reviews at only 60 colleges, or 6 percent of the number for which it was responsible. (At that rate, the commission concluded, a campus was likely to be subject to a complete review only once every 17 years.) As of August 1974, only 13 campuses had been found in compliance; 201 were awaiting action. In addition, more than 700 campuses had not submitted plans.

In footnotes, colleges whose affirmative action plans were approved in fiscal 1973 were listed as Oklahoma Liberal Arts College, the University of Texas-El Paso, Central Seattle Community College, Idaho State University, North Seattle Community College, Oregon State University,

Portland State University, and South Seattle Community College. But most of those plans had been accepted on an "interim" basis because the regulations had since changed.

In addition to Harvard and Washington, campuses whose plans were approved in fiscal 1974 (which then ended in June 1974) were listed as MIT, Einstein College of Medicine, Florida State University, John Carroll University in Ohio, East Texas State University, McNeese State University in Louisiana, Southern Methodist University, University of Texas-Austin, and the University of Oregon. The University of Pennyslvania's plan was approved in July 1974.

In fiscal 1974, HEW rejected plans submitted by the New York University Medical School, Queens College, Brooklyn College, Louisiana Technical University, North Texas State University, Northeast Louisiana University, Oklahoma State University, Oklahoma University, Rice University, Southeast Louisiana University, Texas Christian University, the University of Arkansas, the University of Oklahoma's Health Sciences Center, and Western New Mexico University.

Ironically, the critical report was issued by a civil rights commission now chaired by Arthur Flemming, who had led the delegation of college leaders who had met regularly with Richardson about their issues of concern.

At the start of 1973, Richardson was named secretary of defense while Pottinger was nominated to be assistant attorney general for civil rights. (A few months later, as the Watergate investigations unfolded, Richardson became Pottinger's boss again when he was named attorney general; he resigned in October 1973 after Nixon ordered him to fire the Watergate special prosecutor.)

Pottinger stayed on, and in August 1974, U-M alumnus Gerald R. Ford became president when Nixon suddenly resigned. Fleming immediately reached out to the new president, writing, "You know, I am sure, that there has been an almost complete estrangement between the higher education community and the administration during the last several years." Fleming expressed the hope that "there might be at least a symbolic opportunity to arrange a brief meeting which would indicate that your refreshing attitude toward all major groups in our society extends also to higher education."

A few weeks later White House aide Geoff Shepard sent Ford a memo. The subject line of the draft version read "Robben Flemming [sic]—Stan Pottinger." Shepherd wrote:

In light of your brief comments on this subject last Friday, I thought that you would be interested in a short conversation I had with Stan Pottinger.

Stan has had no dealings with the University of Michigan since leaving HEW in January 1973, so he believes that Mr. Flemming's criticisms probably referred to an investigation by the HEW regional office (Chicago) done about three years ago. He said that like other university presidents, Mr. Flemming was concerned about government intrusion on campus generally, but was also upset about several HEW positions taken specifically with regard to the University of Michigan. Stan said that as he learned of these positions, he agreed that Mr. Flemming's concerns were justified, and took action accordingly. (In fact, although Mr. Flemming probably does not know it, Stan removed the Chicago regional civil rights director from his job because of unreasonable positions taken at the University, as indicated by Mr. Flemming.)

During Stan's tenure at HEW no contracts to the University were terminated or suspended, and he knows of no further problems which have arisen there in the last few years.

With regard to the matter of government-enforced affirmative action at universities generally, Stan has begun the process of preparing new policy options for the Administration.

It is not clear whether Pottinger was referring to Minton, who *was* removed in 1970, or Hodgdon, whose positions Fleming was more likely to have found "unreasonable." It appears that sometime after August 1972, Hodgdon was transferred to HEW headquarters to become acting director of OCR's Higher Education Division. Pottinger may have been referring to investigator Don Scott, whose interaction with Fleming appeared to end after the December 1970 agreement was worked out.

Late in his tenure at HEW, Pottinger asked a public affairs official to produce "a comprehensive list of all women's movement publications," particularly those circulating on college campuses. He said he wanted to explain "our position on some of those issues that keep coming up with women's groups, and solicit their cooperation in communicating with this office before drawing conclusions about our enforcement efforts." The names that were returned included Gloria Steinem, editor of *Ms.* magazine.

"When Pottinger joined the Justice Department he discovered to his astonishment that Justice, unlike HEW, didn't even know there was a 'women's problem,'" Carolyn G. Heilbrun wrote in her biography of Steinem. "So he decided to create a task force in an attempt to change the government's attitude toward women. The first person he thought of was Steinem, whom he had never met, and he called her." In November 1974, he set up a meeting in New York. Afterwards, he drove her to a speaking engagement in Hartford, Connecticut, and a few months later, they began dating. Pottinger was then 34 and newly divorced, and Steinem was 40. Their relationship eventually blossomed into a longtime affair. Pottinger was back in the news in 2019 when he represented women who had accused financier Jeffrey Epstein of sex trafficking.

Esther Lardent recalled that Pottinger "was really quite progressive." But she quickly grew disillusioned over HEW's enforcement efforts and decided to leave the agency. Referring to her colleagues' ability to hold up contracts at Michigan, she said, ". . . You had this amazing power. I mean there was this fabulous remedy, except of course, when we went to go ahead and try to do this, and by this time, you know, I mean it was Richard Nixon's administration that was in. . . . As you can imagine, what happened was this complaint winded its way through what was then HEW—we were overturned. So, it was like having an atom bomb, but you couldn't drop it, and at that point, I decided that I need[ed] to get out."

Reviewing the totality of the Nixon administration's efforts to address sex discrimination, historian Dean J. Kotlowski wrote, "[O]n women's rights, the president and his aides were too steeped in traditional roles to offer anything beyond halfhearted leadership. The result was more action on women's rights than in previous administrations, but also a series of stops and starts on the path to gender equality."

In 1999, near the end of the Clinton administration, Douvan recalled of those earlier years:

> [T]hat was an exciting time and I think was critical in bringing about some of the changes. Now in subsequent administrations in Washington, I think that the [Equal Employment Opportunity Commission] has been so watered down that I'm not sure they would have held up the contracts today. I mean, I just think there's been. . . I guess today they would, but certainly during the Nixon. . . the Reagan era, I think they would have said, "Well, that's just the way it is." By that time, their budget had been cut and they didn't have that many investigators. And I think that was a critical moment in history to bring a suit which would then really bring about some changes. So it was a luck issue partly, a luck of timing.

The 1970s ushered in a period of financial austerity for the University of Michigan that impacted its affirmative action efforts. Larimore recalled that there was a time when the Commission for Women and its committees were supported by multiple staff persons. But "after '75, things began to be cut back. The whole campus went through an era of shutdown. This happened to the minority groups as well. . . . And so the Commission for Women was scaled back and the director was half-time. . . . That is a classic way of shutting initiatives down that you don't want to continue. It's always said that 'there's no money.' But my experience over more than 30 years at this University is that when the University wants to find money, it can."

Still by 1973, the genie was out of the bottle. Two years after her hearings on sex discrimination in higher education, Edith Green guided passage of two laws that were designed to give campus women the civil rights protections they didn't have. In June 1972, Congress amended the Equal Pay Act of 1963 to include executive, administrative, and professional employees. It also passed what became known as "Title IX," a section of the Education Act Amendments of 1972 that prohibited sex discrimination in educational institutions that received federal funding. Once private universities successfully lobbied for language to exempt their gender-based admission quotas, opposition to the bill evaporated. Green shrewdly advised women activists to keep a low profile, and the bill passed—before officials in higher education fully realized the impact that ground-breaking legislation would have.

In 1986, Rose Vainstein told an interviewer: ". . . I have a feeling that if it were not for national legislation forcing affirmative action, forcing equity in whatever way, that if it were not the national kind of pressure plus the fact that there's a little group here kind of pushing, I don't think the [University] administration would on its own ever [have] moved to be concerned about the place of women in academia."

Sue Rasmussen, who later became Michigan's associate director of affirmative action, observed in 2001 that the way the HEW complaint evolved at Michigan demonstrated the effectiveness of what she described as "the three-legged stool": a government agency that gave credence to the women's complaints of discrimination, a moderate group that could implement social change, and what she called "the mob in the courtyard" demanding change. "Whatever they're yelling," she concluded, "tends to make whatever the bureaucrats and the middle are saying look very reasonable."

Over the years, the barriers slowly began to fall at Michigan, and more and more women saw "the first" become part of their institutional descriptors. In 1971, Ann Larimore became the first woman elected to a full term on the governing board of the Rackham Graduate School. Under Dean Donald Stokes, Larimore, Mills, Davis, Gamson, and others produced a major study, *The Higher, the Fewer*, that documented women students' narrowing job opportunities after they earned their advanced degrees. The bulk of the research was done by Martha Hinman, then working as a research associate for Rackham. Larimore recalled that she was a faculty wife with a PhD in German, who was frustrated in her own attempts to get an academic appointment.

In 1974, Carolyne Davis, dean of the School of Nursing, was appointed associate vice president for academic affairs. But it was not until 1985 that Linda Wilson was named vice president for research; after Newell stepped down from the post she had held on an acting basis, it took Michigan 15 years to appoint another woman vice president.

Michigan was also forced to begin disclosing salary information. In October 1979, a few years after the *Daily* filed its lawsuit, and nearly a decade after Davis and Clark used other means to find out what their male colleagues earned, the Michigan Legislature amended the state's

Freedom of Information Act to require state-supported colleges to disclose individual salaries. The university finally abandoned its opposition and began reporting salaries two months later.

But all the progress was not without pain. In what came to be known as "the Cobb Affair," in January 1975 the Regents approved the appointment of Connecticut College Dean Jewell Plummer Cobb, an African-American cell biologist, as dean of LSA. But she was offered a two-year contract instead of the standard five, and the Zoology Department declined to grant her tenure, arguing that she did not meet their standards of scholarship. As a result, Cobb twice turned down the offer. Fleming and Frank Rhodes, then vice president for academic affairs, instead supported the appointment of Acting Dean Billy Frye, who, to complicate the situation, was a tenured zoology professor. The *Daily's* reporting on the Regents' deliberations fueled campus tensions over how Cobb was treated and whether the "old boy's network" was still alive and well. The *Daily* later described the episode as "one of the most embittering and embarrassing disputes in the University's administrative history." A review committee studied what had gone wrong and recommended changes for the future. A new search committee was appointed, and in February 1976, Frye was chosen from a list of 10 finalists.

Cobb's treatment sparked angry protests from many corners of the campus, particularly among women and minorities. The Chicago regional office again said it wanted to investigate and briefly threatened to hold up another half-million-dollar contract. But this time, it was quickly overruled by headquarters. In 1981, Cobb went on to become president of California State University at Fullerton.

The unity that Commission for Women members recalled fondly from their early days also dissipated over time. Eventually a separate Academic Women's Caucus was formed, because, as Larimore remembered, "our employment conditions are so different. There was just not a communality there. There had been a really idealist idea at the beginning that clericals, service workers, professional staff and faculty would all be willing to work on all the problems together, and that every group would have representatives of each group. There was that kind of idealism, egalitarian idealism at the beginning. That just did not work. People put a lot of effort into problems that they had a vested interest in."

From her vantage point, Sandler later observed: "The entire WEAL campaign had cost a few hundred dollars in postage, but hours and hours of time from women in academe who patiently and painstakingly gathered and analyzed data about men and women in their institution, who pressed their representatives and senators for action, organized together and became advocates for change. They are the true unsung heroes of this story. They took enormous risks. Many did not have tenure and as a result of their activities never received it and were lost to the higher educational community. Some became lawyers or found other successful careers. A few went on welfare."

And at Michigan, a few academic superstars moved on in frustration.

Helen Hornbeck Tanner gave up trying to break into the Michigan History Department. But when she died in 2011 at the age of 96, she was remembered as "a major figure in the scholarship often labeled as 'new Indian history.'" Brenda J. Child of the University of Minnesota wrote in the American Historical Association's newsletter: "Her ideas were not always taken seriously by her male contemporaries who had employment and status as historians and anthropologists. . . . Her own experience as a woman in higher education did not cause her to be bitter or to complain, but it may have contributed to her true genius, which was empathy." Working as a research associate at the Newberry Library in Chicago, Tanner received a National Endowment for the Humanities grant to direct a five-year project that resulted in the *Atlas of Great Lakes Indian History*. She became an expert witness and scholar in helping Great Lakes tribes successfully pursue land claims before the Indian Claims Commission and the U.S. Supreme Court. Along with Jean King, Jean Campbell, and a number of women who lived and worked in Ann Arbor in the 1970s, she was later inducted into the Michigan Women's Hall of Fame.

In October 1973, Anne Cowley's complaint was again remanded to her department. The three-man Complaint Appeals Committee who reviewed her case wrote that she was "a highly competent and experienced astronomer who has earned national and international recognition for her basic research in stellar spectroscopy. . . . In all her relations with the University, it has never been suggested that she was denied her desired appointment because of a lack of professional competence or because other persons more competent in her field of specialty were desired." But submitted transcripts reported that some members of the department had voted against her because "they felt that the department should be moving in the direction of different specialties, because they believed Complainant did not have a strong interest in undergraduate teaching, and because they felt her personality was abrasive and her presence in the Department was divisive, or some combination of these reasons." The latter reason was a chilling echo of the kind of comments that had launched Sandler on her mission, four years before.

But the committee sent the matter back to the department, and in November 1973, it again voted against her appointment, and Fleming ratified the decision, noting that the decision of the Complaint Appeals Committee was unanimous, and the departmental vote, overwhelming.

Cowley then decided to pursue her salary complaint. But when Law Professor Joseph Sax was asked whether he would be willing to serve on the complaint committee again, he wrote Fleming on January 31, 1974, to share "my very great disillusionment" on how the case was handled after his committee considered Cowley's promotion complaint:

> After a number of days of extended testimony, it seemed quite clear that Dr. Cowley had been badly dealt with by the Department. . . . I was also persuaded, beyond doubt, that the general atmosphere in the Department had become quite hostile toward her. Challengers of authority are, of course, rarely viewed with affection. I was most sympathetic to Mrs. Cowley's concern that returning her to the Department for further action would be an exercise in futility.
>
> At the same time, I think we all felt the difficulty—in terms of departmental and collegiate self-governance—that would be raised were we to say unequivocally that Mrs. Cowley should be given a professorial appointment.

Sax said the committee had looked for an "intermediate remedy" but could not find one. Nevertheless, it had hoped that the "enlightened administrative officers of the University would put it to the Astronomy Department that they really must come at this matter afresh," that they must "put aside previous feelings," and that a financial inducement might be found to encourage the department to find an appointment for Cowley, "taking into consideration the harm done to the University generally when a hearing had shown even some evidence of sex discrimination infecting a previous faculty appointment process."

Sax concluded that he felt he had been "misused," that the process amounted to "a waste of time," and most importantly, that "Mrs. Cowley has not received justice." He declined to participate on the second committee.

Nine years later, Cowley was part of an international research team that discovered what was only the second "black hole" known to astronomers—and the first outside the Milky Way galaxy. The discovery was heralded for confirming that many black holes existed in space.

Cowley took a sabbatical at Arizona State University (ASU), and in February, 1984, she told the *Daily*, "I think the situation at the University of Michigan is scandalous. There are so few women in the sciences I can count them on two hands." Cowley said that attempts to increase the number of women faculty members were "like beating your head against the wall because the administration doesn't care."

The *Daily* continued:

> Despite the University's explanation that fierce competition for top women professors keeps the number low, Cowley says, the claim masks a lack of commitment. "ASU is a place where things are improving a lot. A place like Michigan is living on its reputation," she says.
>
> Most women I've talked to say they'd think very hard before coming to the University of Michigan. The image outside U of M is that [the University is] resistant to change in this area.

When ASU offered Cowley a professorship, the Michigan Astronomy Department was finally willing to do the same. But Cowley decided to leave. This time she made Michigan wait, refusing to tell them when she planned to return until they forced her to. She spent the rest of her career at ASU.

Shortly after Cowley's departure, Mills told an interviewer that "we were working on [her case] for years and years and nothing happened until she finds a black hole and the University falls all over itself and she's gone off and gotten herself another job and hasn't told them she's not coming back, which I think is absolutely delicious. She's going to let them stew for the maximum of two years. They wouldn't do a thin[g] about getting her a proper appointment."

Over in the Zoology Department, Lowenthal hung on until 1983, when she retired, after 26 years of teaching, as an associate professor, the rank she had held for nearly two decades. The Regents proclamation heralded her teaching skills and her work as a counselor and developer of programs for undergraduates majoring in zoology. She was praised for "consistently demonstrating a warm interest in the students and a concern for their educational progress" and for being "a fluent and forceful interpreter of college and department standards and ideals." Still, the proclamation, in an unnecessary dig, seemed to betray how she was viewed by her male colleagues: "While Professor Lowenthal never developed an independent research program on her own. . . ."

In 1971, a month after Margaret Davis won her fight for back pay but not the acknowledgement she sought that she had been a victim of sex discrimination, she was one of seven women among the 79 names LSA Associate Dean Carruth suggested for appointment to central administrative committees. He described her as "a well-known researcher who is regularly supported by NSF [National Science Foundation]. A leader in the Women's Movement."

But Davis was still angry, and now that she was divorced, it was easier to pursue other options. In 1972, she left to join the Biology Department at Yale. Yale awarded her an honorary master's degree the following year. But, a colleague recalled, she was not happy there, and in 1976, she accepted an offer to become chairman of the Department of Ecology, Evolution and Behavior at the University of Minnesota. She remained there for the rest of her career.

In 1982, she became the first woman to be elected to the National Academy of Sciences from that university. She also served as president of the American Quaternary Association from 1978 to 1980 and president of the Ecological Society of America from 1987 to 1988.

In 2018, Professor Deborah E. Goldberg of Michigan's Ecology and Evolutionary Biology Department was recognized with a Distinguished University Professorship. The professorships are typically named after a "U-M scholar of distinction in the awardee's general research area" and

Goldberg asked that hers be named after Davis, more than four decades after Davis had left Ann Arbor. In addition to being "an amazing scientist," Goldberg said Davis had been "a personal hero of mine because of her refusal to tolerate unfairness," pointing to her fight against sex discrimination.

Ten years after Davis's departure, a sadder-but-wiser Mills reflected on what she had learned after her years on the Commission for Women. She acknowledged that she had gotten "very cynical" about salary surveys "and that kind of stuff." Instead, she said, "I would work on an embarrassment case." If you had a "[Margaret] Davis case that you could get into the papers and do shamelessly," she said, "I would work on that. I think it would have much more use than anything trying to work through the University."

Jean King kept a hand in the fights for gender equality at Michigan. She branched out beyond Ann Arbor, supporting a group called the Flint Feminists at the university's Flint campus. In late 1972, they challenged a decision to restrict a "Pontiac Honor Camp Seminar" (Sociology 299) to men. The class was described as "a sociological perspective on selected social problems such as poverty, race, alienation and mass society, and their relationship to the Criminal Justice System. The development of basic sociological concepts as a means of analyzing social problems" was to be stressed.

In August 1975, she tartly responded to a solicitation directed to Law School alumni: "As soon as the University of Michigan Law School has women professors in reasonable proportion to the number of women law students enrolled, I will be glad to begin contributing to the Fund." Then she added, "Also by that time I might be making money." A review of King's law school class noted that in the five years since she had graduated, the number of women in the entering Class of 1973 had grown to 41, or 9 percent of the total.

In 1985 she filed a complaint on behalf of the Washtenaw County chapter of the American Civil Liberties Union when it was discovered that Michigan's relatively new women cheerleaders were not included when the squad was sent to away games. With the passage of Title IX, King became one of the go-to lawyers for women challenging the barriers they encountered in school and college sports.

In 1978, Mary Pollock, MSU's Title IX coordinator, brought her school's women's basketball team to King's home in Ann Arbor to share their stories of how their team's support lagged behind what the men's team received. Pollock was subsequently fired. King eventually filed a class action lawsuit on the team's behalf, and in 1985, MSU finally agreed to settle. A particularly satisfying twist was that the lawsuit's lead plaintiff, team member Carol Hutchins, was hired by Michigan as the women's softball coach and went on to become the coach with the most victories—man or woman—in U-M athletic history.

But at times, King may have taken on too many causes. Cowley hired her as her attorney to pursue her complaint, but, according to the record of the case, she discharged King in May 1973 after King missed a deadline for filing a brief and failed to seek an extension.

The HEW complaint also inspired other forms of activism on the part of campus women. Marcia Federbush, the faculty wife who wrote an angry letter to Fleming, soon began to challenge sex discrimination in the Ann Arbor public schools and, in 1973, filed a lawsuit over U-M's athletic programs, invoking the new Title IX requirements. Federbush also was later inducted into the Michigan Women's Hall of Fame.

Mary Maples Dunn, the Bryn Mawr history professor who wrote Fleming in the summer of 1970, trying to help him understand the discontent that was brewing on his campus, returned to the world of women's colleges. In 1985, she became president of Smith College and later served as acting president of Radcliffe during the time it merged with Harvard.

Jean King had a competitive streak, and she did not shy away from public recognition. When Robben Fleming published his memoir in 1996, she was infuriated that he made no mention of her complaint and the subsequent HEW investigation. In a 2001 interview, she attributed this to the fact that Fleming "got beaten! On his own territory! He was a labor negotiator, and he was up against somebody that he couldn't negotiate with. . . . What is he supposed to say? . . . He still to this day regards us as very unfair."

There was no love lost between Fleming and King. In a 1999 *Detroit Free Press* profile of King, timed to coincide with Women's History Month, the reporter said Fleming "has criticized King's style, calling it 'not the way to get things done.'" The paper cited a 1996 interview in which Fleming said he "was not trying to resist the federal department's efforts, but thought an internal commission was the best way to deal with the charges."

Sandler said she did not know Fleming personally but believed he was typical of college presidents at the time. Fleming, she observed late in her life, "could have turned it into a public relations advantage. . . there are things he could have taken credit for," such as his role in creating the women's commission. But "it was just not that important to him." Like many men, his attitude was "these are like gnats bothering me." He saw it as "a bunch of women making him and the University uncomfortable."

But women faculty members who remained in Ann Arbor respected Fleming for the way that he managed Michigan during a turbulent time. Larimore observed, "I've often thought that we were very fortunate on this campus to have President Fleming at the helm at that time."

Douvan and others agreed. But Douvan also liked to tell a story about a meeting she had with Fleming and a small group of women that included Varner, Gamson, and Sarah Power, then working for the Commission for Women; Power and Varner later became regents. Fleming, Douvan said, was about to appoint then-LSA Dean Frank Rhodes as vice president for academic affairs "and the women on campus were not wild about that idea." She continued:

So we all met with Mr. Fleming to say, "Please be careful who you appoint." And he must have been living under a lot of strain at that point, and he got very annoyed with us and was really, I would say, edging on rude. He said, "That is none of your business. That is my appointment. I have to clear it with the Regents, but that's my appointment and I don't have to take the advice of any group like yours."

So. . . and then I think he was a little embarrassed about having come back so hard on us. So he said, "You know, women have not had the kind of experience you need to become provost. I mean it's just unlikely that we would have women candidates who would have that kind of background." He said, "For example, when I brought Barbara Newell here from Wisconsin, if you go back and look in the press, or any of the press reports, you'll see that every time Barbara had to make a critical decision, she hadn't really had that experience before. I was there with her. I always backed her. I supported her. I made a visible presence so that she had the support to go through it for the first time."

Nellie Varner, bless her soul, said, "Mr. President, that's all we're asking of you. That you should treat women now the way you treated Barbara at the time, that if we don't have the background, someone has to give us a leg up." Well, it was just a stunning response and he thought about it and was much more positively oriented toward us on the way out than he had been on the way in. Anyway, I thought that was a quite lovely story. And certainly Robben Fleming has done a lot for women.

Even the anonymous PROBE member said of Fleming: "I have to give him a lot of credit for keeping his cool through this whole process because he had nothing but unrest to deal with at that time."

Newell remained friends with Fleming for the rest of his life and recalled visiting him shortly after his autobiography was published. "I was upset that the book is really a focus on the Vietnam War, and he treated very lightly everything else," she said. "I agreed that the women's complaint did not even get the brush. So I jumped on him. I said I was sorry that he had not chosen to do a more complete view of the issues that came up when he was president. His answer was that he was really writing on Vietnam. He really also didn't cover BAM." Fleming did, however, devote a full chapter to the BAM strike and also wrote about his decision to call in the police to end the bookstore sit-in.

Unlike many other campus issues of that era, the HEW complaint was never backed up with protests, strikes, or sit-ins. But as Larimore succinctly observed, "The situation of women was not at all politicized until HEW came on campus. . . . That complaint was a watershed, there's no question that it profoundly affected this University. On the other hand, the effect has to be taken in the context of all the other things that were going on, which were completely really shifting power . . . . "

Over the half-century after FOCUS and WEAL filed their complaints, change eventually happened. Sara Krulwich recalled returning to Michigan Stadium ten years after she was barred from the stadium floor, this time as a photographer for the *New York Times*. "The sidelines looked totally different," she wrote. "There were women cheerleaders, women in the band, women in the security force, women physical therapists, and a woman photographer who happened to be the photo editor at the *Michigan Daily*. By then, no one could even imagine it otherwise."

And indeed, it was easy to forget that it had ever been otherwise. By the 2008–09 academic year, women passed the milestone of earning a majority of the doctoral degrees awarded by U.S. universities. In the 2016–17 academic year, they earned 57 percent of the bachelor's degrees, 59 percent of the master's degrees, and 53 percent of the doctorates. In the engineering discipline, they earned 22 percent of bachelor's degrees; in the field of history, they earned 42 percent of the doctorates. In 2017, U.S. women nudged past men in the numbers attending both law schools and medical schools. At Michigan, 57 percent of Medical School students were women; in the Law School, 54 percent of the entering Class of 2022 were women. Equal numbers of men and women were now admitted to the freshman class; the College Board reported that men and women high school graduates in the state of Michigan did equally well on the Scholastic Aptitude Test in 2019, with men outperforming women on the math part of the test and women outperforming men on the reading and writing exam. After Michigan's administrators fought federal interference in their graduate admissions policies, over the next three decades, the university evolved into a leading proponent of using affirmative action to diversify its student body, defending that approach all the way to the U.S. Supreme Court in 2003.

For a few years beginning in 2009, the university was led by a woman and governed by an elected Board of Regents with a majority of women members. But women on campus—or nationwide—still had not achieved full parity in academic hiring or salaries.

By 2016, women nearly equaled half of the faculty members at U.S. degree-granting institutions. On U-M's Ann Arbor campus, as of November 1, 2018, women represented 44 percent of the "regular" faculty, excluding persons who were adjunct or visiting professors. But the phenomenon of "the higher, the fewer" still persisted to some degree. Women represented 54 percent of the lecturers, and among those who were considered tenured or tenure-track faculty, 47 percent of assistant professors, 39 percent of associate professors, and 28 percent of full professors. But there was still a great range across the university. In the social science departments within LSA, women represented 47 percent of tenure-track full professors in the 2017–18 academic year, but only 18 percent of the full professors in the natural science departments. In Michigan's professional schools and colleges, they represented 34 percent of full professors, but in the Engineering School, only 14 percent.

In 2001, the National Science Foundation began what it called the ADVANCE Institutional Transformation Program to address the underrepresentation of women in academic science and engineering fields. Michigan was part of the first cohort of institutions funded under the initiative. When the grant ended in 2007, the university continued to fully fund the program and expanded it to regularly assess its efforts to promote diversity across the whole university, not just scientific and technological fields. In addition to producing the kind of detailed numbers that it was incapable of tallying a half-century before, the ADVANCE program conducted an annual survey addressing different components of the faculty experience.

The 2018 report studied the leadership and recognition of tenure-track faculty. It noted that "women and URM (Under-represented minority) faculty remain underrepresented at the senior faculty levels, which has important implications for their representation in leadership positions and prestigious named professorships." (The URM category includes African-American/black, Hispanic/Latino, and Native American/American Indian faculty members; the Asian/Asian-American category is tracked separately.)

The 2018 study found that the proportion of department chairs who were women had actually decreased from 34 percent in the 2009 academic year to 30 percent in 2018; in 2018, there were 83 men who were department chairs and 35 women. Women's share of high-level administrative jobs grew from 36 percent in 2009 to 41 percent in 2018, but the number of women serving as deans dropped from eight to five between 2015 and 2018.

Women were equally likely to chair important department, college, or university committees as men were but reported having to serve on more committees than their male counterparts. Despite that, women were more likely than men to report that they felt excluded from participating in important decision-making committees within their departments, colleges, or at the university level.

Women were also more likely to report that they had not been nominated for an award for which they were qualified and were more likely to have considered leaving U-M to garner more respect.

A 2017 survey focused on the "climate" encountered by faculty members, based on their gender and race. Across the university, one-third of women faculty reported experiences of gender discrimination. The report concluded that while "faculty reports of overhearing insensitive and disparaging comments about women" were generally low, they did increase between 2012 and 2017, in some cases by a statistically significant difference. The report found that while the number of instances in which racial-ethnic minorities and/or religious groups had experienced disparaging comments was generally low, the numbers had risen over the five years that were compared.

And as in the rest of the labor market, the salaries of women in academia still lagged behind those of their male counterparts 50 years after the original complaints were filed. Using U.S. Department of Education data, the *Chronicle for Higher Education* reported that the average salary of a male full professor at Michigan was $173,046 in the 2017–18 academic year, compared with $160,271 for a woman. A male assistant professor averaged $96,864, compared with $90,772 for a woman. A male lecturer earned an average of $73,954, compared with $59,563 for a woman.

For the three professorial ranks, women were now making at least 90 percent of what men did, but for lecturers, that figure dropped to 80 percent, the approximate pay gap between men and women generally in the United States. And in 2016, that was the approximate disparity that the College and University Professional Association for Human Resources found between the average salaries of men and women college administrators nationwide. Men still outnumbered women more than 2:1 among college presidents and chief business officers and more than 9:1 among chief facilities officers. The only position in which women occupied the overwhelming majority of positions was that of chief human resources officer, where they outnumbered men by nearly 3:1.

As was the case with faculty members, the study found that the higher a woman rose, the more the pay gap decreased. It also found that among chief facilities managers and chief information officers, where women were greatly outnumbered, women earned 17 percent more than their male counterparts. The study concluded: "This may indicate that—at least in some areas—higher ed institutions recognize the need to recruit and retain women to key leadership positions."

But overall, the study concluded that there was still work to be done. Over the previous 15 years, it found, there had been no narrowing of the pay gap between women and male administrators. And a 2017 study by the American Association of University Women found that women with advanced degrees still earned only 74 percent of what men with those degrees earned.

Sexual harassment had long been a concern in academia, even before women could put a name to it. Cowley recalled her own "very awkward moments at professional meetings—the then president of the AAS (American Astronomical Society) sexually assaulted me in an elevator at a meeting in Italy. I never dared to complain since he had a huge amount of power over me and could have ended my career."

Larimore recalled that when she served on the Rackham board, she was approached by a group of women students who complained they could not get the school to take action against a faculty member who had been harassing them. Larimore suggested they prepare formal letters and helped the women present them to top academic officials, who finally took action. "That," she said, "was satisfactory." Larimore said that when the graduate school developed a grievance procedure, she insisted that "sexual intimidation" be included.

Virginia Nordby, who served as affirmative action director from 1980 to 1988, recalled that during those years, sexual harassment of students and staff "became an issue." Her office developed a "Tell Someone" program, encouraging victims to come forward and instituted procedures for confidential investigations. "There were quite a large number of cases that I personally investigated involving faculty. There was always that commitment to the deans that if there was a faculty member involved, I would personally handle it," she said.

In 2001, Larimore noted that in her experience, only a few complaints had been filed over the ensuing years, because "once you have a procedure. . . it makes a statement." But, she said, sexual harassment was still "an extremely prevalent and deep-seated problem" that won't go away. The 2017 ADVANCE study found that across university divisions, fewer than 15 percent of faculty members said they had experienced any "unwanted and unwanted sexual attention within the past five years." The highest incidence was reported by white women in the arts and humanities. But in 2018–20, just as the #MeToo movement was shining a spotlight on sexual harassment and abuse by powerful men in corporate America, the entertainment industry and journalism, the university was similarly rocked by allegations involving high-ranking administrators and longtime profesors. In some cases, it was alleged that administrators chose to ignore or hide the complaints when they were first made.

In the fall of 2016, Michigan launched a broader, five-year initiative, called Diversity, Equity & Inclusion, through which 49 campus units developed strategic goals for promoting diversity in the ranks of faculty, staff, and students, under the direction of a new Office of Diversity, Equity and Inclusion and a chief diversity officer. By then, the whole notion of diversity had expanded to include considerations of age, disability, native-born status, sexual orientation, first-generation in college status, religion and ethnicity, in addition to gender and race.

In its 2016 surveys of faculty, staff and students, the initiative found no statistically significant difference between the satisfaction levels of male and female staff members with "the campus climate/environment" they had experienced in the past 12 months. But only 61.1 percent of women who were tenure-track faculty reported they were "very satisfied" or "satisfied" with the climate, compared with 78.3 percent of their male counterparts. The student survey found that female students were 52 percent more likely than male students to report "feeling neutral, unsatisfied, or very unsatisfied."

As of the end of 2019, the "History" section of the program's website included a brief chronicle of Michigan's "triumphs and tribulations" in promoting diversity, which it said "serves as an ongoing platform to share how these experiences have shaped our present, and impact our future." Under 1970, the site notes the BAM strike, the establishment of the Center for AfroAmerican and African Studies, the opening of the intramural sports building to women, and the celebration of the centennial of women's admission. Under 1971, the chronicle lists the establishment of the Commission for Women.

There is no mention of the filing of the HEW complaint.

Seven years after they first worked together on the complaint, Sandler wrote King, responding to advice she had given to a woman who was a planning to file a lawsuit alleging sex discrimination: "Your advice was right on target; the problem for many of these women is partially not knowing how the system operates. Of course, many men don't know how the system operates either, but then they don't need to know since it operates to their benefit with or without their awareness. In contrast, the *only* way women can effectively operate within it is to know it for what it is, and in a sense, beat the system at its own game."

But Sandler noted ruefully that judges were still reluctant to interfere in academic cases, no matter what legal protections women now enjoyed. She added, "It is going to take a long, long time. . . ."

In 2000, then-Michigan Provost Nancy Cantor observed: "I think when people say to me, 'Does it matter to have a woman as a provost?' Or, 'Does it matter to have a woman vice president in various areas?' I say, 'What matters most is that you have people in those positions who are likely to have these issues front and center on their radar screen, and that's probabilistically more likely to be the case for someone who has experienced some version of structural obstacles in their lives. So it may be a variety of people who can help each other. But it's just likely that having women and people of color in these positions will be very helpful to the institution."

In its 1975–76 report, the Commission for Women presciently wrote:

Attitudes and behaviors on this campus have changed during these past five years. In a superficial way, the extensive use of "person" instead of "man" says something about attitudes. The effort of many departments to include women on all committees says something about behaviors. Increased numbers of women students in some non-traditional fields, a rise in the number of women graduate students, programs for women interns in administrative and research areas, a few higher level women administrators, more women at least entering the tenure track are encouraging signs that a good beginning is being made.

However, there are still those who feel that "best qualified" means a bright, young man; there are those who do not realize and refuse to recognize the fact when it is explained to them that the "way it has always been done" may be demeaning to women; there are those who still make sexist remarks in classrooms and either do not understand why women students are upset or refuse to acknowledge that they have made a mistake; there are those who do not believe a woman can be serious about career goals; there are those who call a secretary "my girl" and demand that coffee be served; there are those who still see a woman applicant and think of clerical or administrative assistant work but who see a man applicant and think of supervisory and managerial work; there are those on search committees who feel that affirmative action is practiced as long as they interview one woman; there are those who still believe most women work for the extra money in a family and do not realize that there are many single, widowed or divorced women working, who must provide not only for themselves but also have the entire responsibility of children and home. There are still those who find sexism a cause for hilarity; who cannot face the problem of sexism except with a "funny" remark.

"These are some of the attitudes and behaviors which must be changed before we can be seen as truly an equal opportunity University," it added. The task that the Commission for Women set out for itself "is far from done."

AUTHOR'S NOTE

In the fall of 1970, I was a sophomore at the University of Michigan, starting my second semester working on the student newspaper, the *Michigan Daily*. It was anticipated that the university's service employees might go on strike that year, and so I was assigned to a newly created "labor" beat. When the university announced a month later that the U.S. Department of Health, Education, and Welfare had given it 30 days to revise its affirmative action plan to address sex discrimination, the editors decided the story fell onto my beat. I can still remember then-Editor Martin Hirschman taking me aside to patiently explain the extent of federal contracting at the university and why this could become a very big story.

So upfront, I need to acknowledge that this book is both history and memoir, because I lived through these events and became close to some of the protagonists as I reported on them.

From the fall of 1970 until early 1973, I followed the story of sex discrimination at the university along with many of my *Daily* colleagues, particularly women staff members. I switched my major from journalism to history and began writing term papers about the untold stories of American women. I took a seminar on women in journalism created by Marion Marzolf and another one on women's history created by Kathryn Kish Sklar, in the days before women professors organized a formal Women's Studies Department. And when I wrote my senior history thesis on the flapper phenomenon, Kitty served as my thesis adviser.

Jean King would frequently turn up at the *Daily*, eager to provide a tip about the HEW complaint or suggest a new angle that should be pursued. The *Ann Arbor News* once described her as a "hatless Bella Abzug," but in my own experience, the only toes she stepped on were those of her opponents. I got to know many of the women who directed the university's early affirmative action efforts. In the spring of 1972, when one of them learned I was driving to Chicago the next day to interview for a summer internship on *The Miami Herald*, she shared that seven U-M officials—five men and two women—would be there too, attending a conference about implementing the Labor Department's latest affirmative action regulations. Gloria Steinem and Aileen Hernandez, then the president of NOW, were among the scheduled speakers.

Our source warned that we probably would not be permitted to attend the conference but thought it would rattle the male administrators if we were there when they arrived. We agreed. So before dawn the next morning, we climbed into my Ford Maverick and drove to Chicago, where we did, in fact, surprise the university officials. Later in the day, we squeezed in an interview with John Hodgdon, the HEW civil servant who was still in charge of monitoring the university's compliance efforts. We had interviewed him over the phone but had never had the chance to take the measure of the man in person.

It was a heady time to be a woman student at Michigan, and I later reflected how lucky I was to come of age during those years—when *Ms.* magazine began publication, when the National Women's Political Caucus was founded, when the U.S. Supreme Court's *Roe v. Wade* decision gave women greater choices when it came to their reproductive rights. But, in researching this book, I was reminded that it was not such a good time for women who were only a few years older than me, as they struggled to complete advanced degrees and to find a job once they did.

At the end of my summer in Miami, I returned to Ann Arbor to become the first woman to serve as editor-in-chief of the *Daily* when the man who held the job stepped down midway through his term and my peers elected me to take his place. It was a challenging time for me, but I knew that title would create opportunities as I pursued a career in journalism. As for the three other women who drove to Chicago with me, one went on to work for two major U.S. newspapers, one became dean of the College of Arts and Sciences at Roosevelt University, and one rose to become publisher of the Crain Group of business publications and the first woman president of the Detroit Athletic Club.

Flash forward 40 years. In 2010, I was attending an informal women's history roundtable at the Library of Congress as I finished work on my biography of feminist leader Elly Peterson. When I learned that Kitty Sklar would be discussing her new book at the Woodrow Wilson Center that afternoon, I changed my plans so I could attend. At the reception following her talk, I regaled her husband, Tom Dublin, with memories of the times Kitty and I had shared in Ann Arbor. Out of that conversation grew a project on the HEW complaint for "Women and Social Movements in the United States: 1600–2000," the online documents resource that Kitty and Tom founded and co-edited when they taught history at the State University of New York at Binghamton. During my research, I interviewed Jean King, Bernice Sandler, and Kathy Shortridge and discovered the candid oral histories in the Bentley Historical Library that had been collected from women who were involved with the complaint and its aftermath. I wanted to find a way to share more of those stories, and as the 50th anniversary of the complaint approached, this book was the answer. I deeply appreciate the support of the staffs of the University of Michigan Press, the Bentley Historical Library, and the Center for the Education of Women (now CEW+) in helping to make this book a reality. I am only sorry that limits of time and space meant I could not include the stories of more women from that era, some of which may be lost as that generation passes on.

I consider Jean King to be a personal heroine and am grateful that she lived long enough to share in the successes of women who came after her. I enjoyed several visits with Jean when I returned to Ann Arbor in her later years. As I worked on this book, I discovered that she had singled me out among *Daily* reporters in a letter she wrote Eric Stein as he worked on his study of the HEW complaint. (Jean thought I was the reporter who broke the story when HEW held up the first contract, but I was not.) A few years ago, I made a small (by university standards) financial gift so that the women's bathroom off the lobby of the Stanford Lipsey Student Publications Building could be named in Jean's honor.

I did not have as many direct dealings with President Robben Fleming while I was on campus, but in reviewing the *Michigan Daily* file in his presidential papers, I was reminded of an antagonistic exchange of letters we had had over language that I, as editor, had approved for publication in a review of a 1972 movie called *Teenage Fantasies*. Fleming's memoir made clear he was no fan of the *Daily*. In a letter he wrote the then-chairman of the Board for Student Publications about the review, he began by saying, "Periodically we are assured by the editors of the *Daily* that it is the *New York Times* of college newspapers. Thereafter we are given periodic demonstrations of how shallow a claim that is." Fleming contended the review was irresponsible "because we shall now have to fight innumerable battles to convince irate legislators and members of the public that there is something about higher education which lifts it above the gutter. No one wants to censor the *Daily*. Many of us cling to the rather forlorn hope that its editors will some day feel sufficiently secure to act like they really were publishing the *New York Times* rather than a scurrilous scandal sheet."

In my response, I conceded that some readers might have found the review offensive but observed that well-known movie critic Judith Crist had told a campus audience the year before that if critics had begun reviewing X-rated movies when they were first released, they might not have proliferated the way they had in recent years. I confirmed that I had approved the objectionable words and then noted that only two weeks before, the *New York Times*, in its Week in Review section, had described the *Daily* (along with the *Harvard Crimson*) as "the most aggressive and professional" of college newspapers.

Fleming responded that after receiving my letter, "I am more depressed than ever." He told me that I had "the dubious distinction of being the only editor in my five and a half years at Michigan who was willing to go so far." He said he had noticed in the past that *Daily* editors had "an uncanny ability. . . to change the issue." He said he would be more impressed with evidence that "the professional newspaper *men* (my emphasis) on your Board of Publication concurred in your judgment." (All of the board members were, in fact, men at the time.)

Our exchange stopped there. But in hindsight, I wonder if Fleming was shocked that I had chosen to apply the same standards as my male predecessors had. The *Daily* is frequently cited as a source in this book. At least we were among those asking important questions at the time.

In the late 1970s, I ran into Fleming again in Washington, when I was working there as a journalist and he was serving as president of the

Corporation for Public Broadcasting. My entrée to the black-tie event at the Kennedy Center was through my late husband, Walt Wurfel, who was then deputy press secretary to President Jimmy Carter. We had a very pleasant conversation. I made small talk with Sally Fleming about her friendship with my aunt, whom she had met during their time at the University of Illinois. I had, I realized, finally traded in my blue jeans and T-shirts for "the grown-up world."

Despite all of these experiences, positive or negative, I have tried to tell this story objectively, drawing on the skills I gained at Michigan as a journalist and historian, and revisiting these, my college years, from the perspective of an older—and, hopefully, wiser—woman.

NOTES ON SOURCES

This book grew out of a project entitled "What Factors Led to the Success of the Historic 1970 Sex Discrimination Complaint Filed Against the University of Michigan," which the author wrote for *Women and Social Movements in the United States: 1600–2000*, Vol. 17, No. 2, in 2013. Many of the key documents referenced in this book can be retrieved from this Alexander Street online resource, co-edited by Kathryn Kish Sklar and Thomas Dublin.

The bulk of pertinent materials were found in the University of Michigan's archives at the Bentley Historical Library. The author regrets that limits of time and space meant she could not cover the full breadth of Michigan's schools and departments but concentrated her research on the largest unit, the College of Literature, Science, and the Arts (LSA), where most of the activist faculty members taught. There she also reviewed the files of departments where specific sex discrimination complaints came to light.

In the 50 years since the HEW complaint was filed, several projects captured oral histories and other details of the episode. In 1986, the Academic Women's Caucus, an outgrowth of the Commission for Women, conducted a series of interviews, the transcripts of which are in Box 2 of its records. (The author drew from the interviews of Ann Larimore, Harriet Mills, Rose Vainstein, and Zelma Weisfeld.) In 1999, to mark its 25th anniversary, the caucus organized another round of interviews. The author reviewed the interviews of Jean Campbell, Nancy Cantor,

Elizabeth Douvan, Carol Hollenshead, Wilfrid Kaplan, Jean King, Larimore, Mills, Virginia Nordby, Sue Rasmussen, and Rosemary Sarri. (This era is also captured in a video, *Striving Toward Equity at the University of Michigan: 25 Years of the Academic Women's Caucus 1975–2000*, produced by Ruth Barnard in 1999 and 2000.) In 2001, Eric A. Stein conducted another round of interviews when he wrote the 2002 report titled "Women's Activism against Sex Discrimination: The 1970 HEW Investigation of the University of Michigan" for the U-M Institute for Research on Women and Gender. The audiotapes of Stein's interviews are in the Bentley Library; transcripts were prepared of his interviews of King and Bernice Sandler (Sandler authorized the release of her transcript for the author's earlier project.) The author also made use of Stein's interviews of Douvan, Larimore, Barbara Murphy and Mills, Kathy Shortridge, Eugenia Carpenter and Rasmussen, and a member of PROBE who chose to remain anonymous. The Bentley Library released the audiotape of Stein's interview with Robben Fleming for this book.

It was important to both King and Sandler to capture the history of the complaints they filed and both retold their stories many times. King donated her personal papers to the Bentley Library and spent time organizing and annotating them; King also kept clippings of pertinent newspaper and magazine articles. Box 1 of her papers contains biographical information and Box 3 contains documents related to discrimination at Michigan. Sandler's extensive papers were donated to the Schlesinger Library at Harvard University's Radcliffe Institute.

King's key recollections include a March 12, 1994 letter to University of Michigan women's leaders Carol Hollenshead and Virginia Nordby; her December 16, 1999 interview with Elizabeth Duell, found in the Academic Women's Caucus anniversary files; a December 12, 1999 letter to Assistant U-M Provost Kate Soper that she wrote to prepare for that interview; and her June 9, 2001 interview with Stein. This author interviewed her on November 16, 2010, and corresponded with her by mail and email at that time. Yet another source of quotations was a letter that King wrote Stein, commenting on a draft of his report; a copy of this letter can be found in Sandler's papers (Box 69, Folder 11). I am indebted to Sarah Hutcheon of the Schlesinger Library for finding this document. As King got older, she did not always remember all the details of her complaint correctly but usually cautioned her interviewers to double-check the specifics with other sources to make sure they got them right.

Key sources of Sandler's memories are her article "'Too Strong for a Woman'—The Five Words that Created Title IX," which first appeared in the Spring 1997 issue of *About Women on Campus*, what was then the newsletter of the National Association for Women in Education; her essay, "A Little Help from Our Government: WEAL and Contract Compliance," in *Academic Women on the Move*, edited by Alice S. Rossi and Ann Calderwood and published by the Russell Sage Foundation in 1973; and a February 25, 1976 letter to historian Eric F. Goldman, found in Box 3 of King's papers. Sandler provided another overview in *Title IX: How We Got It and What a Difference It Made*, which she wrote for the *Cleveland State Law Review* in 2007. Stein interviewed Sandler on July 17, 2001, and the author interviewed her in Washington, DC, on May 23, 2011.

A good overall study of the university's early response to the HEW complaint, "Equal Opportunity for Women: University of Michigan," was prepared in 1971 by Douglas F. Winslow under the auspices of Harvard University's Institute for Educational Management. Winslow interviewed several key participants, under the supervision of Dean Charles Whitlock, who had served as assistant to Harvard President Nathan Pusey for civic and governmental relations and was involved in responding to HEW's investigation of racial discrimination at Harvard. King received a copy of this study in 1980 from "a friend in California"; it can be found in Box 3 of her papers. More than some of the other sources, this study captures the perspective of high-ranking U-M officials.

Ruth Bordin's 1999 book *Women at Michigan: The "Dangerous Experiment," 1870s to the Present*, published by the University of Michigan Press, is a good reference on the history of women at Michigan generally and developments in the first 25 years after the HEW complaint was filed.

Many key documents, including the letters President Fleming sent to other university presidents and the letters he received from campus women, can be found in Box 24 of his presidential papers in the "Women (Discrimination/HEW)" Folder. A few additional documents are found in the "Affirmative Action" Folder in Box 16, including the correspondence with Mary Maples Dunn. (Because the resolution of the

HEW investigation touched on so many parts of the university, pertinent documents can sometimes be found in more than one place.) After January 1971, most key documents were kept in the records of Michigan's Affirmative Action Office, including subsequent interactions with HEW's Office of Civil Rights and the records of the Commission on/for Women. Materials prepared for the monthly Regents meetings during 1970–71 were found in Boxes 127 and 128 of the Regents records. Minutes of the Executive Officers' weekly meetings during 1970–71 were found in Box 5 of A. Geoffrey Norman's papers in the files of the Office of Research; Norman's correspondence during this period is in Box 2. Documents related to department-level decisions were generally found in the departmental folders of the records of the LSA Dean.

Most documents related to PROBE, the grass-roots women's organization that supported the HEW complaint, can be found in Box 1 of the papers of one of its leaders, Jeanne Tashian, at the Bentley Library. In August 2012, the author exchanged emails with PROBE leader Kathleen Shortridge to get further information about the role she played in filing the complaint and with PROBE.

Some records of the U.S. Department of Labor and its Office of Federal Contract Compliance from this era are available at the National Archives and Records Administration (NARA) in College Park, Maryland. However, related records of HEW's Office of Civil Rights or its Chicago regional office were not available. (Thanks to NARA archivist Tab Lewis for his help in this search.) However, the papers of HEW Secretary Elliot L. Richardson are preserved at the Library of Congress. Boxes 108–73 in Series I cover Richardson's tenure as HEW secretary; the author drew most heavily from the transcriptions of his telephone calls and notations on his appointment calendars. (Unfortunately, Richardson's own handwritten notes on his telephone calls and meetings are generally illegible.) Thanks to the friendly staff of the Library of Congress's Manuscript Division for their help in accessing these papers.

J. Stanley Pottinger donated his papers to the Gerald R. Ford Presidential Library at the University of Michigan. Box 2 includes reports on HEW's Women's Action Project and a folder of "Happy Letters" from some persons involved with the sex discrimination complaints. Box 3 holds two folders on sex discrimination, including the text of Pottinger's December 1971 speech to the American Association for the Advancement of Science. Box 7's "OCR History—Agenda for Secretarial Meeting" Folder is the location of the agenda for Pottinger's December 22, 1970 meeting with Richardson regarding negotiations with Michigan. It also holds a folder of pertinent newspaper clippings about the work of the Office of Civil Rights. Box 8's "OCR History Miscellaneous" Folders hold documents related to the office's work on sex discrimination. Among the many boxes reviewed, Boxes 17 and 19 also held quoted materials. Through a lucky accident, the author met David Kieran, a history professor at Washington & Jefferson College during a visit to Ann Arbor, and his research in the Ford Library turned up President Ford's query to Pottinger about the Michigan investigation in the papers of Kenneth Cole. My thanks to John O'Connell of the Ford Library for locating other documents that clarified the context of this exchange.

For this book, the author conducted telephone interviews with Kitty Sklar, Zelda Gamson, and Marion Marzolf and exchanged documents and email messages with them. She conducted a lengthy interview with Barbara Newell on August 9, 2019, and had additional exchanges with Newell by email. She also exchanged emails with Anne Cowley and with relatives, colleagues, and graduate students of Margaret Davis.

The author expresses her deep appreciation, as an historian and former *Michigan Daily* staff member, to the Kemp Family Foundation for a substantial gift that created searchable online access to all *Daily* issues from 1891 to 2014. Some particularly noteworthy stories are cited below, but *Daily* colleagues who contributed stories and editorials to the day-to-day coverage of the complaint and its aftermath included Lynn Weiner, Martin Hirschman, Rob Bier, Daniel Zwerdling, Pat Bauer, Jan Benedetti, Mary Kramer, Rose Sue Berstein, Tammy Jacobs, Jim Neubacher, Dan Biddle, Sara Rimer, Judy Ruskin, Hester Pulling, Linda Dreeben, Mark Dillen, Debra Thal, Carla Rapoport, Jonathan Miller, Jim McFerson, Lindsay Chaney, W.E. Schrock, Larry Lempert, Marcia Zoslaw, Judy Kahn, Kathleen Ricke, and Penny Blank.

To improve their readability, the author made small editing changes and spelling corrections in transcriptions of some oral histories, interviews, and telephone calls.

Here are citations of particular interest or beyond the key sources described previously.

Prologue

Descriptions of FOCUS were drawn from "Women's Group Hits Cars-well Nomination," an unidentified newspaper clipping (labeled February 1970) in Box 3 of King's papers; Helen Fogel's article, "Women Here Try Phone Drive to Block Carswell," in the *Detroit Free Press* (February 3, 1970, page 1-C) and a Fran Stair article "Traditional Attitudes About Women Challenged by Groups" in the *Ann Arbor News* (March 1, 1970, page 13). Mary Dabbs's letter to the editor ran in the *Michigan Daily* on April 5, 1970 (page 4). This chapter also referenced a March 31, 1970 memorandum from King, "What to do about the Carswell nomination now," in Box 3 of her papers.

The author drew on *The Fifties: A Women's Oral History*, by Brett Harvey (ASJA Press, 1993) and *When Everything Changed: The Amazing Journey of American Women from 1960 to the Present* by Gail Collins (Little, Brown and Company, 2009) for background about the experiences of college women in the 1950s. The full text of Adlai Stevenson's commencement speech at Smith can be found at several places on the internet, including https://wwnorton.com/college/history/archive/resources/documents/ch32_04.htm. The reminisces of Betty Friedan and Gloria Steinem were taken from *COLLEGE: A Smith Mosaic* by Jacqueline Van Voris, published by Smith College in 1975. The text of Hillary Clinton's commencement address at Wellesley was retrieved from https://time.com/4359618/hillary-clinton-wellesley-commencement-transcript/. Sara Krulwich's recollections of her experiences as a photographer at Michigan Stadium are taken from her essay "'No Women' Was No Barrier" in *In the Name of Editorial Freedom: 125 Years at The Michigan Daily*, edited by Stephanie Steinberg and published by University of Michigan Press in 2015. The story originally appeared in the *New York Times Lens Blog* on May 22, 2009.

1: The Eureka Moment

Many details about Bernice Sandler's life came from obituaries written at the time of her death on January 5, 2019. Author Sherry Boschert interviewed Sandler and Vincent Macaluso in 2015 and posted a videotape of their separate interviews on her website (www.sherryboschert.com/

men-fought-fight-title-ix-too/, retrieved September 6, 2019). Sandler acknowledged that it was only after Macaluso retired from the federal government that she was able to identify him by name. More information about their work together was found in "Vincent Macaluso, A Hero of Title IX, Receives VFA's Medal of Honor," Veteran Feminists of America, 2009 Archive (www.veteranfeministsofamerica.org/legacy/VFA2009%20BackPages.htm#VINCENT%20MACALUSO,%20A%20HERO%20OF%20TITL).

For examples of how media coverage of the 1967 Johnson executive order ignored the potential impact on universities, see, for example, "Johnson Signs Order to Protect Women in U.S. Jobs From Bias," by Max Frankel in the *New York Times*, October 14, 1967, page 11, and "LBJ Acts to Promote Women Workers," by Dorothy McCardle in the *Washington Post*, October 15, 1967, page D5.

Sandler did not identify the U.S. Commission on Civil Rights report that contained the footnote about the revised executive order. However, *Jobs & Civil Rights: The Role of the Federal Government in Promoting Equal Opportunity in Employment and Training*, published by the commission in April 1969, fits her description. It can be reviewed at www2.law.umaryland.edu/marshall/usccr/documents/cr11016.pdf.

2: The General

In 2010, Dr. Stephanie Kadel Taras worked with King to complete a short biography entitled *Fighting for Fair Play: Stories from the Feminist Legal Career of Jean Ledwith King*, which was the source of many details about King's childhood and early married life. King was the subject of a lengthy *Detroit Free Press* profile by Maryanne George, "Playing Hardball: Lawyer Is Fearless Champ of Equality in Schools, Sports," published on March 15, 1999. (This was the source of Robben Fleming's critical comments about King's personal style.) The *Ann Arbor News* profiled her in a November 4, 1971 story by Kathleen Hampton, "Meet Ann Arbor's Hatless Abzug." A source on Theodore Newcomb's career was a remembrance, "Theodore Mead Newcomb," written by Philip Converse and published in Volume 64 of the National Academies Press's *Biographical Memoirs* (www.nap.edu/read/4547/chapter/15). Details of Millie Jeffrey's academic career came from her *New York Times* obituary on April 5, 2004. The term "Click Moment" was popularized by Jane O'Reilly's cover story, "Click: The Housewife's Moment of Truth," in the inaugural issue of *Ms.* magazine (Spring 1972).

3: The Complaint

In her 1994 letter to Hollenshead and Nordby, King said she met Sandler when Sandler spoke in Ann Arbor, which Ruth Bordin repeated in her book. However, King later corrected herself. Although Sandler traveled widely during those years, she was not in Ann Arbor in 1970. After the two women met, King became a board member of the Professional Women's Caucus; its activities can be tracked through minutes found in a folder of that name in Box 2 of her papers. Sandler described the caucus's founding meeting in a May 2, 2011 email to the author. *Science* magazine reporter Nancy Gruchow reported on the early status of complaints in a May 1, 1970 article titled "Discrimination: Women Charge Universities, Colleges with Bias." Shortridge's article on sex discrimination at Michigan appeared in the *Michigan Daily Magazine* on April 12, 1970. Hearings about sex discrimination before Michigan's Joint Senate-House Labor Committee were covered by Eileen Foley in "Sex Bias in State Universities Is Charged, which appeared in the *Detroit Free Press* on March 7, 1970.

Initial newspaper stories about the complaint included "Women Charge 'U' with Discrimination" by Lindsay Chaney for the *Daily* on May 28, 1970, and Helen Fogel's story, "U-M Charged With Bias against Women," which appeared the same day in the *Detroit Free Press*. Fogel's follow-up, with U-M's response, "'We'll Try to Do Better,'" appeared on June 4, 1970. Shortridge's letter to the editor of the *Daily*, responding to critiques of her reporting on the admissions policy, appeared in the paper on June 4, 1970.

4: The Times

John Papanek's essay, "1969: The Year of Living Dangerously," was included in Steinberg's anthology of essays about the *Daily*. Fleming's memoir, *Tempests into Rainbows: Managing Turbulence*, was published by University of Michigan Press in 1996. Barbara Newell's quotation about her first day on the job is from Stein's report on the HEW investigation.

Vice President Spiro Agnew's attack on Fleming was reported widely, including in the April 14, 1970 issue of the *Daily*.

Cynthia Stephens's quotation about women in the Black Action Movement was retrieved in early 2019 from the *Ann Arbor Chronicle* at http:// annarborchronicle.com/2010/03/30/open-it-up-or-shut-it-down/. More about the standing of women in the national political parties in 1970 can be found in the author's 2011 book, *Elly Peterson: "Mother" of the Moderates,* published by the University of Michigan Press. Reports about the federal government's investigations of racial discrimination at Michigan included stories by these *Michigan Daily* reporters: Mark R. Killingsworth, "Pentagon Charges 'U' Is for 'Rich, White Students,' Asks Opportunities for Negroes," November 11, 1966; Roger Rapoport, "Clash Over Status of Recommendations," November 12, 1966; and Meredith Riker, "Pentagon Blasts Engin Hiring, Urges 'U' Jobs for Minorities," March 10, 1967. Bruce Currie's interview of Fleming, "U-M's Fleming Guardedly Optimistic about New Year," appeared in the *Ann Arbor News* on August 30, 1970. A clipping is located in Box 1, Folder 1, of Jeanne Tashian's Papers. The column by Rowland Evans and Robert Novak, "Dangerous Precedent at Ann Arbor," appeared in the *Washington Post* on August 19, 1970. Letters generated in response to the column were found in the Robben Fleming Folder of Box 185, Subseries 1970–71 of the LSA Dean's records. Materials related to the Presidential Commission on Campus Unrest are in Box 19 of Fleming's personal papers.

5: *The Summer of 1970*

Details about Edith Green and her career come from her biography on the U.S. House website (https://history.house.gov/People/Detail/14080, retrieved on October 18, 2019) and an oral history conducted by Shirley Tanzer on November 18 and 25, 1978; December 2, 1978; and March 18, 1980. It is found in Box 4, Former Members of Congress, Inc., Oral History Interviews, Manuscript Division, Library of Congress, Washington, DC. Biographical information about Phineas Indritz is from https://now.org/about/history/honoring-our-founders-pioneers/ and https://en.wikipedia.org/wiki/Phineas_Indritz. The transcript of Rep. Green's 1970 hearings and the supporting documents are from

Discrimination against Women, Hearings Before the Special Subcommittee on Education of the Committee on Education and Labor, House of Representatives, Ninety-First Congress, Second Session on Section 805 of H.R. 16098, Parts 1 and 2, U.S. Government Printing Office. The text of the Women's Equity Action League's initial complaint can be found on pages 312-14 of Part 1.

6: The Investigation

Background on Muriel Ferris's career is from her obituary, "Muriel Ferris; Worked for League of Women Voters, Sen. Phil Hart," written by Joe Holley for the *Washington Post*, November 27, 2007. Biographical information about Helen Fogel was taken from her obituary, "Union Activist, News Labor Reporter Helen Fogel Dies," by Kyla Smith, in the *Detroit News* on May 31, 2015. Biographical information on Eileen Foley is from her obituary, "Eileen Foley (1934–2018): Blade Editor, Columnist Known for Tenacity," by Mark Zaborney, in the *Toledo Blade,* September 8, 2018. Helen Fogel's *Detroit Free Press* stories on the initial investigation included "Bias Probe Will Open at U-M," August 17, 1970, page 1-C; "Sex Bias Charges Lack Specifics, Says HEW," August 19, 1970, page 2-D; and "U-M Probe Reveals No Sex Bias," August 22, 1970, page 10-A. Background on Clifford Minton's career comes from "Clifford Minton's War: The Struggle for Black Jobs in Wartime Little Rock, 1940–1946," by Tabitha Orr in the *Arkansas Historical Quarterly,* Vol. 76, No. 1, 2017, pages 23–48. *JSTOR,* www.jstor.org/stable/26281883. Minton's autobiography, *America's Black Trap,* was published by Alpha Book Company in 2001. Esther Lardent's oral history is from the "American Bar Association Women Trailblazers in the Law Project"; she was interviewed by Maureen Thornton Syracuse and Erica Knieval Songer on September 26, 2006; December 16, 2010; March 22, 2011; November 9, 2011; February 22, 2012; and August 3, 2012.

7: The Rebels

Biographical details about Helen Tanner are from her obituary in the *Gainesville Sun,* July 24–25, 2011. Margaret B. Davis's grievance was described by Kathleen Hampton in "Sex Discrimination: The Case of

Margaret Bryan Davis," *Ann Arbor News*, March 19, 1972, (retrieved from https://aadl.org/taxonomy/term/2371). Details on Davis's career are also taken from "Margaret B. Davis, president, 1987–1988," *Bulletin of the Ecological Society of America*, Vol. 68, No. 4, Sept. 1987, pages 490–91, written by Linda B. Brubaker, and emails to the author in 2019 from Davis's colleagues Brubaker, Jane M. Beiswenger, and Patrice Morrow, and Davis's brother, Kirk Bryan Jr.

8: The Findings

James Robertson's observation about the Residential College comes from "A Short History of the Residential College at the University of Michigan," June 2015, written by Charles Bright and Michelle McClellan (retrieved at https://lsa.umich.edu/rc/about-us/history-of-the-residential-college.html). Al Guskin's memo, explaining the tandem teams in the School of Education, is found in Box 11 of the Affirmative Action Office's records. This author's interview with John Hodgdon was reported in "'U' Women's Knight in Shining Armor," in the *Michigan Daily*, March 23, 1972, page 4.

9: The Centennial Celebration

Details on the planning of the centennial celebration came from Box 7 of the records of the Center for the Continuing Education of Women.

10: The Response

Helen Fogel's story, "End Sex Bias, U-M Told," appeared in the *Detroit Free Press* on October 14, 1970, page C-1. "U-M Revises Employment Program" appeared in the *Ann Arbor News* on the same day on page 22. Roy Reynolds's story "Confrontation Politics Irk Fleming" appeared on the local news section front on page 25. Fleming's letter to King and Yourd is found in Box 3 of King's papers. The author conducted a September 6, 2019, phone interview with Joel Berger, a former *Michigan Daily* staff member who joined U-M's News and Information Service in fall 1970.

Details about Elliot L. Richardson's dealings with the universities and his time at HEW come from his papers at the Library of Congress. Most useful were transcripts of Richardson's telephone conversations from 1970–71 (Boxes 124–28). Patricia Reilly Hitt's oral history was conducted September 23, 1997, as part of "A Few Good Women" Oral History Collection, 1938–2000, MGN 984, Penn State University Archives, Special Collections Library, University Libraries, Pennsylvania State University. The *Saturday Review* article on the Nixon administration's desegregation efforts appeared on page 76 of the March 21, 1970 issue. Fleming's observations about Harvard's presidential search were made in a January 11, 1971 letter to Arthur Goldberg, found in Box 14 of his personal papers, in correspondence to friends in 1970–71.

11: *The Contract*

Charles Kidd's memo to members of the Association of American Universities' Council on Federal Relations, is found in Box 3 of Jean King's papers. The *Daily* published the Associated Press's story about the *Chicago Sun-Times'* scoop on the U.S. Civil Rights Commission report ("Commission Report: Bureaucracy Charged with 'Inertia' on Civil Rights Bills") on page 1 on October 11, 1970. Gloria Gladman's letter to Fleming is in Box 24 of his presidential papers, as is the flyer from the Sunday Night Group and his response to it. Details about women in the School of Engineering and national engineering programs come from Ruth Bordin's book (page 9); "Women on Campus: A Symposium, October, 14, 1970," distributed by CCEW at its forum, citing statistics provided by the Statistical Service of the University's Office of the Registrar, from Box 1 of Jeanne Tashian's papers; and the National Center for Education Statistics' *Digest of Education Statistics, 2006*, Table 287: Degrees in engineering and engineering technologies conferred by degree-granting institution, by level of degree and sex of student: Selected years, 1949–50 through 2004–05, http://nces.ed.gov/programs/digest/d06/tables/dt06_287.asp. Richard D. Lyons of the *New York Times* covered the growing number of investigations in "Women Forcing Colleges to Give Job Data to U.S.," November 8, 1970, page 1. The story on the U.S. Agency for International Development contract was broken first by Rob Bier of the *Daily* in "HEW Withholds 'U' Contracts; Bias Dispute Prompts Act," which appeared on page 1 on November 6, 1970. Eileen Foley's *Detroit Free Press* story about Fleming's communications with other college presidents, "U-M Fleming Shared Discrimination Problem," ran on page 1-C on November 24, 1970. Jim Neubacher's editorial, "The 'U and Discrimination: Time for Some Answers," appeared on page 4 of the *Daily* on November 7, 1970. Minutes of the deliberations of the governing board of the Center for Population Planning are from Box 2 of the papers of Professor Leslie Corsa in the Bentley Library. The article, "Six University Officials to Meet with HEW Tuesday," appeared on page 1 of the *University Record* on November 9, 1970. The *Science* magazine article detailing HEW's demands of Michigan appeared in its November 20, 1970 issue on page 834.

12: *The Deadline*

Details about U-M's federal research in 1970 come from "'U' Scientists Engage in Expensive Research," by Lindsay Chaney, and "Classified Research: 'U' and the U.S. Military," by Dave Chudwin, both from the September 2, 1970, *Michigan Daily*, Academics—page 3. Roy Reynolds's story, "University Says HEW Not Holding Up Pacts," appeared in the *Ann Arbor News* on December 2, 1970. Martin Hirschman's story, "Laws, Bureaucracy Weaken HEW Contract Ban," appeared on page 1 of the *Daily* on December 4, 1970. Helen Fogel's story on the December commitment, "Michigan Takes Lead in Bias Fight," appeared in the *Detroit Free Press* on December 10, 1970, page 1-C.

13: *Happy Holidays*

The transcripts of the phone calls of Rep. Marvin Esch and (later) Nathan Pusey to Secretary Richardson are found in Series I: Box 125 of Richardson's papers in the Library of Congress. The transcript of PROBE's meeting with Charles Allmand and William Cash is found in Box 3 of King's papers. The *Detroit Free Press* story, "U-M Sex Bias Plan 'Historic'" appeared on January 20, 1971, on page 3-A.

14: Getting Started

The document "Policy Issues on Sex Discrimination and Employment at the University of Michigan and Potentially Other Universities— ACTION Memorandum" is from Box 12 of the Pottinger papers. Pottinger's notes from his January 19, 1971 meeting with the American Council on Education are in Box 19; his correspondence with Martha Peterson is in Box 2. Daniel Zwerdling's article, "The 'U' Crusade for/ against Women," appeared in the *Michigan Daily's Sunday Daily* magazine on February 14, 1971, page 4. Fleming's letters of recommendation for Newell are in Boxes 13 and 14 of his personal papers; later materials are in Box 17. The directive to the departments regarding affirmative action plans is in Box 7 of CCEW's records. The departmental responses about their affirmative action plans are in Box 183 of the LSA Dean's records. Cheryl M. Fields's article, "Federal Probes into Sex Discrimination Provoke Controversy," appeared in the *Chronicle of Higher Education* on March 22, 1971, page 1. A number of documents, including Dean Frank Rhodes' report on the LSA retreat, were found in Box 212 (Salaries of Women and Allan Smith folders) of the LSA Dean's papers.

15: Sticking Points

The Columbia University folder in Box I: 137 of Richardson's papers was the source of details of Pottinger's negotiations with Columbia in December 1971. Background documents provided to Richardson for his May 1972 speech in Ann Arbor were found in Box I: 164 of his papers. The verse from "Elliott [sic], See!" is from a press release about the floral presentation found in Box 3 of King's papers. In addition to articles in the *Daily*, the Cheryl Clark case was covered by *Science* ("Michigan Wrestles with Equal Pay," by Deborah Shapley, July 16, 1971, page 214), *New York Times* ("Michigan U. Bars Raise for Woman," June 6, 1971, page 43), and *Detroit Free Press* ("U-M Refuses Woman's Equal Pay Bid," by Helen Fogel, June 3, 1971, page 1-D). U-M's announcement of salary increases for women, "Result of Reviews: 100 Women Get Increases," appeared in the February 28, 1972 issue of the *University Record*. The so-called Cluster Reports were summarized in a special edition of the *University Record*, March 20, 1972. Conservative critiques of affirmative action appeared in the *Detroit News* ("HEW Cuts Faculty Quality, Colleges Fear," by John E. Peterson, March 12, 1972, page 22-A) and *Commentary* ("HEW & the Universities," by Paul Seabury, February 1972, page 38). Documents covering Anne Cowley's grievance were found in a dedicated folder of Astronomy Department records in Box 233 of the LSA Dean's records; documents related to the complaints of Helen Tanner, Margaret Davis, and Lois Lowenthal were also found in Box 212 of the Dean's records in the "Salaries of Women," "Allan F. Smith Correspondence," and "Women" folders. Constance Holden's two-part series appeared in *Science* ("Women in Michigan: Academic Sexism Under Siege," November 24, 1972, page 841, and "Women in Michigan: Parlaying Rights Into Power," December 1, 1972, page 962). "Battle of Ann Arbor" appeared in *TIME*, March 12, 1973. James Crump Jr.'s poem appeared in the December 11, 1972 issue of the *University Record*. Meryl Johnson's response followed in the January 8, 1973 issue.

16: The Turning Point

The U.S. Commission on Civil Rights reviewed enforcement efforts at Michigan and three other universities in *The Federal Civil Rights Enforcement Effort—1974: Volume III To Ensure Equal Educational Opportunity*, published in January 1975 (https://files.eric.ed.gov/fulltext/ED102071.pdf). Geoff Shepherd's September 13, 1974 memorandum to President Ford about Pottinger and the Michigan investigation is in the Kenneth Cole papers at the Ford Presidential Library. (The draft version of the memo makes clear that Shepherd was referring to Robben Fleming, despite the misspelling of his last name.) Pottinger's relationship with Gloria Steinem is recounted in Carolyn G. Heilbrun's *The Education of a Woman: The Life of Gloria Steinem*, published by Dial Press in 1995. Dean J. Kotlowski provided a good overview of the Nixon administration's civil rights record in *Nixon's Civil Rights*, published in 2001 by Harvard University Press. Flora Davis's *Moving the Mountain: The Women's Movement in America Since 1960*, published in 1999 by the University of Illinois Press, was among the sources used for describing Rep. Green's strategy for passage of Title IX and the amendments to the Equal Pay Act. *The Higher, the Fewer: Report and Recommendations*, prepared by the Committee to Study the Status of Women in Graduate Education and

Later Careers for the Horace H. Rackham School of Graduate Studies, is available at the Bentley Library. Brenda J. Childs's appreciation of Helen Tanner appeared in the September 2011 issue of the American Historical Association's *Perspectives on History*, (https://www. historians.org/publications-and-directories/perspectives-on-history/ september-2011/in-memoriam-helen-hornbeck-tanner, retrieved on October 23, 2019). Biographies of inductees into the Michigan Women's Hall of Fame are found at http://www.michiganwomenshalloffame. org/inductee database1.aspx (retrieved October 23, 2019). Cowley's reflections on her time at Michigan were captured by Cheryl Baacke in "'U' Women Still Fighting Uphill Battle" in the February 3, 1984 edition of the *Michigan Daily Weekend*, page 1. Deborah E. Goldberg's decision to name her Distinguished University Professorship after Margaret Davis was reported by the Department of Ecology and Evolutionary Biology in a November 21, 2018 press release (https://lsa.umich.edu/ eeb/news-events/all-news/search-news/goldberg-honored-with-distinguished-university-professorship.html). King's response to the Law School solicitation is her August 8, 1975 letter to Samuel Krugliak, found in Box 1 of her papers. U-M Law School's "Class of 1968 Five Year Report" (1973) is available at https://repository.law.umich.edu/ cgi/viewcontent.cgi?article=1076&context=alumni survey reports. Information on the gains made by women in academia in the past 50 years came from U-M's December 3, 2018 faculty headcount report, available at obp.umich.edu/campus-statistics/faculty-staff/. Reports produced by U-M's ADVANCE program were retrieved from https:// advance.umich.edu/#. In particular, the author cited "University of Michigan Tenure Track Faculty: AY2018 Indicator Report" (November 2018) and "Assessing the Academic Work Environment for Tenured/ Tenure-Track Faculty at the University of Michigan in 2012 and 2017: Gender, Race, & Discipline in Department- and University-Related Climate" (October 2018). Other sources included "The Gender Pay Gap and the Representation of Women in Higher Education Administrative Positions: The Century So Far," by Jacqueline Bichsel and Jasper McChesney, published in February 2017 by the College and University Professional Association for Human Resources; *The Chronicle for Higher Education's* survey of faculty salaries for the 2017–18 academic year;

"More Women than Men Enrolled in U.S. Medical Schools in 2017," December 18, 2017 press release from the Association of American Medical Colleges; "The Simple Truth About the Gender Pay Gap," Fall 2018 edition, published by the American Association of University Women; and "Evaluating the Gender Gap," by Allana Akhtar and Rachel Premack, *Michigan Daily*, February 17, 2015. Sammy Sussman's December 10, 2018 *Michigan Daily* investigation of allegations against Professor Stephen Shipps, "Former Students Bring 40 Years of Misconduct Allegations by SMTD Professor," is at https://www.michigandaily.com/section/community-affairs/former-students-bring-40-years-misconduct-allegations-smtd-professor. Reports from Michigan's Office of Diversity, Equity and Inclusion, and its chronology of major University developments, were retrieved from its website, https://diversity.umich.edu/.

INDEX

Association for Women in Psychology, 124
Association of American Colleges, 141
Association of American Medical Colleges, 141, 202
Association of Junior Colleges, 142
Astronomy Department, U-M, xii–xiii, 108, 216, 246–47, 264–66
Atkins, Pat, 161

Beloit College, 46
Bentley Historical Library, U-M, 22, 61, 65, 126
Berger, Joel, 83, 128–29
Black Action Movement, x, 36–40, 45, 49–50, 135, 159, 270, 275
Board of Regents, U-M, xiii, 36, 62, 68, 90, 149, 151, 168–69, 176, 198, 248, 262, 266, 269, 271
Bok, Derek, 232
Bond, Floyd, 218
Booth, Harold, 139, 185
Boston University, 19
Botany Department, U-M, 89–90, 100, 103, 108, 203
Boyer, Elizabeth, 7, 9
Brandeis University, 19, 58, 196
Brazer, Harvey, 22
Brazer, Marge, 22
Brewster, Kingman, xix, 202
Brigham Young University, 196
Brinkerhoff, James, 37, 49–50, 100, 151
Bromage, Mary, 120
Brooklyn College, 1, 52, 199, 257
Broomfield, William, 78
Brown, Dugald, 227
Brown, Garry E., 155
Brown University, 52, 160, 199
Bryan, Kirk, Jr., 88–89

Bryn Mawr College, 46, 268
Bunzel, John, 235
Burns, Kenneth P., 174–75
Burroughs, Robert E., 172–75

Cable, Louella, 22
Cain, Louise, 118, 126
California Institute of Technology, 88
California State University at Fullerton, 262
California State University System, 52
Campbell, Angus, 20
Campbell, Jean, 15–16, 20–21, 126, 187, 207, 225, 263
Canham, Don, 170
Cantor, Nancy, 276
Carnegie Mellon University, 52
Carruth, Hayden, 44, 91, 266
Carswell, G. Harrold, ix–x, xv–xvi, xx, xxii, 70, 124
Cash, William L., Jr., 43–44, 73–74, 77, 164, 188–92, 197, 210, 229
Center for Population Planning, U-M, 156, 159, 200, 223
Center for Research in Conflict Resolution, U-M, 188, 193, 217
Center for the Continuing Education of Women, U-M, xi, 11, 15, 20–21, 71, 87, 118–19, 121–24, 126–27, 153, 248
Central Seattle Community College, 256
Chalmers, Thelma, 108
Chalmers, W. Ellison, 108
Chandler, David, 90–91
Chemistry Department, U-M, 13, 100, 253
Chesapeake Community College, 52
Chesler, Joan, 108
Chesler, Mark, 108

Child, Brenda J., 263
City College of New York, 1–2
City University of New York, 19;
    Graduate School and University
    Center, 236
Clarion State College, 19
Clark, Cheryl, xi–xiii, 224–25, 236,
    244–46, 248, 250, 261
Clark University, 52
Clinton, Hillary Rodham, xx
Cobb, Jewel Plummer, xiii, 262
Cohen, Wilbur J., 178–79
Coleman, Mary Sue, xiii
College and University Professional
    Association for Human
    Resources, 273
College Entrance Examination Board,
    63, 271
College of Engineering, U-M, 27, 41,
    123, 152–53, 272
College of Literature, Science, and
    the Arts, U-M, xiii, 21–22, 26, 30,
    41, 44, 47–48, 64, 87, 91, 107–08,
    122–23, 153, 219, 222–23, 227, 230,
    241, 249, 251, 262, 266, 269, 271;
    Executive Committee of, 65, 90,
    244, 247
Collins–Robson, Mary Jean, 222
Columbia University, 52, 58, 72,
    238–39; Barnard College at, 204,
    206, 232
Columbia University's Women's
    Liberation, 9, 58, 73
Commission for Women, U-M, xii,
    239, 242–43, 246, 248, 251, 267,
    275–77; Cluster Communications
    Committee of, 240–41 (see also
    Commission on Women, U-M)
Commission on Women, U-M, xi 127,
    155, 161, 166, 180, 187, 189–90, 192,
    207–9, 211–12, 214, 218–22, 225–26,

231, 234, 236, 240, 262 (see also
    Commission for Women, U-M)
Connecticut College, xiii, 262
Cook, Marlow, xvi
Cornell University, 5, 55, 212, 216
Cosand, Joseph, 142, 200
Cowley, Anne, xii–xiii, 216, 246–47,
    263–66, 268, 274
Cowley, Charles, 246–47
Crafton, Helen, 242
Crouch, Gaye, 193–94
Crowfoot, Dale, 108
Crowfoot, James, 108
Crump, James, Jr., 253
Cuyahoga Community College, 8

Dabbs, Mary, xvii
Darrow, Peter, 15
Davis, Carolyne, 261
Davis, Margaret B., x, 87–93, 99, 108,
    110, 154, 215, 226, 229–30, 236,
    244–46, 250, 261, 266–67
Davis, Rowland H., 89
DePauw University, 19
Dixon, Marlene, 124, 128
Douvan, Elizabeth (Libby), 22–24,
    123, 126, 135, 157, 242–43, 260, 269
Dowding, Nancy E., 8
Drouyer, Gertrude, 22
Duke University, 232
Dunn, Mary Maples, 46–48, 268

East, Catherine, 9, 124
Eastern Illinois University, 52
Eastern Michigan University, 25, 54,
    249
East Texas State University, 257
Ecology and Evolutionary Biology
    Department, U-M, 266
Economics Department, U-M, 120,
    242

Edwards, Harry T., 225
Einstein College of Medicine, 257
Electrical Engineering Department,
    U-M, 174
English Language and Literature
    Department, U-M, 26, 100, 105,
    107–08
English Language Institute, U-M, 216
Equal Employment Opportunity
    Commission, 6, 39, 260
Esch, Marvin L., 70, 179, 183–84,
    249
Evans, Keith, 100, 107, 109, 155, 166

Far Eastern Languages and
    Literature Department, U-M,
    207–08, 216, 253
Fauri, Fedele, 164–66, 179–80, 185,
    188, 195, 206, 208–09, 211, 219,
    240, 246
Federbush, Marcia, 176–77, 268
Ferris, Muriel, 70, 176
Fields, Cheryl, 222
Finch, Robert, 30, 69, 136–38, 143
Fine, Sidney, 13, 15, 215, 227, 228–29
Fisher, Justine, 74
Fisk University, 191
Fleming, Robben, 20, 28, 64–66, 68,
    73–74, 77, 100, 117–19, 128, 140,
    142, 145–47, 160, 164–65, 172, 174,
    176, 191, 203, 210–12, 218, 220,
    226, 231, 235, 240, 249, 257, 262,
    264; communication with other
    college officials, 132–36, 148,
    169–70, 179, 181, 198, 200, 232;
    correspondence, meetings with
    HEW, x–xi, 42–43, 79, 81, 88, 96,
    98, 99, 114, 148, 155–56, 158, 175,
    178–86, 194, 197–98, 202–05, 236,
    250, 252, 258; correspondence
    with women, 86–87, 127, 151,
    153, 176–77, 228, 268; creation of

Commission on Women, 187–89,
    192, 208, 212; management of
    student protests, 35–38, 50, 131,
    269–70; views on discrimination,
    45–46, 48, 93, 99, 130, 136, 163,
    234, 244–45, 269–70
Fleming, Sally, 46, 74
Flemming, Arthur, 142–43, 181–82,
    198, 200, 257
Flint Feminists, 267
Florida State University, 257
Florida State University System,
    52
FOCUS on Equal Employment for
    Women (Ann Arbor), 22, 57, 61,
    68, 74, 80, 122, 151, 153, 157, 189,
    232–33, 240; complaint against
    University of Michigan and, x,
    xvi, 29–30, 40, 45–46, 51, 53, 70,
    73, 75, 147, 270; founding of, x,
    xxii, 21
FOCUS on Equal Employment for
    Women (U.S.), xvi, 124
Fogel, Helen, 71–72, 75, 78, 80, 82–83,
    131, 166–67, 180
Foley, Eileen, 71–72, 135
Ford, Gerald R., 257, 258
Ford, William D., 70
Forestry Department, U-M, 108
Fredericks, Marshall, 64
Freehling, Williams, 188, 207
Freeman, Jo, 9
Friday, William, 202
Friedan, Betty, ix, xvi, xix, 5, 8
Frostburg State College, 52
Frye, Billy, 262

Gamson, Zelda, 22, 107–08, 261, 269
Gardner, Emily W., 207
Gardner, Jo-Ann E., xvi, 57, 124–25
Gaston, Dale, 175
General Motors Co., 165, 237

Geography Department, U-M, 79, 108, 242–43
Geophysics Laboratory, U-M, 174–75
George Washington University, 52, 56, 159
Georgia Southern College, 204
Georgia State University, 199
Georgia Tech University, 199
Germanic Languages and Literature Department, U-M, 100, 106, 146, 261
Gibson, Charles, 229
Gifford, William L., 70
Ginsburg, Ruth Bader, 15, 18
Gladman, Gloria E., 151, 153–54
Goheen, Robert, 202
Goldberg, Deborah E., 266–67
Goldstein, Murray, 140
Gordus, Adon A., 253
Graduate School of Business Administration, U-M, 218
Great Lakes Research Division, U-M, 89–90
Green, Edith, 51–61, 78, 106, 137, 145, 154, 237, 260
Green, Saul, 32
Greene, Walter R., 40–41
Griffin, Robert P., xvii
Griffiths, Martha, 21, 30, 124
Groesbeck, Byron, 28
Guskin, Alan, 108–09
Guskin, Judith, 108–09

Haber, William, 41–42, 44
Hamilton, Jack, 135
Hamlin, Albert T., 186, 195
Harrington, Fred H., 77, 141, 202
Harris, Ann Sutherland, 58
Harris, Martha, 250
Hart, Philip A., 70, 78, 80, 226
Hartwick College, 52
Hartwig, Marie, 13

Harvard University, x, xx–xxi, 19, 21, 37, 55–56, 88, 134, 140, 142, 159, 185, 196, 199–200, 204–05, 221, 232–33, 238, 255, 257, 268; Harvard College: Board of Overseers and, 140, 201; HEW investigation at, 72, 83; Institute for Educational Management at, 96; School of Law at, 15, 202
Hatcher, Harlan, 13, 41
Hathaway, William D., 58–60
Hayes, Edward C., 100, 107, 109, 155, 164, 166, 192–93, 207, 210, 218, 220–21, 230
Haynsworth, Clement, xv, 70
Heebink, David, 206, 240
Heilbrun, Carolyn G., 259
Henry, David, 142, 170, 179, 181, 198, 200
Highway Safety Research Institute, U-M, 224–25
Hiltner, W.A., 216
Hinchey, Mary Catherine, 229
Hinman, Martha, 261
History Department, U-M, x, 86–87, 100, 103, 105, 107, 215, 227–29, 242, 263
Hitt, Patricia Reilly, 56, 137–39, 143
Hodgdon, James D., 69
Hodgdon, John, 78, 81, 86, 88, 96, 116, 148, 160, 165, 167–68, 180, 185, 226–28, 234, 239–40, 258
Hoffman, Lois, 108, 123, 223
Hoffman, Martin, 108, 223
Hook, Sidney, 235
Hucker, Charles C., 216–17
Huebner, Gertrude V., 119, 161–62
Huitt, Ralph K., 132–33, 135, 142
Human Genetics Department, U-M, 207
Hutchins, Carol, 268

Idaho State University, 256
Indritz, Phineas, 53
Institute for Social Research, U-M, 20, 188, 192, 207, 221
Institute of Labor and Industrial Relations, U-M, 108
Interior Department: U.S. Geological Survey, 185
Internal Revenue Service, 83, 101

Jackson State College (University), 37
John Carroll University, 257
Johnson, Lyndon B., x, 5, 14, 39, 133, 148, 178
Johnson, Meryl, 253
Journalism Department, U-M, 24, 103, 242

Kaplan, Rachel, 108
Kaplan, Stephen, 108
Kauper, Thomas, 15
Kelsey Museum of Archaeology, U-M, 253
Kennedy, Richard, 117
Kent State University, 37
Kidd, Charles, 133, 147, 202, 204–05, 208
Kiely, Owen, 55–56, 70, 78, 156, 160, 174, 186, 198–99, 204–05, 226
King, Jean L., 18–23, 38–40, 46, 54, 61–62, 66–68, 71–73, 86, 120–22, 131–32, 135, 136, 139, 153–54, 162, 167, 180, 193–94, 208, 222, 242–43, 249, 252, 263, 267–68, 276; biography of, 11–17; complaint against University of Michigan and, 24, 29–33, 91; correspondence with members of Congress and, 68–70, 145, 179, 254; investigation of University of Michigan and, 75–76, 78, 82;

organization of FOCUS and, xvi–xvii; tracking U-M contracts and, 155–57, 172, 176
King, John, 12–13
King, Martin Luther, Jr., 37
Klamp, Margaret, 22
Knauss, Robert, 63, 149
Kolars, John, 79, 108–9, 243
Krulwich, Sara, xxi, 270

Laird, Melvin, 202
Landscape Architecture Department, U-M, 20
Lardent, Esther, 74, 82, 87–89, 94–96, 99, 110, 145, 239, 246, 259
Larimore, Ann (Kolars), 79–80, 82, 95, 108–10, 145, 242, 243, 260, 261–62, 269–70, 274
Leland, Carol, 63
Lemmer, William, 164, 210
Levi, Edward, 77, 124
Lincoln University, 52
Lloyd, Helen, 188
Lohman, Anita, 108–09
Lohman, John, 108–09
Louisiana, 137, 196
Louisiana Technical University, 257
Lowenthal, Lois, 226–30, 266
Loyola University, 233
Loyola University of Chicago, 159
Loyola University of Los Angeles, 199
Lutz, Gilbert, 163

Macalester College, 142–43
Macaluso, Vincent, 6–10, 11, 23, 69–70, 148
Macomber, William B., Jr., 136
Manhattan Community College, 56, 199
Marcus, Melvin G., 80, 82

Queens College, 257

Rackham Graduate School, U-M, 28, 48, 102, 122, 261
Radcliffe College, xix, 19, 55, 88, 268
Radical Lesbians, 121–22, 124, 151, 170
Radock, Michael, 168, 198
Rasmussen, Sue, 97, 261
Reade, Maxwell, 176
Reed College, 212
Rees, Mina, 236
Reister, Russell W., 100, 187
Residential College, U-M, 86, 103, 107–08, 228
Revelli, William D., 136
Rhodes, Frank H.T., 223, 262, 269
Rice University, 257
Richardson, Elliot L., xi, 55, 69, 133, 136–43, 147, 178–79, 181–85, 196–98, 200–03, 206, 226, 238, 249–50, 257
Riegle, Donald W., 70
Riesman, David, 28
Robertson, James, 108
Robinson, Jean M., 207
Rockefeller, Nelson, 238
Rodgers, Mary Ann, 126
Rogers, Lorene, 133
Ross, Arthur M., 21, 164
Royster, Preston M., 55–56
Ruppe, Philip E., 70
Rutgers University, 18–19, 52

Sandler, Bernice, 11–12, 14, 16, 18–19, 21, 28, 30, 32, 39, 68–70, 72–74, 78, 104, 106, 138, 146–47, 154, 167–68, 199, 219, 222, 235, 263, 269, 276; biography, 1–10; Green hearings on sex discrimination and, 52–55, 57–58, 60–61

Sandler, Jerry, 2, 3
Sanford, Terry, 232
San Jose State College (University), 235
Sarri, Rosemary, 188
Sax, Joseph, 264–65
Schelkun, Ruth, 22
School of Business Administration, U-M, 120, 123, 153, 219
School of Dentistry, U-M, 219
School of Education, U-M, 30, 57, 108, 123, 142, 178, 194, 241
School of Law, U-M, 15–16, 29, 39, 63, 121, 123, 195, 225, 231, 241, 264, 267, 271
School of Library Science, U-M, 30, 40, 58, 84–85, 103, 145, 188, 219, 244
School of Medicine, U-M, 21, 27, 29, 123, 153, 219, 271
School of Music, U-M, 122, 136
School of Natural Resources, U-M, 123
School of Nursing, U-M, 30, 32, 123, 219, 261
School of Public Health, U-M, 159
School of Social Work, U-M, 2, 11, 30, 58, 123, 164, 241
Schottland, Charles, 196, 202
Schultz, Jean, 207
Scott, Ann, 20–21, 154, 222
Scott, Don F., x, 81, 83, 96–100, 118, 128, 131, 134, 145, 148, 154–55, 165–66, 174, 178–79, 180–81, 194, 210, 258
Scott, Mary P., 207
Seabury, Paul, 235
Senate Advisory Committee on University Affairs, U-M, 63, 115, 146, 170, 187–88, 193, 207
Shepard, Geoff, 258

Shortridge, Kathleen, 39, 120; *Michigan Daily* investigation and, x, 24–29, 58, 64; PROBE leadership and, 61, 84
Shulman, Mary Alice, 120, 242
Shultz, George P., 8, 19, 29, 69–70
Sklar, Kathryn Kish, 107
Smith, Allan, xii, 32, 41, 48, 63, 77, 99, 100, 119, 164–65, 195–96, 204–05, 209–11, 218–19, 229, 239, 242, 245, 248, 254
Smith College, xviii–xix, 19, 268
Social Psychology Department, U-M, 13–14
Sociology Department, U-M, 44, 107–08
Sociology Department, University of Chicago, 124
Southeast Louisiana University, 257
Southern Illinois University, 19, 159
Southern Methodist University, 257
South Seattle Community College, 257
Sponberg, Harold, 249
Spurr, Stephen, 48
Stadler, Carole M., 226
Stanford University, 238
State University of New York system, 154
St. Cloud State College, 212, 231
Steinem, Gloria, xix, 259
Stephens, Cynthia, 40
St. John's University, New York, 199
Stokes, Donald, 45, 261
Survey Research Center, U-M, 13, 20, 161, 207
Susquehanna University, 52
Sussman, Alfred, 48, 65, 90–92, 222–23, 226, 229, 243, 247

Takeshita, John, 159
Tanner, Helen Hornbeck, x, 86–87, 108, 215, 227–29, 263
Tanter, Raymond, 202
Tashian, Jeanne, 61, 194, 249
Tentler, Adrienne, 121
Texas Christian University, 257
Theater Department, U-M, 244
Thieme, Frederick P., 198
Thorburn, Andrew, 170–71
Thrupp, Sylvia L., 228
Tobias, Sheila, 232
Townes, Henry, 108
Townes, Marjorie, 108
Trinkhaus, Charles, 242
Tufts University, 52, 199, 233

Ullman, Betty M., 207
University Computer Center, U-M, 192
University Health Service, U-M, 29
University of Akron, 77
University of Arkansas, 257
University of Buffalo (State University of New York at Buffalo), 20, 154
University of California at Berkeley, 233, 235, 256
University of California at Riverside, 212
University of California at Santa Barbara, 37
University of Chicago, 9, 77, 82, 110, 124, 128, 233
University of Colorado, 198
University of Connecticut, 52, 141
University of Georgia, 52, 160, 199
University of Hawaii, 212
University of Illinois, 142, 148, 160–61, 169–70, 179, 181, 198, 200, 204, 233

University of Maryland, 2, 3, 8, 10, 19, 55, 82, 159, 168, 233; College of Arts and Sciences at, 9; Department of Counseling and Personnel Services at, 2; Psychology Department at, 2–3; School of Education at, x, 9

University of Massachusetts, 52

University of Miami, 52

University of Michigan, 12, 16, 35, 38–39, 46–50, 57, 61–67, 70, 85–89, 183, 201, 212, 229, 260, 276; admissions policies of, 26–27, 103, 204; advertising job openings at, xii, 111, 114, 248; affirmative action plans at, ix, xii–xiii, 42–44, 97–98, 114, 129, 150, 155, 200, 206, 213–14, 218–19, 227, 230, 231, 233–34, 238–39, 241, 249, 254; analysis of employment data at, 190–93, 220–22; anti–nepotism policies at, 107–10, 115, 206–07, 219–20, 247; centennial celebration of women's admission at, xi, 118–27, 161; complaint procedures at, 221, 223–25, 235; federal contracts and, 11, 145–49, 155, 172–76, 198, 258; graduate school admissions and, 155, 166, 178–81, 195–97, 203, 213, 271; Hayes–Evans response to HEW and, 100–02, 105–07, 109–10, 112–14, 166; HEW investigation at, 74, 82–84, 92, 128, 163, 255, 258, 275–76; hiring of student, faculty wives at, 130, 211; male traditions at, xxi, 152, 161, 208; negotiations with HEW at, 178–79, 180–82, 186, 192, 194–98, 240, 250; privacy concerns at, 167; progress regarding women at, 271–75; racial discrimination compliance at, ix, 40–41; reputation for addressing discrimination and, 222, 252, 261; salary adjustments for women at, xii, 129, 155, 178–79, 197, 224, 230, 235–36, 241–42, 245–46, 261; sex discrimination evidence at, 25–30, 94–117, 122–23, 200, 228, 232, 261, 263, 265, 267; sexual harassment at, 274–75; standards for recruiting women faculty at, 155, 178, 180, 196–97, 204, 219

University of Michigan–Flint, 267

University of Minnesota, 52, 77, 263, 266

University of Nebraska, 134, 169

University of Nevada, 212

University of New Hampshire, 52

University of North Carolina, 19, 55, 202

University of North Carolina–Wilmington, 52

University of Northern Iowa, 212

University of Notre Dame, 49

University of Oklahoma: Health Sciences Center, 257

University of Oregon, 142, 257

University of Pennsylvania, 257

University of Pittsburgh, 10–11, 19, 159–60, 167, 199, 230, 233

University of Rhode Island, 52

University of San Francisco, 199

University of Southern California, 205; School of Medicine, 140

University of Tennessee, 19

University of Texas at Austin, 133, 233, 257

University of Texas at Dallas: Medical School, 199